THE 2001 TOUR DE FRANCE

THE 2001 TOUR DE FRANCE
LANCEx3

John Wilcockson
with Charles Pelkey, Bryan Jew and Lennard Zinn

VELO
press®

Boulder, Colorado

The 2001 Tour de France: Lance x 3
© 2001 Inside Communications

Printed in the United States of America

Distributed in the United States and Canada by Publishers Group West

10 9 8 7 6 5 4 3 2 1

International Standard Book Number: 1-931382-01-8

Library of Congress Cataloging-in-Publication Data
Wilcockson, John.
    The 2001 Tour de France : Lance x 3 / John Wilcockson with Bryan Jew, Charles Pelkey, and Lennard Zinn.
        p. cm.
    ISBN 1-931382-01-8
    1. Tour de France (Bicycle race) 2. Armstrong, Lance. 3. Cyclists—United States—Biography. I. Jew, Bryan. II. Pelkey, Charles. III. Zinn, Lennard. IV. Title.

GV1049.2.T68 W545 2001
796.6'2'094090511—dc21   2001046808

VeloPress
1830 N. 55th Street
Boulder, Colorado 80301-2700 USA
303/440-0601; Fax 303/444-6788; E-mail velopress@7dogs.com

To purchase additional copies of this book or other VeloPress books, call 800/234-8356 or visit us on the Web at velopress.com.

Cover and interior photos by Graham Watson
Interior design by Paula Megenhardt

To Jacques Goddet (1905–2000)

The Tour de France lost its spiritual "father" in December 2000, when Jacques Goddet died in Paris at age 95. He was the Tour race director for half a century until well into his 80s. Goddet was the son of Victor Goddet, the man who founded the French daily sports newspaper *L'Auto* (now called *L'Équipe*) in 1900, and helped establish the Tour de France in 1903, sponsored by his newspaper. Jacques Goddet was born two years later. He would become editor-in-chief of *L'Équipe* and follow 54 Tours de France.

CONTENTS

Preface

AN OLD-FASHIONED TOUR
WITH A TOTALLY MODERN WINNER

In winning the Tour de France for a third consecutive time, Lance Armstrong became only the eighth man to take the world's most famous bicycle race three or more times. His 2001 Tour victory was arguably the most complete of the three, because he proved that not only was he the best prepared rider in the race, but also the most powerful climber and the fastest time trialist. Despite that, his dominance did not make the Tour a bore. Far from it. Before the American took the overall lead on the 13th of 20 stages, the crowds on the roadside and the fans watching on television (broadcast live for the first time in the U.S.) were treated to a very open race, which saw five different riders wearing the leader's yellow jersey. The unpredictability continued throughout the three weeks, as the event took on a no-holds-barred style of racing that evoked the best Tours of years past.

As in 1999 and 2000, the story of the race revolved around Armstrong, the man who came back from advanced testicular cancer to become professional cycling's dominant performer. Before cancer, he was already a phenomenal athlete: the winner of the world professional road championship at age 21; a two-time winner of "America's Tour de France," the 10-day Tour DuPont; and one of the top-five riders in Europe's one-day classics, winning the Clasica San Sebastian and Flèche Wallonne, and twice taking second at the rugged Liège-Bastogne-Liège. After he came through the surgery and chemotherapy, Armstrong set his sights on returning to the top level of his sport; but even he didn't realize that the 15 pounds or so of body mass he shed during his illness would allow him to not only ride strongly on the short hill climbs of the classics, but also excel on the long mountain climbs that characterize the Tour de France.

That realization first came midway through his comeback season of 1998, at the four-day Tour of Luxembourg. And that's why we open this book with a look back at that race through Armstrong's eyes. The rest of Part One traces the progress of Armstrong and his U.S. Postal Service through the 2001 season, from the year's first training camp in Arizona to their final pre-Tour race, the Tour of Switzerland. Then comes a look at all the Americans in the race, the race favorites and the teams selected for the Tour.

Part Two includes detailed reports of every stage of the 88th Tour de France, complemented by route maps and elevation profiles, along with detailed results and two 16-page spreads of color photography by famed shooter Graham Watson. Adding an insider element to the race story are the rider diaries of Tyler Hamilton, Armstrong's close friend and teammate; Kevin Livingston, a former Armstrong teammate, who had joined the Deutsche Telekom team of rival Jan Ullrich; and the American road champion Fred Rodriguez, who raced on the Belgian-based Domo-Farm Frites squad.

The book's Part Three includes an analysis of Armstrong's victory and the dynamics of the 2001 Tour de France; a post-race interview with the winner on his return to the United States; a report on the media's skepticism over Armstrong's assertion that drugs did not play a part in his Tour-winning performances; and a chapter on the part played by technology in the Tour's time trials. Finally, to help readers better understand the Tour, there is a glossary of cycling terms, which includes explanations of mountain climb categories and how the various competitions are scored.

With another win behind him, Armstrong's next target—though he wouldn't admit it—was to join the exclusive group of riders that has won the Tour five times: Jacques Anquetil, Eddy Merckx, Bernard Hinault and Miguel Induráin. Maybe three-time runner-up Ullrich, who's a couple of years younger than Armstrong, would have something to say about that in 2002....

Acknowledgments

Just as a Tour de France winner needs expert teammates to help build a victory, so an author needs a professional, experienced team to turn a raw manuscript into a completed publication. And I believe that the team working on this fourth Tour de France book from VeloPress has created yet another winner. First of all, I would like to thank all the people who make traveling with the Tour such an exciting experience—particularly the racers, Tour organizers, fans and fellow journalists.

In 2001, Tyler Hamilton of the U.S. Postal Service team, Fred Rodriguez of Domo-Farm Frites and Kevin Livingston of Deutsche Telekom wrote about their experiences in their race diaries. Bryan Jew again contributed to Part One of the book, and he safely drove our press car around France for 23 days in July, while Charles Pelkey—who wrote the chapter on drug use—was the mastermind of the velonews.com Web site at the Tour. All three of us would like to thank our wives, Rivvy Neshama, Cori Jew and Diana Denlson, for their understanding and patience. The Tour was also made more pleasurable (and more interesting!) by our traveling companions, *VeloNews* technical guru Lennard Zinn—who has contributed the chapter on Tour tech—and his wife, Sonny Zinn, Rupert Guinness of *The Australian* newspaper and David Walsh of *The Sunday Times* of London.

Once again, Graham Watson shot all the photos that illustrate the book, including an extra 16-page section this year; Rivvy Neshama did another polished copyediting performance; and Paula Megenhardt did the interior design. Thanks also are due to the VeloPress design team for helping create the individual stage maps and the cover design, and to VeloPress editors Amy Sorrells and Theresa van Zante for keeping us all on track.

John Wilcockson

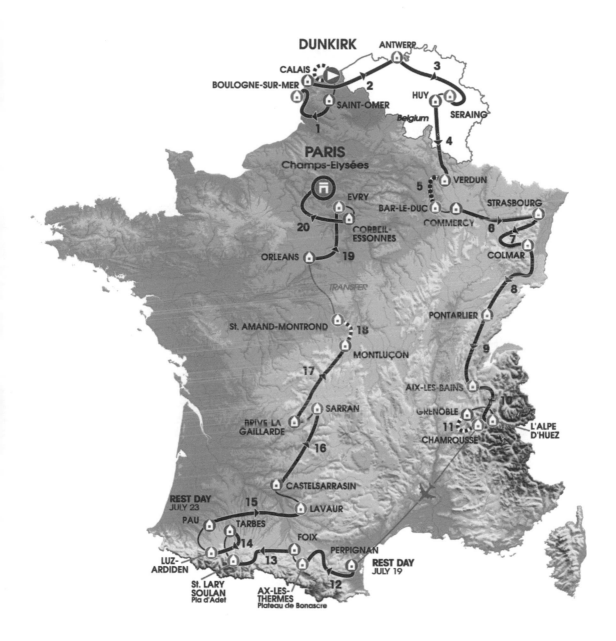

DUNKIRK
ANTWERP
CALAIS
BOULOGNE-SUR-MER
2
SAINT-OMER
HUY
3
SERAING
1
4
PARIS
Champs-Elysées
VERDUN
5
STRASBOURG
EVRY
BAR-LE-DUC
20
COMMERCY
6
CORBEIL-
ESSONNES
7
ORLEANS
19
COLMAR
8
Belgium
TRANSFER
PONTARLIER
St. AMAND-MONTROND
18
9
MONTLUÇON
17
AIX-LES-BAINS
SARRAN
10
GRENOBLE
BRIVE LA
GAILLARDE
11
L'ALPE
D'HUEZ
16
CHAMROUSSE
CASTELSARRASIN
REST DAY
JULY 23
15
LAVAUR
PAU
TARBES
FOIX
14
PERPIGNAN
LUZ-
ARDIDEN
13
REST DAY
JULY 19
St. LARY
SOULAN
Pla d'Adet
AX-LES-
THERMES
Plateau de Bonascre
12

© Société du Tour de France

PART ONE
The Road to the Tour

A Taste of Tours to Come

LANCE ARMSTRONG'S RETURN FROM CANCER
AND HIS PATH TOWARD WINNING HIS FIRST
TOUR DE FRANCE BEGAN IN LUXEMBOURG IN 1998

The powerful voice at the other end of the transatlantic wireless phone link sounded exhilarated, tired and relieved. "We're driving to the airport," Lance Armstrong shouted over the din of a fast-moving car. "We won the race!"

The race was the Tour of Luxembourg, June 1998—more than a year before Armstrong won his first Tour de France, and a long three months after the recovered cancer patient had almost quit cycling for good.

Recalling his early departure that March from the week-long Paris-Nice—during a cold, torrential downpour on the very first road stage—Armstrong said on his cell phone, "When I pulled over and stopped, I said to myself, 'That's the last time I'll ever race a bike.' But that wasn't how I wanted to go out … it didn't have any dignity. So I took a couple of weeks to re-think things...."

"At Paris-Nice, I was disappointed with how I was racing. But looking back, it was stupid to expect to be at the same level [as before cancer]."

Stupid, maybe. But on his return to big-time European racing—18 months after he left it in October 1996, on learning that he had an advanced form of testicular cancer—Armstrong wanted to prove to other cancer survivors (and to himself) that he could perform

3

at the same level as he did before the surgery, chemo and rehab. Yes, he was impetuous. No, he couldn't wait.

Even before that fated Paris-Nice, Armstrong wasn't pleased with his form: In his very first post-cancer race, February '98's five-day Ruta del Sol in Spain, he placed 15th overall. To a stunned world, that was a phenomenal showing. To a hyper-ambitious Armstrong, it was a failure. He wanted to "show" the continental cycling establishment that it was mistaken in discarding him. It still hurt the former world champion that he was picked up for a song by U.S. Postal, after not one European directeur sportif had been willing to take over the high-priced contract he'd signed with French team Cofidis prior to his cancer.

For all these reasons, Armstrong attacked the opening-day time trial at Paris-Nice determined to shine. That he failed to win it contributed to his abandoning the race the next morning in bewildering circumstances. Armstrong appeared to be quitting not only the race, but cycling itself. That judgment was later confirmed by his close friend and U.S. Postal Service teammate Frankie Andreu, who was there when Armstrong climbed off his bike.

Andreu was there again in June '98, when Armstrong returned to European racing at the 58th Tour of Luxembourg, a four-day race won in the past by grand tour winners like Bernard Hinault (1982), Freddy Maertens (1974) and Louison Bobet (1955). Armstrong's name was about to be added to that list....

"The win comes as a complete surprise," said Armstrong on his way to the Brussels airport. "This is the first time I've worn the [leader's] jersey—and it's my first win—in a European stage race." He didn't consider his 1991 victory at the pro-am Settimana Bergamasca, when he was a 19-year-old amateur, in the same league.

The impetus for the Luxembourg success came from the previous week's racing in the United States, where victories for Andreu (at Lancaster, Pennsylvania) and George Hincapie (in Philadelphia) restored the confidence that the Postal Service team had been lacking since leader Armstrong had left the peloton in March. Even so, Armstrong felt sluggish at the First Union USPRO Championship in Philadelphia on June 7. He said it was "like I was dragging a manhole cover" in the race, which he put down to his lack of competition. Nonetheless, Armstrong was the catalyst that ignited his team: Hincapie took the stars-and-stripes championship jersey thanks to the unselfish riding of his six teammates, especially Armstrong.

"I wanted us to carry that solid team riding over to Europe," Armstrong continued. "Before the first stage [in Luxembourg], I told the guys that we had to cover every break." They followed his orders.

There were many attacks on the hilly opening stage, which, at 190km, was the longest of the race. And, as Armstrong requested, a rider from the Postal Service went with every move. Despite the aggression, the pack regrouped each time, until just before halfway—when Frenchman Philippe Gaumont of Cofidis attacked with Estonian Lauri Aus of Casino. This time, it was Armstrong's turn to respond, and he jumped across alone to the two leaders. Working well together, this leading trio soon created the biggest gap of the day.

The pace was too much for Gaumont, who was dropped about 20km into the attack, leaving Aus and Armstrong to ride the remaining 80km together. "We rode pull for pull," reported the American, who said his heart rate averaged 160 bpm for the stage. "When we had a lead of about seven-and-a-half minutes, Mapei and Telekom began the chase. But they only closed to about five or six minutes, and then gave up."

By the finish, Armstrong and Aus were four minutes ahead of the first chase group. "The sprint was slightly uphill with a strong head wind," Armstrong reported. "It was a short sprint, and he led out." This was how Armstrong wanted it, and he came around Aus to take the stage *and* the jersey. With bonuses, the American led the Estonian by five seconds on G.C.

Four of those seconds were lost by Armstrong in a crash-filled finale the next day. "There were circuits every stage at the finish," Armstrong noted, "usually on small roads. And it rained. With about four or five kilometers to go, the entire Telekom train fell in front of me. I got up quickly, but my chain was off. It was a nightmare trying to chase back...."

Given the hard work the Postal team had exerted in defending the jersey, it was decided not to fight for all the time bonuses on the third day's two short road stages. As a result, Aus took over the lead in the morning stage, which ended in a field sprint taken by the GAN team's Aussie Stuart O'Grady. That afternoon saw Telekom control the finish—without crashing this time—to give the win to its sprinter, Erik Zabel.

And so the final day began with Armstrong two seconds down on Aus—a deficit he could win back in the intermediate sprints—and with the next riders still four minutes back.

"It was a really aggressive race," said Armstrong. "At the second time bonus, there was one rider away, leaving a two-seconds bonus for second. Frankie led me out for a kilometer for the sprint, which was a little uphill. We caught them by surprise, and I got the two seconds. That made us even."

If Armstrong and Aus had remained tied until the finish, the win would probably have gone to the Casino rider, who had better overall stage placings. But the American and his team weren't going to rely on time bonuses.

After the bonus sprint, Andreu went on the attack in a small group that included teammate Marty Jemison and Rabobank's Dutchman Erik Dekker. Then, on a challenging 6km climb, Armstrong went across to the leaders in another group, one that contained teammate Tyler Hamilton and Cofidis team leader Francesco Casagrande—but not race leader Aus. "I thought that was it," Armstrong later said. "But Casino chased hard and came back."

All this attacking led to a lull in the pace, until the pack reached a first short, steep climb on the finishing loop at Diekirch. Andreu again went away, this time with Dekker and a few other riders. It seemed that the Postal Service team was in control ... until the break gained three-and-a-half minutes. With Dekker only four minutes behind on G.C., the race was in jeopardy of going to Rabobank. So, "the second time up the steepest climb, we attacked with about 20 other guys," Armstrong said.

There were still roughly 50km to go, with heavy rain showers continuing through the finish. In the counterattack with Armstrong were his teammates Hamilton and Jemison, along with riders like Casagrande and Lotto-Mobistar's Andreï Tchmil. Once again, Aus was left behind. But in the Armstrong chase group, no one was willing to share the work with the USPS men. This caused Jemison and Hamilton to ride like heroes, setting the tempo and snuffing out the Dekker danger by closing to within 42 seconds of him by the finish. Even more importantly, Aus and the peloton lost nine minutes, leaving Armstrong as the undisputed winner.

In front, Andreu attacked on the last big climb, 20km from the line, and won the stage on his own, 37 seconds ahead of the chasers, to complete the American triumph.

"We won the race," Armstrong repeated on the phone, the enthusiasm palpable in his voice. His comeback was finally underway, and that victory in Luxembourg began the roll that set the Texan on course to winning that much bigger national tour in France.

Building a New Team

THERE WAS AN OPTIMISTIC START TO THE 2001 SEASON
FOR LANCE ARMSTRONG AND THE NEW RIDERS ON HIS
U.S. POSTAL SERVICE TEAM AT A TRAINING CAMP IN ARIZONA

His training clothes sodden, his face flushed from riding in two hours of glacial rain, Lance Armstrong burst into the lobby of Tucson's swank Westin La Paloma hotel, dropped off his Trek with a bellhop and, shivering from the cold, asked for his room key. "That was the coldest my hands have ever been," the Texan said later.

Across the sprawling, hillside resort, Roberto Heras was headed for his bathroom. "He sat in a boiling tub for about a half-hour ... still shivering," reported roommate Tyler Hamilton. The only time that Hamilton himself could remember being colder was racing in a blizzard at the 1999 Flèche Wallonne. That was Belgium. *This* was southern Arizona....

It seemed like a great idea when the U.S. Postal Service team management chose Tucson, with its 360 days a year of sunshine, for its main U.S. get-together and sponsor weekend in January 2001. Certainly a better choice than California, where, 12 months earlier, winter storms whipped in from the Pacific to make Postal's coastal retreat near San Luis Obispo a very soggy affair. But when the 100-plus representatives from the team's two dozen sponsors showed up on January 12 at La Paloma, sitting high on a hillside overlooking Tucson, instead of seeing a backdrop of sun-streaked peaks beyond the hotel's

7

palm-fringed pools, they saw, through a shroud of sheeting rain, snow dusting the jagged outline of the Santa Catalina Mountains.

For the team, the bad weather turned what should have been a long, pleasant weekend of gentle riding, schmoozing with sponsors, posing for photos and getting to know their other 20 teammates, into a more character-building experience. The serious training would happen at the squad's Spanish camp later in the month, but this was a nice dose of reality for Postal's new-look, bigger-budget formation.

Great things were expected in this new season from newcomers like 2000 Vuelta a España winner Heras; his ex-Kelme teammate José Luis (a.k.a. Chechu) Rubiera; and the talented Colombian rider Victor Hugo Peña. On the debit side, Postal's road captain Frankie Andreu had retired and climber Kevin Livingston had transferred to the Telekom squad of Armstrong's main Tour de France rival, Jan Ullrich.

Livingston's defection definitely shocked Armstrong. "I think it's like Colin Powell going to [work for] Communist China," he bluntly stated during an interview at the hotel. "It was very hard to believe. It wasn't devastating—because I think from a team standpoint we're obviously gonna be very good—but from a friendship standpoint, I was disappointed.

"I still care for Kevin a lot—I don't talk to him very much—but ... I don't understand those actions. I think everybody understood the first part [accepting an offer to lead the Linda McCartney team—which didn't work out]; I don't think *anybody* can understand the second part [joining Telekom]. What he left behind here was a winning team, great friends—not just me. Tyler, George [Hincapie], *everybody* here.... That's odd."

When asked if he would have taken Livingston back after the McCartney misstep, Armstrong replied emphatically: "In a heartbeat ... absolutely."

Despite his disappointment, Armstrong said he was confident that even with Livingston's help and the Telekom team's "Operation Yellow Jersey" program, Ullrich wouldn't beat him at the 2001 Tour.

"If he does it just right, he'll be hard to beat," conceded the Texan. "But I know that I don't have to ride any faster than I've already ridden—[to] climb at my speed and to time trial at my speed will always be enough. That's not to say that I won't crash, I won't be sick, I won't have whatever problems....

"I think that by Ullrich getting back to his best form of whenever that was—I personally think his best form was in 1996—is not good enough. Getting to his '97 form is not good enough. Not '98."

Armstrong argued that Telekom could publicize its Tour-winning operation as much as it liked, but he and his Postal squad would quietly get on with what they'd been doing so successfully for the past two years: "Everybody knows our ambition. We don't need to talk about it. It is what it is, and we want to win the Tour for the third time...."

To reach that goal, Postal had what was potentially the strongest lineup for a Tour since Eddy Merckx and his Faema team ruled the roads of France 30 years before. "We're always trying to get good riders," Armstrong explained, "but now we're in a position, since the budget is stronger, that we can get [those] riders."

Indeed, winning two Tours de France had done wonders for the team—and its budget. In its sixth year as the title sponsor, the U.S. Postal Service had increased its annual expenditure on the American squad to an estimated $4.5 million, which was 60 percent of the team's budget. The major co-sponsors were Thomas Weisel Partners, Visa, Yahoo!, Trek, Nike and, now for 2001, Interwoven Software—which added about a further $3 million, for an estimated $7.5 million total.

Team leader Armstrong then gave a quick run-down of the team's exciting acquisitions. Heras is "the next great hope in cycling. A great climber, a good kid. Seems like he has plenty of room to improve and grow even from there—especially for the big tours with his time trialing, which we've already worked on. The wind tunnel will tell you he's lost already [two] minutes on one time trial ... with equipment, helmets, position."

Then there was Rubiera, whom Postal contacted after the Spaniard's great Giro d'Italia, through his agent Tony Rominger. "He can climb well, can time trial well, he's a team guy," Armstrong said. "He's also a very intelligent guy.... After cycling's done, this is just a small part of his life, which is a very cool thing."

And Peña? "He also had a great Giro, won the time trial there." Elaborating, the Tour champion continued, "The good thing about Chechu [Rubiera] and Vic [Peña] is they can both really time trial and climb ... but I think the base of me, Roberto, Chechu, Vic and Tyler is a pretty good start."

Building on that start, Postal could look to balance its Tour team with riders like Viatcheslav Ekimov, George Hincapie, Steffen Kjaergaard, Benoît Joachim and newcomer Matt White. Regarding White, Armstrong said, "I've seen what he can do. And he's so committed to the Tour de France. That's why he came here ... but I don't want to name the team now, because that's not fair. Things happen."

If having such powerful teammates weren't enough, Armstrong said he was having no trouble getting motivated for a third Tour win. "This year I have a lot of motivation," he said, "Oh yeah. I'll always find something.... Last year, it was Bartoli, and Vandenbroucke, a lot of guys that discredited my victory. The first year was normal enough—I was hungry to come back, and hungry to prove I could do it. The next year, everybody said, 'It's not really a victory because I wasn't there.' Pantani said that, Ullrich said that, Bartoli [and] all these people said that; so that's plenty of motivation. But that's not really deep, deep motivation. That doesn't get you through January, February, March, April.... That's just, sort-of *French* stuff."

So would his motivation for the 2001 Tour come from the judicial inquiry being made by a Paris judge into Postal's possible use of "doping substances" at the 2000 Tour?

Armstrong's observation on the continued attempts by the French media (and judicial system) to discredit him was: "The best thing we could do to relieve the pressure ... is to *lose* the Tour de France. The more we win ... if we win again ... we saw it happen in '99. We're seeing it happen now. It will always happen to us, to cycling, to sport. This is the era that we live in. Everything is questioned.

"Like Cédric [Vasseur] told me yesterday.... I said, 'What's the deal here?' 'Lance, you don't understand,' he said. 'People in France don't like the winner. *They* like the guy who's second.'

"So, it's tough. The only thing I'll say about that *affaire* is that we have nothing to hide. And we're very excited that they are testing the samples. End of story. And I think when the results come back, it will truly be the end of the story—the end of *this* story, the end of this chapter."

Armstrong added that neither he nor the U.S. Postal Service team had been officially informed of the French investigation, or the judge's proposal to test for EPO in the team's urine samples that were frozen after the 2000 Tour. "The only thing we know is what we read [in the media]. It's unbelievable," he said. "[When] they test the samples, hallelujah! I wanted them to test the samples after the Tour de France. The only disclaimer I'll say is that they need to do an incredible and professional job.... But I'm confident they'll do it right."

End of one story, maybe. Still, as Armstrong noted, "It will always be something. Always. And that's unfortunate."

Did the continued questioning of his success and the drugs allegations bug Armstrong? "In '99 ... when this stuff first hit, it bothered me," he stated, "just because there'd been a lot of inaccurate things written and reported....

"This [current] stuff is absurd. And the tactics used were cheap. I mean ... come on. But it's been stressful, a very stressful winter. There's been ... issues like that, issues like Kevin's ... very stressful issues."

Then, briefly referring to his fight with cancer, Armstrong added, "Obviously, that's why I'm lucky, because I've had to deal with winters that were a helluva lot more stressful."

As a result of the continued negativity emanating from France, allegations were made in the winter that the Postal team was going to boycott French races, and that Armstrong was going to move his European home from Nice, in the South of France, to somewhere in Spain. Any truth to those rumors?

Regarding his Nice home, the relaxed, fit-looking Texan said, with a chuckle, "We're keeping our house in Nice. It's a beautiful house. My wife loves it. And ... I love that home. That home and that community and that city has done a lot for my career ... so to sell it and to move away completely is not an option."

But what about the schedule of races that the team had chosen? The Tour of Switzerland instead of the Dauphiné Libéré; Tirreno-Adriatico instead of Paris-Nice. Wasn't that proof of boycotting France?

Not so, according to Armstrong.

"For me, the biggest reason for doing the Tour of Switzerland is the uphill time trial [similar to the one scheduled in the 2001 Tour de France]," he said. "I did one two years ago in Dauphiné. I did one, it seems like a decade ago, in the Tour of Switzerland. I just have no experience of that ... and the Dauphiné doesn't have it [this year].

"There's a lot of reasons—there's the uphill time trial ... it's something new ... it's a big, big race, probably the fourth biggest in the world ... we can go there and try to win the race with one of our guys, something we've never done ... Tony Rominger is now part of the (race) management; he's a very good friend of mine. It's a good way to support him.

"So many people want to make something of—'Well, there's no French races' or 'They're skipping France'—but that's not the case."

This was confirmed by Postal directeur sportif Johan Bruyneel, who said, "Everybody says now you're hiding from France, but it's not true. In the month of May, we're riding there, at Dunkirk and the Tour de l'Oise."

Armstrong added, "I had scheduled Paris-Nice last year, and got sick, didn't do it. But it's not a statement. If you really wanted to avoid [France], then you would just try and avoid the Tour de France. Which is obviously not an option."

Besides the Tour, the U.S. Postal Service had other clear goals. Bruyneel said, "I think this year is the year that George [Hincapie] has to explode. I'm sure he has the potential of winning a World Cup classic—Milan-San Remo, Tour of Flanders, Paris-Roubaix, Amstel Gold Race. And I think we have a strong team for those classics; that's the main objective for the beginning of the season. Then, everything is focused on the Tour de France and, after the Tour, with Roberto Heras as team leader, the Vuelta a España. And, throughout the year, we want to be more represented at the American races … and having Frankie Andreu as U.S. director is a big step forward, I think."

Indeed, Postal was stepping forward on several fronts, and looked as though it was headed toward its most successful season to date. The Tucson get-together was a first step, particularly that cold, wet ride around the Saguaro National Monument. Bigger challenges awaited, but after weathering that winter storm together, Armstrong and his 20 teammates would be ready for anything that came their way as the year unfolded.

Heading Toward July

BESIDES THE HEAVY WORKLOAD OF TRAINING FROM
JANUARY TO JUNE, LANCE ARMSTRONG HAD A
FOCUSED RACING PROGRAM THAT ACCELERATED
AS THE TOUR DE FRANCE GOT CLOSER

Despite the enormous publicity their battles engender in July, Tour de France contenders rarely compete against each other in the months beforehand. That's why certain races have greater bearing in giving them a feel for their upcoming opponents prior to the big confrontation in July. For Lance Armstrong, some of the most important build-up races in 2001 were the French classic Paris-Camembert in April, the Spanish stage race Bicicleta Vasca in May, and the one-day Classique des Alpes and 10-day Tour of Switzerland in June.

Paris-Camembert

At Paris-Camembert on April 17, Armstrong and his U.S. Postal Service team lined up with riders like Bobby Julich of Crédit Agricole, British standout David Millar of Cofidis and Frenchman Didier Rous of Bonjour. They all came to the start line with something to prove.

Armstrong was nearing the end of his phase-one race preparations for the Tour, and he wanted to improve on the second place he took at Paris-Camembert in 2000. "It's a beautiful race, and the hills at the end are pretty demanding," said a smiling Armstrong as he left his hotel at Meulan, 50km west of Paris, on the morning of the race.

Julich, too, was after a win. "This and Liège-Bastogne-Liège on Sunday are my big aims for the spring," he said before the start at Mantes-en-Yvelines. "Then I go back home [to Reno, Nevada] for four weeks of training at altitude prior to my Tour build-up." And Millar—who defeated Armstrong in the 2000 Tour's opening time trial and held the yellow jersey for three days—was eager to continue the winning streak he had started the previous week with two stage wins and the overall victory at the Circuit de la Sarthe.

This was the 62nd edition of Paris-Camembert, a 208km race that heads west from Mantes into the farm country and rolling hills of Normandy. It's a bit like an early stage of the Tour, mainly flat until the final 80km, which includes seven climbs around the rural town of Vimoutiers. The final 20km features the two most difficult hills on a loop of narrow back roads in the Camembert cheese countryside. There's the 16-percent Côte du Moulin Neuf, and then the 17-percent Mur des Champeaux, 10km from the finish. As the race approached this difficult finale, a 40-second lead was held by two counterattackers of an early 17-man break: Frenchmen Stéphane Bergès of AG2R and Jérôme Bernard of Jean Delatour. It was time for Armstrong to step up the pace.

"Lance was feeling good," his Postal teammate Levi Leipheimer later reported, "so with about 25km to go, he told me to start riding on the climb before the last circuit. So I started setting tempo, and then the rest of the guys came up and we really started to dial it up...."

It was like seeing a mini-rehearsal of the team for the Tour, the sort of effort that prepares the riders for their July dateline. In fact, Leipheimer, Tyler Hamilton, Cédric Vasseur, Steffen Kjaergaard and Jamie Burrow rode so hard at the head of the pack that they split the peloton and brought back the breakaway, just as the second-to-last climb began.

"The team was at the front at the bottom," Armstrong said, "and then Cédric [Vasseur] did a great job. He was flying up the first steep hill—he basically made the selection to 15 guys. I could hardly come around him."

Armstrong *did* come around, and his surge saw him cross the summit in first ahead of Frenchmen Laurent Brochard of Jean Delatour; Bonjour's Rous, the race's defending champion; and Team Fakta's on-form Aussie, Scott Sunderland. Also in the split were both Julich and Millar, along with Mercury-Viatel's Italian Fabrizio Guidi—who was racing for the first time since sustaining a concussion when he crashed into a truck at the Three Days of De Panne two weeks earlier.

At the day's toughest climb, the Champeaux "wall," Millar, the 24-year-old Cofidis rider from Scotland who was starting to fulfill his huge talent, decided to make his move. "I attacked at the bottom, 'cause I came from farther back," Millar said. "Then I got caught halfway up and lost ground at the top."

The first to come past Millar was Brochard, with Guidi glued to his wheel. But his lack of racing caused the Italian to cramp, allowing Brochard to take a 50-meter solo lead, while Guidi dropped back to a chase group led by Armstrong. Just behind the action was Sunderland, who had crashed on the steep descent from the Moulin Neuf climb and was chasing on his own. "I picked up David Millar with about 8km to go," said the 34-year-old Aussie, "and we both came back [to the group] together."

By now there was a 13-strong chase group on the mainly descending roads 100 meters behind Brochard. The former world champion, who comes from nearby Le Mans, had previously finished fourth, third and second in Paris-Camembert. This time the 32-year-old Frenchman—aided by teammates Patrice Halgand and Stéphane Goubert who were defending his slim lead in the chase group—hung on for first. And the two men who caught back, Millar and Sunderland, dominated the uphill sprint to take second and third respectively, nine seconds behind Brochard, while Guidi cramped again, taking fourth.

As for the top two Americans, Julich, pleased with his form, was 11th, and Armstrong 13th. Afterward, Armstrong answered a few questions before being whisked away for a massage and a flight that evening to Spain, where he started the Tour of Aragon the next day. That five-day race would be followed by his only spring classic, the April 28 Amstel Gold Race, where he finished second, before devoting the month of May to his trademark training camp rides over the key stages of the Tour de France.

And Millar? He said he was happy with his second place, having rediscovered the sprint he used to win many races as an amateur. His Tour prep would include the early-May Four Days of Dunkirk, June's Dauphiné Libéré and, like Julich, he would head the following day to Belgium for Liège-Bastogne-Liège. The next time these two and Armstrong would all be racing against each other would be at the Tour de France prologue in Dunkirk on July 7.

Bicicleta Vasca

With the Tour de France only a month away, many of its likely contenders—including defending champion Lance Armstrong—chose the tough little Bicicleta Vasca, May 30–

June 3, to test their form. And one of the American's top rivals, local Basque star Joseba Beloki of ONCE-Eroski, almost pulled off a sensational final victory. But Beloki's strong attack on the last two climbs of the final stage came up short, leaving iBanesto.com's Juan Carlos Dominguez the overall winner.

It was the third major win of the year for Dominguez, who earlier took the Tour of Aragon and Tour of Asturias. He had clearly been the signing of the season. After a winless 2000, the 30-year-old Spaniard had sprung back to his form of 1999, when he had six wins, including the overall titles at Aragon, Asturias and the Tour of Rioja.

Another man on the comeback trail, ONCE's Mikel Zarrabeitia, won the Bicicleta Vasca's opening stage. He did so by using his local knowledge in a late attack at Urnieta, to finish seven seconds clear of the remnants of a seven-man break. Zarrabeitia kept the leader's blue jersey after the next stage, which was won by second-year pro Jorge Capitan of Colchon Relax—the lone survivor of a three-man break that went just 4km into the 158km stage. Remarkably, Capitan's younger teammate Juan Antonio Flecha pulled off a similar move on stage 3. After an all-day effort, the 23-year-old Spaniard's only company was Belgian Dave Bruylandts of Domo-Farm Frites and Euskaltel-Euskadi's Roberto Laiseka. They were a couple of minutes clear starting the difficult climb to the finish at the Virgen de Oro Sanctuary, where Flecha won by 17 seconds from Bruylandts and Laiseka. Beloki showed his form by climbing strongly to finish only two seconds later, just ahead of ONCE teammate Igor Gonzalez de Galdeano and Dominguez. Zarrabeitia was another five seconds back, and he lost the race lead to Flecha.

Some of the U.S. Postal riders had come straight from a road camp in the Pyrénées— including José Rubiera, who finished at Virgen de Oro with Zarrabeitia in eighth place (at 24 seconds), Tyler Hamilton 16th (at 32 seconds), Armstrong 51st (at 2:18) and Roberto Heras 69th (at 3:27).

After three stages in the Basque mountains, the sprinters were glad of a short respite on the morning of day 4. Italian Alessandro Petacchi of Fassa Bortolo easily took the 50-man sprint in Abadino, ahead of Sweden's Glenn Magnusson of Domo. Interestingly, fifth over the line was Cofidis's Millar—who would be center-stage in the afternoon's 21.2km time trial, taking the stage at almost 49 kph. The winner of the 2000 Tour's opening time trial raced almost five seconds faster than runner-up Dominguez, who took over the race lead, while Armstrong showed that he, too, was not far from his July peak by going fourth

16

fastest, 15 seconds behind Millar. And just behind in fifth was the Texan's training partner Hamilton, with Mercury-Viatel's Floyd Landis in sixth.

After starting the last stage in fifth, 25 seconds down on Dominguez, Beloki attacked on the second-to-last climb to join a small breakaway. It was from this group that Italian Fassa Bortolo rider Ivan Basso escaped on the descent and gained 1:30 before the final ascent, while Beloki dropped the others to take second on the stage, 1:20 down on Basso. Dominguez fought back to lead in a seven-man chase group at 1:42—which was just enough for him to beat Beloki by three seconds overall!

Mercury's Pavel Tonkov rode solidly for fifth overall, but with his team not riding the Tour, the Russian star would have to focus his attention on the Dauphiné Libéré. For Armstrong, it was a satisfactory workout that yielded a solid 20th overall, while Hamilton hung tough in the final stage to take eighth overall. Good signs heading into June and the Postals' final prep for the Tour.

Classique des Alpes

There were 25km left in the 175km Classique des Alpes on June 9, and the recent Midi Libre winner Iban Mayo appeared to be cruising to an easy victory in this mountainous Cat. 1 French classic. The 23-year-old Basque phenom had a huge solo lead of four minutes over a small group of chasers, and all that remained was a 7km climb up the Col du Granier, followed by a twisting 16km descent and a short run-in to the finish in Chambéry.

Piece of cake, right? Well, not exactly.

First, low cloud and rain showers were adding to the difficulties of the race's seven climbs and descents in the thick pine forests of the Chartreuse massif. Second, Mayo had already been on the attack for more than two hours, first with Kelme-Costa Blanca's Oscar Sevilla over climbs No's. 3, 4 and 5, then alone over No. 6, the Col du Cucheron. And third, Mayo had just one Euskaltel-Euskadi teammate—Venezuelan Unai Etxebarria—trying to control a chase group that was led by U.S. Postal's Tour de France champion Lance Armstrong and Mercury-Viatel's former Giro winner Pavel Tonkov.

The southern approach to the Granier is nowhere near as tough as the eastern side that the race had tackled three hours earlier, but Mayo's four-minute cushion soon started to tumble after Tonkov attacked. Armstrong went after the Russian, accelerated past him and set off on a solo pursuit of the leader.

17

"I wanted to test myself," Armstrong said later. Some test!

In the last 5km of the Granier climb, Armstrong took 2:30 out of Mayo, to cross the mist-shrouded 3720-foot summit 90 seconds down, and a half-minute ahead of Tonkov. The Texan's chase continued on the technical, tree-lined descent of the Granier's northern slopes, and the gap dropped to a minute....

"I didn't know Armstrong was on his own chasing me," said Mayo. "I thought it was still a group. It was cold [and] I didn't know the roads very well. It was hard."

These were just the sort of challenging conditions that can sometimes descend on Tour mountain stages. But this wasn't the Tour, and with the *grande boucle* still four weeks away, Armstrong would have been foolish to totally hang it out on that treacherous descent. So he backed off a little, Tonkov caught him, and the Postal leader finally took the two-up sprint for second place, 1:12 behind a delighted Mayo.

Besides being a great workout for Armstrong, the 11th edition of this alpine classic—organized by the Tour de France people—was also a challenging test for Postal's back-up riders, particularly finishers Hamilton, Victor Hugo Peña and Kjaergaard.

Hamilton and Kjaergaard, along with Mercury's Landis, were in the race's first big move. They joined a group headed by two-time race winner Laurent Jalabert (CSC-Tiscali), which then bridged a 30-second gap to Sevilla and iBanesto.com's Ramon Gonzalez Arrieta, descending from the opening peak, the Col des Près. And by 57km, at the foot of the first Granier ascent—the hardest uphill of the day—this group was two minutes clear of the still-100-strong peloton.

With two teammates ahead, Armstrong decided to test his climbing legs for the first time, and he easily bridged to the leaders on the 12km climb. The lead group over the summit was 13-strong, including the three Postals, Jalabert, Landis, Mayo, Etxebarria and iBanesto.com's Francisco Mancebo, the best young rider at the 2001 Tour de France.

This break was soon joined by four others and took a one-minute lead over 18 chasers led by Tonkov and Crédit Agricole's Julich—who was racing for the first time after his four-week training stint back home in Nevada. All these riders eventually regrouped on the long descent after the Col du Grapillon and Col des Egaux, where Mayo and Sevilla made their escape.

The two breakaways had more than a five-minute gap before the Col du Cucheron, where Armstrong sent his Postal guys into full Tour mode, pounding away up the stair-step

12km climb. At the same time, Mayo rode away from Sevilla, while Armstrong, Tonkov, Mancebo, Etxebarria, Benoît Salmon of AG2R and Felix Cardenas of Kelme dropped the rest of the rain-sodden group.

Now it was time for the dramatic finale, a finale that confirmed the talent and determination of Euskaltel's Mayo, the ascendant form of Armstrong a week before starting the Tour of Switzerland, and the good form of Mercury's Tonkov a day before heading into the Dauphiné-Libéré.

The fourth consecutive Spanish winner of the Classique wouldn't make his Tour debut in 2001, but when Mayo does graduate to the Tour, he's bound to remember this breakthrough win in the Alps. Especially since the man he beat was Lance Armstrong.

Tour of Switzerland

If you had dropped in any day at the 65th Tour of Switzerland in late June, you could have been fooled into thinking that either this was the Tour de France, or Lance Armstrong and his U.S. Postal Service squad were conducting another road camp to perfect their stage-racing performance. Why so? Well, Armstrong started out by winning the opening time trial in convincing fashion, and even after losing the race leader's golden jersey on stage 3, the Texan and his team continued to ride the event as if they were in the driver's seat, always staying at the front to make sure that no dangerous rivals would take time out of them before the vital uphill time trial three days from the end of the 10-day race.

That Armstrong's form was going to be hot in Switzerland was foretold by his second-place finish at his previous race, the single-day Classique des Alpes. Ten days later, after some more training, this time in the Swiss Alps, the Postal leader was ready to test himself in the Tour of Switzerland's opening 7.9km time trial at the Europapark theme park in Rust, Germany. On a completely flat course that featured 12 sharp turns and a similar number of sweeping curves, Armstrong demonstrated just how to ride a prologue-type time trial.

As usual, Postal team director Johan Bruyneel first obtained kilometer splits for Tyler Hamilton, who set what was the initial fastest time of 9:49—later improved by a split-second by CSC's French star Laurent Jalabert, before Armstrong came to the line.

"After one kilometer, Johan shouted to Lance that he was already five seconds down on Tyler," reported Armstrong's coach Chris Carmichael, "so he really had to go hard."

Not only did the Texan make up his five-second deficit, he went on to win the stage by an impressive five seconds over Jalabert, with Hamilton in third.

"This win shows that I have good condition, because you had to accelerate so much on this course," said Armstrong, who added, "I'm also happy that my team is on form." So much on form that besides taking first and third, Postal placed Viatcheslav Ekimov in fourth, George Hincapie in seventh and Steffen Kjaergaard in 13th.

Armstrong retained his lead on the opening road stage to Basel, taken in a mass sprint by Erik Zabel of Telekom, his 15th win of the season. The next day, Tour of Flanders winner Gianluca Bortolami of Tacconi-Vini Caldirola and Austrian Peter Wrolich of Gerolsteiner emerged 92km from the finish in Baar, after first escaping in a group led by Jalabert and shadowed by Hamilton. Once that danger passed, Postal was content to ride a steady tempo, allowing Bortolami and Wrolich to gain over nine minutes. The gap was still 2:53 at the end, where Bortolami led out the sprint, won the stage and took over the race leadership.

No climber, Bortolami wasn't expected to hang onto the golden jersey on the stage 4 summit finish to Wildhaus. This 10km climb out of the Rhine Valley, near Switzerland's border with Austria, provided an insight into how Armstrong would tackle the later mountain stages in the Swiss Alps.

After the Postal team's tempo had condemned a long breakaway by Aussie Robbie McEwen of Domo-Farm Frites and local rider Christian Heule of Post Swiss, Hincapie led the pack up the first part of the finishing climb. A 19-strong group resulted at the front, with Postal's Armstrong and Hamilton riding steadily near the back, content to watch the developing attacks. In the end, recent Tour of Germany winner Alex Vinokourov of Telekom got away with Giro d'Italia winner Gilberto Simoni; Vinokourov jumped Simoni in the flattish final kilometer to claim the stage win; and a dynamic Jalabert left the chase group and almost caught Simoni on the line.

Armstrong rolled home with the group 12 seconds down in 11th place, while Hamilton was another four seconds back in 19th. As for the surprising Bortolami, he jumped away from the main pack to take 32nd, 2:21 down, and save his jersey by 14 seconds over Vinokourov.

There would be no chance of such heroics on stage 5, the longest and toughest of the race, which crossed the Cat. 3 Flims and Cat. 1 Oberalp Pass before tackling two climbs of the imposing *hors-categorie* St. Gotthard Pass. The finish was at the 6860-foot mountain road's summit, after ascending the infamous 38 switchbacks of the mainly cobblestoned old road up the side of the Val Tremola.

For the fifth day running, hot sunshine and clear blue skies greeted the race, and within 27km a group of seven riders sped clear, heading up the deep valley of the Rhine. It was the start of a five-plus-hour adventure for Fassa Bortolo's Russian veteran Dmitri Konyshev, who led the break over the first two climbs, then left them in his wake on the St. Gotthard's northern approach.

By the summit, with 29km to go, Konyshev, 35, was alone and retained more than six minutes of what had been a maximum 12-minute lead. Again, Postal did much of the chasing, assisted on this first St. Gotthard climb by Rabobank's Swiss brothers, Beat and Markus Zberg.

After a fearless descent, Konyshev tackled the near-8-percent, 13km climb to the finish with 6:30 to spare. That gap was less then five minutes when he entered the final 5km, as the Russian faltered on a difficult 17-percent stretch. Behind him, a chase group of five eventually emerged: Lampre's Simoni and Juan Manuel Garate, Fassa Bortolo's Wladimir Belli, Mapei's Manuel Beltran … and Armstrong. Again, the American didn't push himself, but kept his steady rhythm as Simoni, Belli and Beltran pulled clear with 3km to go.

Konyshev held on to win the stage, while 1:57 later Simoni outsped Belli for second place. But it was Belli who took the race lead by one second over his Italian rival. Fourth and fifth places went to Spaniards Beltran and Garate, while Armstrong was caught by Beat Zberg, and they crossed the line together, 37 seconds behind Simoni. A surprising Jalabert, not known for his climbing ability above the 2000-meter contour, hung in to take eighth place, only 1:05 behind Armstrong.

The giant stage had done its damage, but not broken the peloton's spirit, as the next day's hilly loop course in sunny Mendrisio, close to the Italian border, saw the race's fastest stage. Jalabert was again lively, breaking away on the final climb with Vinokourov and the promising Swiss rider, Alexander Moos of Phonak; but this trio was caught on the run-in by Russian champion Sergei Ivanov, who sprinted home to give Fassa Bortolo its second consecutive stage win.

Vinokourov and Jalabert moved up to seventh and eighth overall, respectively 1:09 and 1:19 behind leader Belli—but the dangerman was still Armstrong, lurking in third, just 25 seconds back.

Stage 7 on June 25 went over the 8130-foot Nufenen Pass—higher than any of the climbs the riders would face in the Tour de France. Midway through the 156km stage, and halfway up the long, long climb, solo breakaway Stefano Garzelli of Mapei-Quick Step was 15:24 ahead of the main group: a hefty lead for a former winner of this race and the Giro d'Italia. But the shaven-headed Italian climber had been allowed his freedom because he was lying only 39th overall, 19:29 behind race leader Belli.

On the steady 5.5-percent grade of the Nufenen, Belli was riding near the head of the pack with a couple of teammates, and Armstrong was also there with all seven of *his* teammates. In fact, by the stage finish, only one Postal rider, Vasseur, wouldn't be in the front group with their team leader. Postal's strength cut Garzelli's winning margin to less than eight minutes; but, more importantly, the U.S. squad was able to close down a dangerous counterattack by Austrian Georg Totschnig. Formerly with Telekom, now with Division II Gerolsteiner, Totschnig made up the two minutes he was behind Belli and then some, before Postal went into action, riding in an echelon against a head wind in the upper valley of the Rhône.

His team's collective effort was just the reassurance Armstrong needed before the next day's vital uphill time trial from Sion to Crans-Montana—a 25.1km stage that was a near mirror of the Tour de France's upcoming test to Chamrousse. The Texan didn't hold anything back in the time trial, using it as a dress rehearsal for the Tour. He beat race leader Belli by almost two minutes, while second-place Simoni, Lampre's Giro winner, was a massive 1:26 slower than the Texan. Just as encouraging for Postal was Hamilton's third place in the stage, just a second slower than Simoni, a performance that confirmed Hamilton's good form approaching July.

With a comfortable overall lead heading into the final two stages, Armstrong and his team simply had to control the tempo and avert unexpected attacks—just as they had done in the previous two editions of the Tour de France. They did their job well, according to Postal team director Johan Bruyneel, who said, "Having to defend the jersey the last two days was good training for the Tour de France. We had not taken on that type of responsibility in any other race yet this year."

The team's only concern was raised by a thunderstorm making the roads slick when the race crossed the last significant climb, the Col des Mosses, on stage 9. But it soon blew through. Team Phonak's Bert Grabsch (younger brother of Telekom's Ralf Grabsch) started a solo break here that took him nine minutes clear at one point. He was caught on the run-in to Lausanne, where Telekom's Erik Zabel outsprinted Gerolsteiner's Saulius Ruskys and Domo-Farm Frites' Robbie McEwen, to take his second stage of the race, and his 16th of the year.

The final day, sunny like most of the previous nine, saw a bold attempt by 2000 race winner Oskar Camenzind of Lampre-Daikin to become the first Swiss stage winner of the race. The former world champion succeeded in getting into a five-man break at half distance on the out-and-back loop from Lausanne. Camenzind was the best-placed of the five on G.C., but more than eight minutes down on Armstrong. At the finish, the gap was down to 2:56 when Camenzind achieved his goal by outspeeding Emmanuel Magnien of La Française des Jeux and Christian Poos of Post Swiss.

So Armstrong took his first prestigious victory of the year ... and it looked as though more would follow at the Tour.

In Pursuit of the Three-Peat

WINNING A THIRD CONSECUTIVE TOUR IS NO SHOO-IN,
BUT GOING INTO THE 2001 EDITION ARMSTRONG AND
HIS POSTAL TEAM WERE CONFIDENT OF SUCCESS

Until 2001, only four men in the 98-year history of the Tour de France had managed to win the race three times in succession: Frenchmen Louison Bobet (1953-55), Jacques Anquetil (1961-63), Belgian Eddy Merckx (1969-71) and Spaniard Miguel Induráin (1991-93). Lance Armstrong was about to attempt to join those four greats of the past.

Of the four, you would have thought that the insatiable Merckx would have had the easiest passage to his three in a row. He had won the Tour in 1969 and 1970 by huge margins of 17:54 and 12:41 respectively. Nonetheless, his 1971 ride proved to be the least glorious of his eventual five Tour victories. After wearing the yellow jersey for the first 10 days, Merckx developed back pains and was in trouble in the Alps, losing the lead by a few seconds on the stage to Grenoble. Then, on the Côte de Laffrey, a modest opening climb of the short, 133km stage from Grenoble to Orcières-Merlette, Merckx was unable to follow an attack by his main rivals. He did recover, and hauled in all except two of them, but in taking third place on the stage he lost 8:42 to Spaniard Luis Ocaña, who took over the yellow jersey.

Merckx fought back, yet only retrieved the race lead after Ocaña crashed in a thunderstorm descending the Col de Menté in the Pyrénées. Ocaña slid out on a slick switchback and another rider landed on him, knocking him semi-conscious and displacing several vertebrae. His Tour was over.

Merckx went on to take that third consecutive triumph in Paris, but his troubles that year demonstrate that even the winningest champion can expect to have problems in a race as long, demanding and unpredictable as the Tour. "There are too many factors you have to take into account that you have no control over," Merckx stated. "The most important factor you can keep in your own hands is yourself. I always placed the greatest emphasis on that."

Merckx taught that lesson to his good friend Armstrong, who at the 2000 Tour also experienced a bad patch in the Alps. While not as serious as the back pains that Merckx had in 1971, the American's hunger bonk on the Joux-Plane climb emphasized how fragile even a several-minute lead can seem when a rider is in trouble. Armstrong was able to recover and went on to beat Jan Ullrich by 6:02, compared with the 7:37 with which he overcame Alex Zülle in 1999. Now, what would this 2001 Tour produce?

If results and preparation going into the race meant anything, then Armstrong could win the 2001 Tour by a Merckx-like 10 minutes or more. The U.S. Postal Service team leader knew what he had to do to win; his teammates were ready to ride hard all day, every day to keep him as fresh as possible for the serious climbing efforts he'd have to make in the Tour's five consecutive summit finishes (L'Alpe d'Huez, Chamrousse, Plateau de Bonascre, Pla d'Adet and Luz-Ardiden); and his preparation had been as near perfect as could be.

Armstrong is such a fine-tuned athlete that he and his coach Chris Carmichael have almost daily conversations on the minutiae of the rider's physical state. Carmichael relayed a typical chat after Armstrong came in 11th on the first mountaintop finish at June's Tour of Switzerland. "Lance said he was not feeling good today," he said. "But he was perfect in the time trial the first day, so I keep second-guessing. Have we done too much time-trial training and not enough climbing? Or is it too much climbing and not enough time trialing?"

This almost-obsessive questioning was just one part of the grand plan that kept Armstrong totally focused on his Tour preparations. In fact, Carmichael, Armstrong and the Postal team's Belgian team director, Johan Bruyneel, treated their annual assault on the Tour as a year-long, almost military-like campaign.

Like any successful campaign, it first needed a substantial investment of both money and time. Armstrong received those commitments from the U.S. Postal Service team and, in particular, its management company, Tailwind Sports. Tailwind is the latest incarnation of the group set up by San Francisco financial magnate Thom Weisel and managed by 1984 Olympic gold medalist Mark Gorski. It was with the resources of Tailwind and sponsors, which collectively provided some 40 percent of the team's $7.5 million budget, that Armstrong and Bruyneel were able to strengthen the Postal team for 2001.

Planning for the 88th Tour de France actually started at the race a year earlier, as the team analyzed its strengths and needs. Among the factors that needed to be addressed were the team's faltering performance toward the end of the team time-trial stage; Armstrong's "isolation" on the final two climbs of the tough mountain stage to Hautacam; and his lack of immediate climbing support when hunger knock put his yellow jersey in danger on the Col de Joux-Plane in the Alps.

Even while the 2000 Tour was still on, Bruyneel contacted Australian rider Matt White, who was then one of the top team riders for Vini Caldirola's world No. 1 Francesco Casagrande. White later signed for Postal and was targeted for Postal's Tour team. Early contact was also made with two riders on Spanish teams: Colombian Victor Hugo Peña of Vitalicio Seguros, a team about to lose its sponsor; and José Luis Rubiera of Kelme. Both of these seasoned pros had won time trials and shown their strength as climbers, and they were signed to add power to Postal's team time trial squad and ride hard for Armstrong in the mountains.

The fourth new rider that Bruyneel contacted—and eventually signed after buying out his contract with Kelme—was an even bigger coup: Spain's new pin-up boy, Roberto Heras. Heras, one of the world's elite climbers, had won the 2000 Vuelta a España after coming in fifth at the Tour de France (ironically, he was the rider who was attacking on the Joux-Plane climb when Armstrong fell back).

With these reinforcements, Postal had taken care of any potential weaknesses in Armstrong's team for the 2001 Tour. The next part of the squad's Tour campaign involved bringing together the team's old and new players at winter training camps in Texas, Arizona and southern Spain, to build camaraderie and plan the new season. Other teams do similar things, but none of Armstrong's expected rivals at this Tour—Telekom's Jan Ullrich and ONCE's Joseba Beloki—had the same capacity to focus their training and racing programs on reaching a peak for the three-week Tour. So while Armstrong raced occasionally through February, March and April, the other contenders had very different programs.

The Telekom team paid lip service to a "new" Ullrich, talking about an Operation Yellow Jersey, signing former Armstrong lieutenant Kevin Livingston, and sending their German phenomenon to South Africa at Christmas to prevent him from eating his mother's delicious cakes. It didn't work. Throughout the spring, Ullrich was struggling to lose weight and gain fitness in a variety of stage races in Spain. And while Armstrong was scouting the Tour's difficult stages in late May with his teammates Tyler Hamilton, Heras, Peña and Rubiera, Ullrich was still struggling at the three-week Giro d'Italia to gain the fitness he would need at the Tour.

The Giro was meant to be the major season goal for Casagrande, but a broken wrist on the first road stage sent him home to Tuscany. Prior to his Giro accident, Casagrande had shown ever-improving form that saw him play a major role in the Liège-Bastogne-Liège classic and win the five-day Giro del Trentino (including taking a stage with a mountaintop finish).

Casagrande's former teammate, White, had an interesting assessment of the Italian, who looked like he could be one of the biggest threats to Armstrong's winning a third consecutive Tour. "On his day, he's one of the best climbers, if not the best climber, in the world," White said about Casagrande. "But it could be to his detriment that he has such a passion to win. He's probably got 90-percent form for 90 percent of the season, whereas [Armstrong and Ullrich] can come to 100-percent form just when they need to."

Furthermore, Casagrande had not focused on the Tour de France since 1998. That year, he was the leader of the French team Cofidis, but he crashed out on the first mountain stage. So the last Tour that Casagrande finished was in 1997, when he was with Saeco. He came in sixth overall, despite not being Saeco's designated leader.

Now, as the leader of Fassa Bortolo, Casagrande was expected to have his team's full support. Since 1997, he had lost weight—he was now 132 pounds at 5-foot-7—to improve his climbing. But that gain came at the expense of his time-trialing capabilities ... and in this 2001 Tour de France, climbing and time trialing had equal emphasis, and would often come together.

The 8.2km course for the prologue time trial at Dunkirk on July 7 was completely flat, but sprinting out of its 10 or so turns and fighting the likely crosswinds on the seafront finish straightaway would demand the explosiveness and cadence that Armstrong had developed in his climbing. Then the 67km team time trial to Bar-le-Duc on July 12 was on a rolling course with a stiff 2km climb to the finish line. Again, flexibility and power would both be essential.

This Tour's most vital time trial, of course, would come on July 18. Its 32km course was almost all climbing, with a 5000 foot elevation change. This was steeper and longer than the Sion to Crans-Montana time trial that Armstrong won on June 26 in the Tour of Switzerland. There, he averaged 31.823 kph to beat Gilberto Simoni, Lampre-Daikin's Giro d'Italia winner, by 1:26.

The same day that Simoni and Armstrong were battling in the Swiss Alps, Casagrande was riding the difficult final stage of the Route du Sud in the Pyrénées, and took his first win since crashing out of the Giro. His long hours of training after rehabilitating a broken wrist had certainly paid off, as Casagrande needed power, stamina and climbing ability to win the Route du Sud stage atop the Plateau de Beille—which is a similar climb to the nearby Plateau de Bonascre mountaintop finish that the Tour riders would tackle on July 20.

Besides Casagrande, ONCE's Beloki was also busy racing in the countdown to the Tour. The young Spaniard won the Tour of Catalonia after winning the hilly third stage at Barcelona and the final one, a mountain time trial in Andorra.... Meanwhile, Ullrich was training, training, training. The German came out of the Giro in reasonable shape, but had failed to show himself in the mountain stages. So the second half of June saw him training with climber teammates Kevin Livingston, Andreas Klöden and Giuseppe Guerini in the French Alps—where he previewed L'Alpe d'Huez and the time-trial course to Chamrousse.

It looked like it would be quite a showdown for the Tour's yellow jersey. Armstrong was the big favorite, but he wouldn't need reminding of the pitfalls that can happen to even the greatest champions. The Chamrousse time trial would start in Grenoble—where Eddy Merckx's problems began in 1971. And later in the 2001 Tour, on July 21, the field would have to negotiate the potentially treacherous descent of the Col de Menté, where Ocaña fell those 30 years before. If Armstrong could survive similar pitfalls, then his hat-trick chance would still be alive....

Americans at the Tour

ONLY ONE AMERICAN TEAM,
BUT THERE WOULD STILL BE EIGHT
U.S. RIDERS AT THE TOUR'S DUNKIRK START LINE

There would be only one American team at the 2001 Tour de France, Lance Armstrong's U.S. Postal Service formation. The expected debut by Mercury-Viatel was thwarted in May by the Tour organizers' chauvinistic wild-card choice of two extra Division II French teams, as opposed to a second Division I team from the U.S. Despite that, there were still eight Americans on the start line in Dunkirk. Here is a quick look at each of them, with a review of their 2001 preparation and prospects.

LANCE ARMSTRONG

Age: 29
Height: 5 ft. 11 in. Weight: 165 lbs.
Hometown: Austin, Texas
Team: U.S. Postal Service
Number of Tours: 6

To say that Armstrong was a shoo-in to win a third straight Tour would minimize the opposition and belittle the Tour de France. And the Texan himself was not about to underestimate either his rivals or the enormity of the Tour. That meant that the Postal team

31

leader and directeur sportif Johan Bruyneel took Armstrong's preparations for this Tour just as seriously as they did in 1999 and 2000.

His schedule for the 2001 Tour was this:

1. A solid base of winter miles and gym work, introducing extra abdominal work and an hour of stretching each day.

2. Meaningful race-situation tests, including strong performances on the mountain summit stage finishes at the Setmana Catalana in March and Tour of Aragon in April.

3. A glimpse of the opposition with his lone World Cup ride, when he finished second in the Amstel Gold Race.

4. Road training camps in May to explore the Tour's key stages in the Vosges, Alps, Pyrénées and Massif Central.

5. Final build-up, including climbing power tests, and his last pre-Tour races: the Classique des Alpes on June 9 and Tour of Switzerland, June 19–28.

Unless Armstrong experienced one of the training crashes that plagued his 2000 season, he would be ready both physically and mentally for the challenges that awaited him in the *grande boucle*, or "big loop," as the French like to call their favorite annual sports event.

TYLER HAMILTON

Age: 28
Height: 5 ft. 8 in. **Weight:** 140 lbs.
Hometown: Marblehead, Massachusetts
Team: U.S. Postal Service
Number of Tours: 4

When you meet Tyler Hamilton, you think, "This guy's too nice to be a pro bike racer." His dark, wavy hair is neatly barbered, his eyes twinkle, and his mouth always has a hint of a smile. And with his calm, polite demeanor, the slightly built 28-year-old New Englander looks more like a banker sitting down to discuss a line of credit, than he does an elite athlete about to embark on his fifth Tour de France.

Hamilton might well have become lost in the corporate world, as he majored in economics at the University of Colorado. But while studying at the Boulder campus, he transitioned from downhill skiing into cycling, winning the national collegiate championship in

1993. Within two years he was a professional cyclist with the Subaru-Montgomery team, which morphed into the U.S. Postal Service squad the following season, 1996.

His compact build and sometimes fragile health give no clue to what lies inside this longest-standing member of the Postal squad: a big heart and infinite determination. Those qualities enabled Hamilton to perform some amazing feats over his first four Tours de France, mainly in the service of others—particularly current team leader, Lance Armstrong. Who could forget the way Hamilton performed in the Alps during the 1999 Tour? One day after crashing heavily on a rain-slick descent just before the finish of the stage to Sestriere, Hamilton was the only Postal rider left with Armstrong to set the pace on Alpe d'Huez and enable his leader to ward off threats to his yellow jersey.

As he planned for *this* Tour, Hamilton followed his usual slow and steady build-up. "The spring for me is more about just being patient, listening to my body," he said. "My focus is on races all in the summer months. It's important for me not to get frustrated: 'Okay, I'm not getting results here in March or April.' You know, there are not too many guys that are going well in March, and still going well in June, July and August."

This 2001 season had seen Hamilton's form start to improve in April, especially at the Circuit de la Sarthe, where, he said, "I felt stronger, felt I played a part in the race, whereas I was pack-fill, more or less, in the early-season races. You need little things like that just to build up the confidence."

There can also be little things that set you back, like the crash Hamilton suffered at Liège-Bastogne-Liège in late April. Luckily, the broken bone in his elbow had time to heal before his next scheduled race, Spain's Bicicleta Vasca in late May. Prior to that, he and Armstrong set off on their annual training road trips, riding the Tour's key stages, including Alpe d'Huez.

"I train with Lance pretty much every day, as we're normally on the same race schedule," Hamilton said. "For me, that's a big bonus, being able to train with the best rider in the world." And a bonus for Armstrong was that Hamilton would again race into the red zone at the Tour for his training partner from Texas.

GEORGE HINCAPIE

Age: 28

Height: 6 ft. 3 in. **Weight:** 175 lbs.

Hometown: Greenville, South Carolina

Team: U.S. Postal Service

Number of Tours: 6

This popular American racer rode his first Tour de France in 1996 with Motorola when he was just 23, and he had been a fixture at the July race ever since. In his first year, Hincapie had a bad crash and didn't finish, but he made steady progress in each of the following years. In 1998, the spring classics' specialist had one of his best Tours from an individual standpoint, narrowly missing a chance to wear the leader's yellow jersey after featuring in a winning breakaway on stage 3.

The next two years, however, weren't about individual goals. There was no pursuit of an early yellow jersey for Hincapie, nor any other individual honor such as the green jersey or a stage win. When your teammate is Lance Armstrong, the Tour means one thing: working for the boss.

For Hincapie, who had been in the paid ranks since age 19, his approach to the Tour was definitely that of a seasoned pro. Each year, the early part of his season was dedicated to those spring classics—specifically the Tour of Flanders, Ghent-Wevelgem and Paris-Roubaix—where he'd shine as the U.S. Postal Service's team leader.

Once the classics were over at the end of April, Hincapie had to switch gears completely. He had to go from super-intense one-day races in demanding spring weather over cobblestone roads, to the different rigors of a three-week Tour over terrain that ranges from flat, windy plains to the high mountains. Before ramping back up, he first took a short break back home in South Carolina.

"I go back to America and take a couple days, a week easy, not riding much, and then start training for Philadelphia [the USPRO Championship in early June], but basically for the Tour ... and use Philadelphia more as a build-up," he said. "Once I get to the Tour, I know it's going to be hard work trying to keep Lance ready, so there's definitely a lot of training to be done in May, hard training!"

Hincapie doesn't shy away from all that hard work, because whether it's April when he's the Postal team leader, or July when he's Armstrong's protector, the man is a pro. It's that simple.

34

BOBBY JULICH

Age: 29

Height: 6 ft. **Weight:** 150 lbs.

Hometown: Reno, Nevada

Team: Crédit Agricole

Number of Tours: 4

Remain healthy and avoid crashes. That was Julich's mantra ever since allergies wrecked his preparations for the 2000 Tour de France, in which he finished a disappointing 48th overall. The native Coloradan wanted to retrieve the form and consistency that saw him finish third at the 1998 Tour, and he was determined to avoid another crash like the one that eliminated him from the '99 Tour on the stage 8 time trial. Part of his "rehabilitation" was to move his U.S. home back from the Philadelphia area to the West, near Lake Tahoe, Nevada. That's where he spent four weeks until late May, doing the type of altitude training—honing his climbing and time trial skills—that he hoped would bring him to optimum fitness by the time the Tour started on July 7.

During the spring, Julich showed signs of his former self, placing top 10 in some time-trial stages and testing himself in long breakaways, like the one he shared with eight others for most of the last 80km of the Liège-Bastogne-Liège classic. His hard work looked likely to be rewarded when the Tour raced on some of the same roads in Belgium, and in the subsequent tough stages before the Alps.

Following his weeks of altitude training, Julich returned to racing at the Dauphiné Libéré, but he didn't feel good. "I just didn't have the legs to go with the front guys," he said. "It was frustrating…. Maybe I did too much [training], or my body wasn't ready for the massive amount of work and intervals I was doing."

Julich ended the Dauphiné by taking third on the final stage and finishing 29th overall. Then he went to his last race before the Tour, the Tour of Catalonia, in which he still didn't have the climbing power he had anticipated. He could only hope that his heavy training load would finally pay off at the Tour.

KEVIN LIVINGSTON

Age: 28

Height: 6 ft. **Weight:** 155 lbs.

Hometown: Austin, Texas

Team: Telekom

Number of Tours: 4

In 1999 and 2000, Livingston built a reputation as one of Lance Armstrong's most trusted teammates. Indeed, ever since riding in his first Tour in 1997 (for Cofidis), Livingston, a Missouri native, had played the role of a top lieutenant. In 1998, he helped Cofidis teammate Bobby Julich finish on the podium. But in that same Tour, Livingston placed 17th overall, proving he had the talent to be a major G.C. threat on his own.

So it came as only a small surprise when Livingston was ready to accept an offer in late 2000 to assume a leadership role on the Linda McCartney team. The British squad was on a recruiting drive and Livingston was a solid choice as a team leader for a major tour. Providence (or good sense) intervened and Livingston's deal fell through—two months before the team itself collapsed under the weight of serious financial troubles. Livingston was almost immediately snatched up by Telekom, the team of 1997 Tour winner Jan Ullrich.

"Right away, it clicked," Livingston said. "He's a quiet guy, to be sure, but at the same time he's easy to talk with and he's fun to be around. I like him and that makes it a lot easier to do the job."

With a new team and a new boss, Livingston rode the Giro d'Italia for the first time. "I've never done this sort of race program to get ready for the Tour," he said. "It's a lot to do.... Instead of the very safe approach I've always taken to the Tour. I was always very careful not to overdo it. But this year, doing the Giro and then the Tour, it's a lot to do, but maybe it can bring me up another level."

Livingston quickly added that moving up another level does not mean that his goals include adding stage wins to his own résumé. "That's not in the team plan," Livingston said. "It was the same at Postal. It was never in the plan that I or anyone other than Lance would go for a stage win. We were there to work for Lance, and this year I'll be there to work for Jan. That's my job. To set personal goals of trying to stay at the front after doing the work on the climb—that's sort of dreaming. I knew what my role would be. It wouldn't do anyone any good to make these crazy announcements about my personal ambitions. My only objective has to be to help Jan win the Tour. And we can do that, I'm sure."

A top lieutenant, again.

FRED RODRIGUEZ

Age: 27
Height: 5 ft. 10 in. **Weight:** 150 lbs.
Hometown: Emeryville, California
Team: Domo-Farm Frites
Number of Tours: 1

Riding in his first Tour de France in 2000 for Mapei-Quick Step, Fred Rodriguez took care of business, helping deliver sprinter Tom Steels to two early stage wins and Stefano Zanini to victory on the final stage in Paris. And when he had a chance to ride for himself on stage 17 around Lake Geneva, the Californian managed a third-place stage finish in Lausanne.

Now riding for the new Domo-Farm Frites squad, Rodriguez wouldn't have Steels to lead out, but could find himself working to set up world champion Romans Vainsteins.

With Domo's powerful classics squad at work all spring, Rodriguez was able to prepare for the Tour at lower-key spring races, before heading back to the States to defend his USPRO Championship in Philadelphia. He won the U.S. title for the second year, and then headed back to Europe, where he won the opening stage of the Tour of Luxembourg, and appeared ready to have an outstanding Tour.

CHRISTIAN VANDE VELDE

Age: 25
Height: 5 ft. 11 in. **Weight:** 150 lbs.
Hometown: Boulder, Colorado
Team: U.S. Postal Service
Number of Tours: 1

In his first Tour de France in 1999, the then-23-year-old Vande Velde was a key teammate for race winner Armstrong. He was looking forward to filling that role again in 2000, but an infected spider bite just before the start of the Tour left him out of the mix.

His Olympic-year disappointments continued in the fall, when he traveled to the Sydney Games but could muster only a 12th-place finish in the individual pursuit.

With his focus 100 percent on the road in 2001, Vande Velde was again living up to his promise in the spring, taking fourth place overall at the Three Days of De Panne, 17th at the Tour of Flanders and 22nd at the Amstel Gold Race. He also had an outstanding ride at Liège-Bastogne-Liège, finishing just behind the winning break.

With a strong few months behind him, Vande Velde would once again be called on as one of Postal's main workers at the Tour—especially after the retirement of Armstrong's long-time lieutenant Frankie Andreu.

JONATHAN VAUGHTERS

Age: 28
Height: 5 ft. 11 in. **Weight:** 135 lbs.
Hometown: Denver, Colorado
Team: Crédit Agricole
Number of Tours: 2

The 28-year-old Vaughters is one of the top climbing talents in the world, as he proved in 1999 when he set the course record for climbing Mont Ventoux in the Dauphiné Libéré. He has the talent to go head-to-head with *anyone* in the mountains of Europe.

Unfortunately, when it comes to the Tour, he has had nothing but bad luck. In 1998, a crash before the Tour prevented him from starting. And then, at his first Tour in '99, Vaughters crashed and abandoned on the treacherous Passage du Gois on stage 2. The Coloradan crashed out again in 2000, on the epic Dax-Hautacam stage, just as the race hit the mountain roads that he craved.

In 2001, the Crédit Agricole rider had enjoyed a quiet spring, before returning home at the end of April. Most of his Tour preparation took place at altitude in Colorado, and was followed by a mixed performance at the June 10–17 Dauphiné: Vaughters won the stage 4 time trial, but failed in the next day's mountain stage and pulled out on stage 6. His climbing legs were better in Spain's Tour of Catalonia, where the American finished 12th overall.

It was a promising build-up to the Tour, in which he'd be one of his French team's main hopes.… But for Vaughters, the main goal would be getting to Paris for the first time.

A Tour with Fewer Favorites

THE ORGANIZERS' REJECTION OF SEVERAL
NON-FRENCH TEAMS CUT THE LIST OF CHALLENGERS
TO LANCE ARMSTRONG'S TOUR CROWN

In selecting eight French teams, including five from Division II, and excluding Division I teams such as Mercatone Uno and Saeco of Italy, Mercury-Viatel of the U.S. and Team Coast of Germany, Tour de France director Jean-Marie Leblanc seemed to devalue the 88th Tour de France. On May 2, Leblanc announced the five wild-card selections—not four as originally indicated—to create a field of 21 teams.

The teams added to the original list of 16 named in January were BigMat-Auber 93 and La Française des Jeux of France, CSC-Tiscali of Denmark, Euskaltel-Euskadi of Spain and Lotto-Adecco of Belgium.

"To invite 21 teams is a circumstantial measure," said Leblanc, explaining that French cycling needed a boost. For a team like La Française des Jeux, it was a matter of survival. Being excluded almost certainly meant the end of the team, which needed exposure from France's biggest sporting event to justify sponsor investment. And so the six-man selection committee from the Société du Tour—Leblanc and five other Frenchmen—added two Division II squads, La Française des Jeux and BigMat, to the six French teams already named.

Incredibly, at a time when French pro racing was at an all-time low (the highest-placed pro on the UCI world rankings was Christophe Moreau of Festina in 29th place), Leblanc had included the highest-ever number of home teams. Even when the French led the world of cycling in the 1960s and 1970s, no more than six home teams ever started the Tour.

In making this decision, Leblanc and his committee closed their eyes to the Tour's worldwide audience. There has been no more popular racer than Marco Pantani, and yet he and his Mercatone Uno team were excluded. Just as surprising was the exclusion of Mario Cipollini and the Saeco squad, and Alex Zülle and Fernando Escartin of Coast. And for American cycling, Leblanc's shunning of Mercury-Viatel was a decision that threatened the future of the first-year Division I squad.

Mercury-Viatel's French directeur sportif Alain Gallopin was blunt: "This will cause problems, that's certain." But apparently, Tour boss Leblanc was more eager to deal with domestic problems than include an exciting overseas team like Mercury, which boasted potential stage winners in Leon Van Bon, Gord Fraser and Peter Van Petegem, and potential top-10 contenders Pavel Tonkov, Niklas Axelsson and Chann McRae.

More shocking was the exclusion of Pantani's Mercatone Uno squad. "This team is currently last in the Division I rankings," explained Leblanc. "Its worth is based solely on its leader, who didn't finish the last Tour de France, nor the other races since. We haven't seen Marco Pantani, professional cyclist, for eight or nine months."

This view was shared by Bernard Hinault, who told a French newspaper: "Pantani cannot be invited because there was too great a chance of his being disqualified at any time. Not to invite him is the logical decision for us and the Tour."

Another five-time Tour winner, Miguel Induráin, disagreed. "It upsets me that such great riders as Pantani are not going to the Tour de France," said the Spaniard. "The organizers ... are a separate entity and they have acted in their own private interests."

In response to those sentiments—and similar sentiments from UCI president Hein Verbruggen—Leblanc said, "The Tour has chosen to show confidence in young riders, to favor development. We have [in BigMat and La Française des Jeux] teams that have chosen that course. We decided unanimously to give a chance to these two teams, to show our support of French cycling in a concrete manner. This is also a sign of breaking from a [former] cycling era."

This last comment was a reference to his committee's exclusion of many of the top stars of the 1990s: Pantani, Cipollini, Zülle and Escartin. But Leblanc *did* include another aging star who was then short on form and fitness. His name? Laurent Jalabert, leader of the Danish team, CSC-Tiscali. And yes, he's French....

Without traditional contenders like Escartin, Pantani and Zülle, the list of favorites was shorter than usual. These were the riders that topped most lists of Tour contenders:

Lance Armstrong (U.S. Postal Service)

No crashes, no new media accusations and twin babies on the way (Kristin Armstrong was expecting in December), everything seemed to be going right for the Postal team boss as he headed toward another yellow-jersey defense. About the only thing that went wrong during Armstrong's spring build-up was the crash of his right-hand man Tyler Hamilton in Liège-Bastogne-Liège. But even that was just a memory as the July 7 Tour start drew closer.

Armstrong placed second at the mountainous Classique des Alpes on June 9, and then headed to the Postal's final Tour tune-up: the 10-day Tour of Switzerland, June 19–28. In the opening time trial, the Texan and his team proved that they were right on target: They placed four riders in the top 10, and Armstrong rode into the leader's yellow jersey. The Texan then won the mountain time trial to clinch the overall victory in Switzerland. If things could have gone any smoother for the American heading into the Tour, it's hard to imagine.

TOUR RECORD: 2000: 1st; 1999: 1st; 1996: DNF; 1995: 36th; 1994: DNF; 1993: DNF.

Jan Ullrich (Deutsche Telekom)

As the man most likely to challenge Armstrong, Ullrich took a different approach to his Tour preparations. For the first time in his eight-year career, the German chose to ride the Giro d'Italia to get himself fit for the Tour. While his results were insignificant (two third places in semi-mountain stages and 52nd overall), he definitely got in the training miles he was seeking—spending long stretches driving the pace at the front of the peloton on the flats, and riding steadily over the high mountains of the Dolomites.

Following the Giro, Ullrich and three Telekom teammates retreated to the Alps for some Tour-specific climbing training, but he wasn't able to completely escape the media spotlight. First he had to explain that the drugs found in his room during the June 6 police blitz at the Giro were simply antihistamines he used to counteract asthma and allergies; and then, in mid-June, he was dogged by accusations raised by former Festina soigneur

41

Willy Voet and former Festina team manager Bruno Roussel, who respectively claimed that no recent Tour winners had won without drugs, and that in the '97 Tour Ullrich accepted a $15,000 bribe to lose the Courchevel stage to Richard Virenque. Ullrich flatly denied both allegations.

Meanwhile, his preparations looked to be falling into place when he won the German national championship on the Sunday before the Tour.

TOUR RECORD: 2000: 2nd; 1998: 2nd; 1997: 1st; 1996: 2nd.

Francesco Casagrande (Fassa Bortolo)

After Casagrande crashed and broke his wrist on stage 1 of the Giro, he set his sights on the overall at the Tour de France. But by the time the Giro had finished, new problems had emerged. His Fassa Bortolo teammate Dario Frigo pulled out of the race after being caught in possession of banned drugs; and another teammate, Wladimir Belli, was tossed when he slugged a spectator, who turned out to be race leader Gilberto Simoni's nephew. With all of the turmoil surrounding his team and Italian cycling in general, Casagrande had a tough time focusing on the Tour. But he *was* undertaking six-hour training runs in his native Tuscany, prior to his return to racing at the June 23–26 Route du Sud in the French Pyrénées. There, he won the final stage, but he then caught a stomach bug that prevented him from racing his national championship six days before the Tour. A big question mark hung over the man who could most threaten Armstrong in the climbs.

TOUR RECORD: 1998: DNF; 1997: 6th.

Joseba Beloki (ONCE-Eroski)

Like his former Festina teammate Christophe Moreau, the 27-year-old Beloki had a breakout Tour performance in 2000, finishing third behind Armstrong and Ullrich. And so there would be plenty of eyes on Beloki to see if he could repeat or improve on his 2000 performance. At the May 30–June 3 Bicicleta Vasca in Spain, Beloki nearly pulled out a win, showing off his best climbing form. His final tune-up was another Spanish race, the Tour of Catalonia, June 21–28, which he won in impressive fashion.

TOUR RECORD: 2000: 3rd.

Christophe Moreau (Festina)

Moreau put in the best finish by a French rider in three years in 2000, with his fourth place at the Tour, but there were still some questions about his ability to be a real contender for the overall. He answered some of those questions with his winning performance at the 2001 Dauphiné Libéré, in which he showed the ability to ride up front in the high mountains, sticking with challenger Pavel Tonkov on the key alpine stage over the Croix-de-Fer, Télégraphe and Galibier passes.

TOUR RECORD: 2000: 4th; 1999: 27th; 1998: excluded for drugs; 1997: 19th; 1996: 75th.

The 21 Teams and 189 Riders

U.S. POSTAL SERVICE (USA)

1 Lance Armstrong (USA)

2 Roberto Heras (Sp)

3 Viatcheslav Ekimov (Rus)

4 Tyler Hamilton (USA)

5 George Hincapie (USA)

6 Steffen Kjaergaard (N)

7 Victor Hugo Peña (Col)

8 José Rubiera (Sp)

9 Christian Vande Velde (USA)

ONCE-EROSKI (Sp)

21 Joseba Beloki (Sp)

22 Santos Gonzalez (Sp)

23 Alvaro Gonzalez De Galdeano (Sp)

24 Igor Gonzalez De Galdeano (Sp)

25 Ivan Gutierrez (Sp)

26 Jörg Jaksche (G)

27 Mikel Pradera (Sp)

28 Carlos Sastre (Sp)

29 Marcos Serrano (Sp)

DEUTSCHE TELEKOM (G)

11 Jan Ullrich (G)

12 Udo Bölts (G)

13 Giuseppe Guerini (I)

14 Jens Heppner (G)

15 Andreas Klöden (G)

16 Kevin Livingston (USA)

17 Alex Vinokourov (Kaz)

18 Steffen Wesemann (G)

19 Erik Zabel (G)

FESTINA (F)

31 Christophe Moreau (F)

32 Florent Brard (F)

33 Angel Casero (Sp)

34 Pascal Chanteur (F)

35 Felix Garcia-Casas (Sp)

36 Pascal Lino (F)

37 Luis Perez (Sp)

38 Arnaud Pretot (F)

39 Sven Teutenberg (G)

FASSA BORTOLO (I)

41 Francesco Casagrande (I)
42 Fabio Baldato (I)
43 Ivan Basso (I)
44 Wladimir Belli (I)
45 Sergei Ivanov (Rus)
46 Nicola Loda (I)
47 Alessandro Petacchi (I)
48 Oscar Pozzi (I)
49 Matteo Tossato (I)

LOTTO-ADECCO (B)

61 Rik Verbrugghe (B)
62 Mario Aerts (B)
63 Serge Baguet (B)
64 Jeroen Blijlevens (Nl)
65 Fabien de Waele (B)
66 Guennadi Mikhailov (Rus)
67 Kurt Van De Wouwer (B)
68 Pol Van Hyfte (B)
69 Stive Vermaut (B)

MAPEI-QUICK STEP (I)

81 Daniele Nardello (I)
82 Michele Bartoli (I)
83 Paolo Bettini (I)
84 Davide Bramati (I)
85 Paolo Fornaciari (I)
86 Stefano Garzelli (I)
87 Bart Leysen (B)
88 Tom Steels (B)
89 Stefano Zanini (I)

RABOBANK (Nl)

51 Michael Boogerd (Nl)
52 Bram de Groot (Nl)
53 Steven de Jongh (Nl)
54 Erik Dekker (Nl)
55 Maarten Den Bakker (Nl)
56 Marc Lotz (Nl)
57 Grischa Niermann (G)
58 Geert Verheyen (B)
59 Marc Wauters (B)

COFIDIS (F)

71 David Millar (GB)
72 Daniel Atienza (Sp)
73 Iñigo Cuesta (Sp)
74 Andrei Kivilev (Kaz)
75 Massimiliano Lelli (I)
76 Nico Mattan (B)
77 David Moncoutié (F)
78 Christophe Rinero (F)
79 Guido Trentin (I)

iBANESTO.com (Sp)

91 Francisco Mancebo (Sp)
92 Santiago Blanco (Sp)
93 Thomas Brozyna (Pl)
94 José Vicente Garcia-Acosta (Sp)
95 Eladio Jimenez (Sp)
96 Denis Mentchov (Rus)
97 Jon Odriozola (Sp)
98 Javier Pascual Rodriguez (Sp)
99 Leonardo Piepoli (I)

CRÉDIT AGRICOLE (F)

101 Bobby Julich (USA)
102 Frédéric Bessy (F)
103 Sebastien Hinault (F)
104 Thor Hushovd (N)
105 Christopher Jenner (F)
106 Anthony Morin (F)
107 Stuart O'Grady (Aus)
108 Jonathan Vaughters (USA)
109 Jens Voigt (G)

AG2R (F)

121 Benoît Salmon (F)
122 Christophe Agnolutto (F)
123 Stéphane Bergès (F)
124 Alexandre Botcharov (Rus)
125 Ludovic Capelle (B)
126 Sébastien Demarbaix (B)
127 Jaan Kirsipuu (Est)
128 Gilles Maignan (F)
129 Ludovic Turpin (F)

JEAN DELATOUR (F)

141 Laurent Brochard (F)
142 Jérome Bernard (F)
143 Gilles Bouvard (F)
144 Stéphane Goubert (F)
145 Patrice Halgand (F)
146 Christophe Oriol (F)
147 Laurent Roux (F)
148 Eddy Seigneur (F)
149 Olivier Trastour (F)

EUSKALTEL-EUSKADI (Sp)

111 David Etxebarria (Sp)
112 Angel Castresana (Sp)
113 Iñigo Chaureau (Sp)
114 Txema Del Olmo (Sp)
115 Unai Etxebarria (Ven)
116 Iker Flores (Sp)
117 Roberto Laiseka (Sp)
118 Alberto Lopez De Munain (Sp)
119 Haimar Zubeldia (Sp)

CSC-TISCALI (Dk)

131 Laurent Jalabert (F)
132 Michael Blaudzun (Dk)
133 Francisco Cerezo (Sp)
134 Marcellino Garcia (Sp)
135 Nicolas Jalabert (F)
136 Nicolay Bo Larson (Dk)
137 Jakob Piil (Dk)
138 Nicki Sørensen (Dk)
139 Rolf Sørensen (Dk)

KELME-COSTA BLANCA (Sp)

151 Santiago Botero (Col)
152 Felix Rafael Cardenas (Col)
153 Laurent Desbiens (F)
154 Aitor Gonzalez (Sp)
155 José Enrique Gutierrez (Sp)
156 Javier Pascual Llorente (Sp)
157 Oscar Sevilla (Sp)
158 Antonio Tauler (Sp)
159 José Angel Vidal (Sp)

BONJOUR (F)

161 Didier Rous (F)
162 Walter Bénéteau (F)
163 Franck Bouyer (F)
164 Sylvain Chavanel (F)
165 Damien Nazon (F)
166 Olivier Perraudeau (F)
167 Franck Renier (F)
168 Jean-Cyril Robin (F)
169 François Simon (F)

LA FRANÇAISE DES JEUX (F)

181 Sven Montgomery (Swi)
182 Jimmy Casper (F)
183 Jacky Durand (F)
184 Frédéric Guesdon (F)
185 Emmanuel Magnien (F)
186 Bradley McGee (Aus)
187 Christophe Mengin (F)
188 Daniel Schnider (Swi)
189 Nicolas Vogondy (F)

BIGMAT-AUBER 93 (F)

201 Stéphane Heulot (F)
202 Guillaume Auger (F)
203 Ludovic Auger (F)
204 Christophe Capelle (F)
205 Thierry Gouvenou (F)
206 Xavier Jan (F)
207 Loïc Lamouller (F)
208 Alexei Sivakov (Rus)
209 Sébastien Talabardon (F)

LAMPRE-DAIKIN (I)

171 Marco Serpellini (I)
172 Raivis Belohvosciks (Lat)
173 Rubens Bertogliati (Swi)
174 Ludo Dierckxsens (B)
175 Matteo Frutti (I)
176 Robert Hunter (SA)
177 Marco Pinotti (I)
178 Jan Svorada (Cz)
179 Johan Verstrepen (B)

DOMO-FARM FRITES (B)

191 Romans Vainsteins (Lat)
192 Enrico Cassani (I)
193 Servais Knaven (Nl)
194 Axel Merckx (B)
195 Marco Milesi (I)
196 Johan Museeuw (B)
197 Fred Rodriguez (USA)
198 Max Van Heeswijk (Nl)
199 Piotr Wadecki (Pl)

PART TWO
The 88th Tour de France

GRAHAM WATSON

CAPTURES THE ESSENCE OF **THE 2001 TOUR DE FRANCE**

Jan Ullrich looked ready for the upcoming battle as he led out his Telekom troops at the team presentation on the eve of the Tour's start in the port of Dunkirk.

Frenchman Christophe Moreau lit up a murky evening in Dunkirk with a sparkling prologue.

More than a million Belgians (above) greeted the peloton on stage 2, while the next day one fan (left) showed his support for Lance Armstrong's U.S. Postal team.

Marc Wauters's win in Antwerp (top left) earned him the yellow jersey and created a hot market for his fan club's yellow T-shirts on the next day's stage in his hometown of Lummen.

Racing through the rain to Bar-le-Duc, race leader Stuart O'Grady led his Crédit Agricole squad to a stunning victory in the team time trial.

On stage 4, Postal's Viatcheslav Ekimov (No. 3) got a helping hand from teammates Steffen Kjaergaard (6) and Victor Hugo Peña (7).

Christian Vander Velde (leading above) was a key player in Postal's team time trial performance, despite a crash; and two days later, with his leg still bandaged, he collided with a lamppost (right) and was forced to abandon the Tour.

Stage 8 winner Laurent Jalabert was home and dry in Colmar (left),
while the next day he was cold and wet in the peloton that finished
at Pontarlier more than a half-hour behind a 14-man break (top), which
was powered by Andrei Kivilev of Cofidis, Erik Dekker of Rabobank
(who took the stage) and a frigid O'Grady (who retook the yellow jersey).

An unusual sight nearing the top of the 2000-meter Col de la Madeleine: No sign of rider No. 1 in the first half of the front group. Was Lance Armstrong struggling—or maybe bluffing—on stage 10 to L'Alpe d'Huez?

Turns out that Armstrong
was bluffing. He was
all alone climbing the
Alpe (left), and crossed
the line punching the
thin air, almost two
minutes ahead of Ullrich.

On the uphill time trial to
Chamrousse, stage winner
Armstong used custom
clip-ons that allowed him
to pull on the central part
of the bars as well as the
brake hoods.

Joseba Beloki was left gasping in seventh place on the steep climb to Plateau de Bonascre, but he would hang tough in the last two mountain stages to repeat his third place overall of 2000.

Eighteen years after his brother Pascal wore the yellow yersey, François Simon fought hard in its defense on the climbs of the Pyrénées.

WEEK 1

Hidden Dangers

To the casual observer, the Tour de France is all about the mountains, where puny, mortal bicycle racers overcome giant, immortal climbs, and the winner emerges wearing the yellow jersey. There is, of course, an element of truth to this simplistic view, but before the race even *reaches* the mountains all manner of obstacles and potential dangers lie in wait. Recent followers of the Tour would remember 1999 and the stage 2 pileup on the infamous tidal causeway, the Passage du Gois, that cost Lance Armstrong's main challenger, Alex Zülle, six minutes. Tour history is full of such first-week setbacks: crashes, mechanical misfortunes, unexpected breakaways, mistaken strategies, sickness and injuries.

In this 88th Tour, most of the 189 starters would likely fall victim to one of these pitfalls. One rider, Belgian Fabien de Waele of Lotto-Adecco, suffered his misfortune even before the race kicked off, when he crashed while training on the morning of the first day's prologue. He would ride the prologue, finish last and later discover that he had broken his hip. His Tour was over before it really began.

There would be many such tales in the opening week-and-a-bit, made up of the prologue and nine stages, preceding the first serious mountain climbs in the Alps. In fact, almost half of the race's 3458.2 kilometers (2148.8 miles) would be raced in this opening stretch, which, from the start at Dunkirk on the North Sea coast of France, took the peloton in a broad arc across Belgium and then south and east across the French provinces of Lorraine, Alsace, Franche-Comté and the Jura to Aix-les-Bains.

Unlike many recent Tours, these early stages seemed to offer few chances for the bunch finishes that thrust sprinters like Mario Cipollini into the daily headlines. In 1999, for example, all of the first seven stages resulted in field sprints, four of them won by Cipollini. Such a scenario looked very unlikely in 2001, since the run-up to the Alps had four hilly days, one semi-mountainous stage and a team time trial, but only three stages where mass sprints looked a possibility.

Along with the daily quest for glory, this opening sector also held the potential for breakaways that could affect the whole Tour. That's why the main contenders needed to be in top form going into the race. And given the challenges of this unusual Tour beginning, riders short of racing miles—like Italian contender Francesco Casagrande—wouldn't be able to ride themselves into shape as they could in a more conventional first week. For Armstrong, this was not a problem. The American came to the Tour fully prepared, because his final race, the 10-day Tour of Switzerland, which finished just over a week before the Tour, brought him a resounding victory. His chief challenger, Jan Ullrich, didn't come to France with much recent competition behind him, but he had used a well-thought-out approach. A month before the Tour, the German raced the three-week Giro d'Italia to lose weight and bring him some much-needed focus, and then he trained in the mountains, adopting Armstrong's strategy of riding several of the Tour's key stages.

A first indication of the relative form of Ullrich, Armstrong, Casagrande and all the other contenders would come at Dunkirk, in the short, individual prologue time trial....

PROLOGUE: IN THE GIANT'S SHADOW

Every year in February, the people of Dunkirk celebrate a three-day "Carnaval" that has its origins in the 14th century. It centers around a benevolent giant named Reuze, the mythical patron of Flemish maritime life who protected the fleets of herring fisherman that set sail from Dunkirk for the rich waters of distant Iceland.

What's that got to do with cycling? Well, Reuze was at the start of this 88th Tour de France's prologue time trial, or rather his effigy was, standing in the bows of a make-believe boat. Some 20 feet tall, he had a rugged face with chiseled beard and mustache, wore a plumed silver helmet and a coat of armor, and carried a hefty sword at his hip. The giant Reuze towered over his four larger-than-life, papier-mâché companions: a helmeted warrior and his wife, a second, younger soldier, and a child in a white bonnet.

Dunkirkers revere their Reuze, so it was only natural that he'd be looming above the prologue start house, watching each of the 189 cyclists set out on their three-week journey. Also watching, lining the barriers around the 8.2km counterclockwise circuit, were an estimated 100,000 fans, some dressed in shorts and T-shirts after a month of summerlike weather, others toting umbrellas, wary that an overnight rain might return on the strong west winds blowing in

from the North Sea. Maybe Reuze had a hand in it, for the rain held off until after the last rider, Armstrong, had finished, shortly before 7:30 p.m. on a murky, muggy evening.

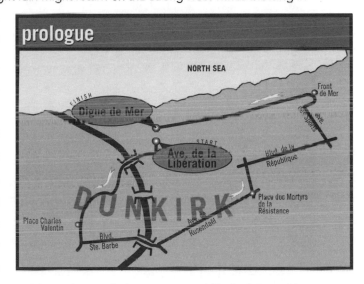

The two-time defending champion was, of course, the big favorite to win this prologue—and the Tour. In fact, the Texan was as dominant as Reuze in the pre-race predictions: The prestigious *L'Équipe* sports newspaper that morning had made Armstrong its five-star favorite; and no one had four stars. Next in line, with three stars, was Ullrich, followed by Spaniards Joseba Beloki of ONCE-Eroski and Armstrong's teammate Roberto Heras, with two stars apiece. Showing an uncustomary lack of chauvinism, *L'Équipe* gave home standout Moreau, 2000's fourth-place finisher, just one star, along with Italy's Casagrande and Stefano Garzelli of Mapei-Quick Step, and one more Spaniard, Angel Casero of Festina.

To see how all these contenders would fare in the prologue was one of the more fascinating prospects of the day; and, along with the chance to see every rider up close, that's the reason the fans so enjoy coming to Tour time trials.

As is traditional in prologues, the team leaders all raced at the end of the day, while their lieutenants went off early to give the teams an indication of the best gears to use and the likely time splits. For Telekom, that meant making Tour debutante Andreas Klöden its first starter. The skinny 26-year-old German had been tipped as Ullrich's potential successor, and he duly posted a solid time of 9:39, just two seconds down on the early leader and former world under-23 TT champion, Norwegian Thor Hushovd of Crédit Agricole. Postal's designated greyhound was Tyler Hamilton, but a loosening seat bolt hampered his performance and negated his usefulness to Armstrong. That wasn't the case with his teammate Steffen Kjaergaard, the other Norwegian in the race, who went through the halfway point in 4:34, a time split that would hold up as the fastest of the day.

That fast start came back to hit the hard-working Kjaergaard on the course's demanding finale. After riding either with the wind through downtown, or sheltered by the brick buildings along Dunkirk's narrow city streets, it was a shock for every starter to emerge onto the seafront and be hit by a three-quarter head wind for the final 1.8km straightaway. Kjaergaard did "okay" by finishing up with a 9:36, but that was already two seconds off the pace of two new leaders: the precocious Spaniards Carlos Sastre of ONCE and tall Toni Tauler of Kelme-Costa Blanca.

Sastre's 9:34 wasn't matched by any of the next 83 riders until Festina's Florent Brard stopped the clock in 9:27—eventually good enough for fifth. Riding his first Tour at age 25, the youthful Brard had had a breakthrough year, including beating teammate Moreau to win the previous week's French national time-trial championship. There were still 45 riders to finish, and half of those came in before another race rookie—ONCE's Igor Gonzalez de Galdeano, the younger of two Basque brothers in the race—beat Brard's time by a huge four seconds.

The Basque rider—who finished second to Ullrich at the 1999 Vuelta a España—was clearly a man to be watched in this Tour, as he could climb as well as ride strong time trials. But after a poor 2000 season with the now defunct Viatalicio team, his performance here was something of a stunner. That was proved five minutes later when one of the prologue favorites, Brad McGee of La Française des Jeux, crossed in only 9:35—after running out of gas in the last, challenging kilometer.

It was just before hitting the seafront that an even hotter favorite, Cofidis's David Millar, came to grief. "My rear tire exploded in the second-to-last corner and I fell," said the tall Scot, who until then was right on schedule to challenge the best time. "It was a new experience for me, as I've never crashed in a time trial before."

Millar's misfortune was a big letdown for the hordes of British fans who had crossed the Channel in hopes of seeing their hero take the first yellow jersey for the second year running. But with Gonzalez de Galdeano still in the driver's seat, the stage seemed to be coming down to the dramatic finish everyone was hoping for: a winning effort by one of the 2000 Tour's top four finishers.

The first of these four was Moreau, who hung out his tongue for most of an impressive-looking ride that saw him fail to catch his minute man, Casagrande, by only 15 seconds. Moreau blasted through the finish, lit by the following cars' lights that pierced the "two hours before sunset" gloom, in 9:20.58. "Best time!" shouted the delighted French race announcer, Daniel Mangeas.

"Prologues were my only strength at the start of my career," Moreau said later, "but I've worked hard at my climbing and flexibility these past two years. I treated today like a double pursuit and rode lower gears—mostly 54 x 14—at a higher cadence, 100 rpm, to keep something in reserve for the finale, when I used 54 x 13."

After Moreau came his teammate of the previous year, Beloki, who was fresh from winning the final time trial and overall title at the mountainous Tour of Catalonia. But that TT was up a mountainside in the Pyrénées, while this one was completely flat. So Beloki's 9:33, among the 10 fastest of the day, was right on target.

And that left two. The big two. Jan and Lance. The only men in the race to have won the Tour. The two men the fans had been waiting for all day. A battle of the giants. Or would Lance be the only true giant, the race's Reuze, and Jan one of those lesser beings?

On this night, the battle was close. Ullrich, six days after taking a Telekom-dominated German championship—the same thing he did prior to winning his only Tour, in 1997—looked solid and smooth. He barely moved his head and torso as he raced up the straightaway in the shelter of the crowds lining the barriers above the beach. Appearing calm and composed, he powered a much bigger gear than either Moreau or the following Armstrong. The crowd cheered as the flush-faced Teuton flashed beneath the finish banner. A solid time, but seven seconds off Moreau's pace, and just a fraction faster than Brard's.

"I've never won a prologue in my life, not even in lesser races," Ullrich noted. "So I am happy to be so close to the best."

Would Armstrong be that best? He *did* win the Tour prologue in 1999, to don his first yellow jersey in a tear-filled ceremony. But that was at Le Puy du Fou on a prologue course that contained a stiff climb and a technical descent—perfect elements to showcase his top skills and strengths. Less favorable elements met him here on the windswept seaside at Dunkirk.

Armstrong was in his full 100-plus-rpm cadence, but he was taking no chances: He rode in

Tyler's diary: Prologue

July 7, 2001

DUNKIRK: *Getting underway at the Tour de France is always a nerve-wracking ordeal.* Having to arrive early for health exams and the team presentation means we all spend the final days leading up to the start cooped up in our hotel rooms. Although this probably forces us to rest like we should, it also leaves us with lots of time to consider the job ahead. And with this being my fifth start, I know all too well the pressure and the pain that lies ahead.

The team presentation was a little rough yesterday. It was the first time I remember our team ever being booed. That's not to say there weren't many supporters in the crowd as well, but there certainly were some angry Frenchmen out there who made it clear they were unhappy about Cédric Vasseur being left off our Tour team. Cédric's first amateur team was based here in Dunkirk, and his French fan club is huge, so I guess it should be no surprise that the team has received a little "feedback" here.

My bib number for this year is "4", which is kind of strange given that it was my number last year as well. Usually the team assigns numbers alphabetically, after the leader who assumes the first in the lot. But Roberto Heras is number 2, and we all fall out in order after him. It's quite a big deal having two grand tour champions riding for the same squad. Roberto is the biggest reason why a lot of folks are saying the U.S. Postal team looks more threatening this year. There's no doubt he's strong. I just wish his butt was a little bigger, because I have to ride behind him in the team time trial. At 58 kilos (128 pounds) he's not much of a draft. I think I'm going to have to talk to him about stuffing a watermelon in the back of his skinsuit....

I was the second Postal guy off in the prologue this afternoon. My first three kilometers were good—I was riding like I wanted to be, strong and feeling secure on the bike. But then my seat slipped. The nose of the saddle just dipped forward. I had my seat adjusted just before the start, which probably wasn't a great idea in retrospect. When I tried to adjust it a little bit, the seat slipped again, and after that my cadence was off. Knowing the bolt was loose, I wound up concentrating more on balancing my weight on my pedals instead of on my seat. With both my position and confidence a little rattled, my split times were considerably slower on the second half of the course. But these things happen, and the Tour de France is a long race. By this time tomorrow, today's prologue will be a distant memory.

the center of the concrete-brick-paved finish straightaway, catching the wind rather than risking a punctured tire in the right-hand gutter. And as he pedaled to the line—between the salty twang of the North Sea waves and the pungent aroma of french fries emanating from La Pataterie café—the aero-helmeted Texan triggered a readout of 9:24.64. Third place. One second slower than Gonzalez, four behind Moreau. The *maillot jaune* went to the rider who had left the 1998 Tour in drug-swoop disgrace as one of the Festina nine....

The media was rightfully mobbing the 30-year-old, seventh-year pro, one of a record 51 French starters. He flashed his dental-perfect smile, while answering endless questions about his ride, his hopes, his past, his future ... as the giant Reuze looked on, and another giant, Sir Lance, rode by, happy to avoid the crush of cameras and mikes and head to the sanctuary of his team's greystone castle, remote in the green hinterland.

The Carnaval known as the Tour had begun.

STAGE 1: THE NEW SPRINTERS—AND ZABEL

Going into this first road stage of the Tour, the question on many people's minds was, Who will be the new sprinters? The question was given emphasis because the dominant sprint winner of the past decade, Mario Cipollini, was absent. As for Cipollini's regular rivals, Tom Steels was present but not fully recovered from a spring bout with extreme fatigue syndrome; fre-

quent stage winner Jeroen Blijlevens no longer seemed to be a threat; Robbie McEwen's team didn't select him; and Marcel Wüst had retired after almost losing an eye in a post-Tour 2000 crash.

So, except perhaps for the aging Jaan Kirsipuu, the only sprinter of the older generation still firing on all cylinders was five-time Tour points champion Erik Zabel— which explains why he came into the Tour already with 16 season wins to his credit.

Ready to challenge the 31-year-old Zabel was a short list of younger riders who had shown promise in recent Tours, or were making

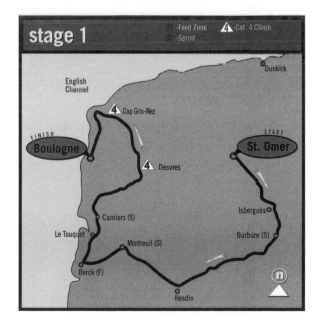

their debut here after good results in other races. Of this younger generation, the names most frequently being mentioned were world road champion Romans Vainsteins, 28, and his Domo teammate Fred Rodriguez, 27; Fassa Bortolo's Alessandro Petacchi, 27; La Française des Jeux's Jimmy Casper, 23; and Crédit Agricole's Thor Hushovd, also 23. And of these half-dozen contenders, the most promising, long term, appeared to be Casper....

A couple of years ago, when Casper was just 21, he astounded the cycling world at the Tour of Germany by winning four stages—all of them in mass sprint finishes ahead of Zabel. Casper then debuted at that year's Tour de France with hopes of taking at least one stage success. But in the world's biggest bike race, his best finish was fifth on stage 2 and he quit before the mountains. The fast, flashy Frenchman needed to gain some experience and endurance.

Casper didn't get a chance to improve in 2000, as he was on the injured list with an infected wound for much of the year and didn't ride the Tour. But he knew what he had to do. "I trained hard last winter and came into the season much stronger," he said. Good results soon came, including a stage win at February's Mediterranean Tour. However, on that race's final sprint, the rider from Picardy fell in a spectacular crash, colliding with the crowd barriers at top speed. Six weeks out with a broken collarbone put a dent in his spring program, yet perhaps gave him more reserves coming into this Tour.

In any case, Casper appeared to be the most relaxed man in the peloton as the race gathered for its opening road stage in the ancient city of St. Omer. A steady drizzle kept many of the riders in their team buses and campers until the last minute, but not Casper. He was sitting on his bike, his foot on a crowd barrier, an umbrella over his head, as he chatted with some friends around the corner from the start area. Nice and relaxed.

Five hours later, Casper—along with Hushovd, Petacchi, Vainsteins, Kirsipuu and

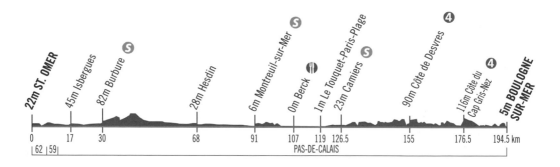

Zabel—were all in the 160-strong pack that came together when the day's 125km-long breakaway by Casper's teammate Jacky Durand and Jean Delatour's Christophe Oriol was caught. After the rain cleared early on, the wind had been the breakaways' enemy, a wind so strong that the swallows flying along parts of the course were dipping beneath the roadside hedgerows to avoid the gusts.

Once reeled in, Durand and Oriol were replaced by incessant counterattackers, and as the field eventually hurtled down a steep hill into Boulogne, it was closing on the last of those: a flying Laurent Brochard of Jean Delatour. Brochard, one of race leader Moreau's former disgraced Festina teammates, had broken away into the stiff wind that was whistling over the grassy bluffs high above the English Channel. As he descended toward the choppy gray waters of Boulogne's port, with less than a kilometer to go, it was clear that the lone rider would be caught and that the stage was going to end in a furious sprint.

With a fast drop so close to the end and Brochard not being swallowed until 350 meters from the line, there was no time for any team to organize a leadout train. The newly crowned Belgian champion Ludovic Capelle was doing his best to clear the way for his AG2R team leader Kirsipuu on the right side of the smooth, slightly curving street, with Zabel and Crédit Agricole's Stuart O'Grady among those in their wake. Across on the left, and slightly behind, Vainsteins was getting some help from Domo teammate Piotr Wadecki, with the big Norwegian Hushovd and the compact Casper behind them.

In the final few seconds, Zabel calmly accelerated away from the right-hand wave— "There's no sense in going too early," he later said—while Vainsteins did the same on the left.

With no show of emotion, Zabel cut the finish plane and looked left to see he was a bike length ahead of Vainsteins, while Casper's late charge between the world champion and the barriers gave him third place, with Hushovd in fourth. The new generation was close, but on this day, old-man Zabel showed them what they still had to learn.

Stage notes

■ Starting the stage within 15 seconds of the yellow jersey, O'Grady and Kirsipuu both went for bonus seconds in the three intermediate sprints. Kirsipuu picked up eight seconds, O'Grady two, to move respectively within eight and 11 seconds of leader Moreau.

■ A group of 24 riders finished almost six minutes behind the pack, after losing contact when the field split into three groups after the day's last climb of Cap Gris-Nez. Among them were Steels and Jonathan Vaughters. Steels said he just didn't have the legs on the climb, while Vaughters dropped his chain and was at the wrong end of the peloton when it split.

STAGE 2: ONE FOR THE BELGIANS

They came in hundreds of thousands to see the Tour return to Belgium for the first time in five years … and for its first stage finish ever in Antwerp. Lining the narrow brick streets or sitting in roadside cafés in town, perched on farm tractors or hay bales in the countryside, the crowds were never ending on the meandering 220.5km course from the English Channel coast to the banks of the Schelde River.

Those fans in the flatlands of Flanders created the frenzied atmosphere that raised the adrenaline level in the peloton and saw the local men play a leading role in every move that mattered.

The conventional wisdom for such a stage put the odds on all the attacks being swept up by the finish, with the stage probably ending in a mass sprint. But with the only Belgian who could win such a sprint, Steels, still under the weather, attacking would be his compatriots' motivation for the day.

After a quiet opening hour, raced at just 39 kph, and a bonus-sprint win for Kirsipuu over O'Grady in the streets of Dunkirk, the stage caught fire. The remaining 181.5km were covered at a stunning average speed of 50.5 kph, the pace never dropping as break after break went clear. Admittedly, the wind was favorable, but this was a course littered with sharp turns, bad road surfaces and numerous, plateau-like speed bumps in every town. And there were a lot of towns.

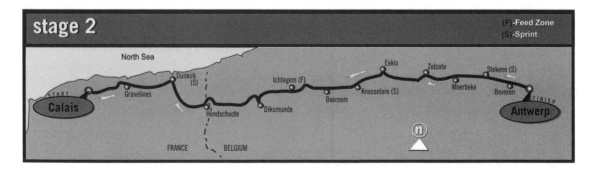

Just before the race left France to head onto the rugged, sometimes rough, concrete roads of Belgium, a first serious group went clear. It was a break that included the real Lion of Flanders, multi-titled Johan Museeuw of Domo, and 12 others. The ferocity of the ensuing battle can be gauged by its statistics: The break lasted 30km, but never had more than a 43-second gap.

Next out of the box was a nine-strong move initiated, ironically, by two Frenchmen: Guillaume Auger of BigMat and Christophe Agnolutto of AG2R; but its real impetus came from the Belgians Ludo Dierckxsens of Lampre-Daikin and Stive Vermaut of Lotto. This was their land, and they didn't mind that their efforts were taking the likes of U.S. champ Fred Rodriguez on a wild 55km-long ride that took them 2:35 clear at one point.

Rodriguez later said, "Only stupid riders would have worked in a break like that ... there was so far to go." Stupid or not, the break fired up Vermaut's fans who were waiting for him near his village—and, not understood by a New World rider like Rodriguez, it is attacks like this that the local fans will remember for years. The American would have known that if he had skimmed a special supplement produced by an Antwerp newspaper for this momentous day in Belgian cycling. It was packed with sepia-style photos from the 1950s through to modern images of Belgians doing great things in Belgium in the Tours of the '90s. No doubt, a ride like Vermaut's would be on the short list for inclusion in a future edition.

Appropriately, the day's winning move began when Lotto's Pol Van Hyfte was allowed to escape the peloton to have time to stop and greet his family near Eeklo, 65km from the finish. After stopping for some quick hugs and kisses, Van Hyfte was joined by the attacking Jens Voigt of Crédit Agricole, Servais Knaven of Domo and Matteo Frutti of Lampre. This quartet gained 45 seconds on a furiously chasing peloton before a counterattack was launched by the Rabobank tandem of Dutchman Erik Dekker and Belgian Marc Wauters. They in turn were chased by 10 others—including, remarkably, three more Crédit Agricole

Tyler's diary: Stage 2

July 9, 2001

ANTWERP: You hear people complaining about having one of those "days." Well, I think I might be having one of those "seasons." There's nothing more frustrating than working hard, sacrificing and staying dedicated, only to find yourself trapped under a pile of cyclists. And while there's no time at that moment to ask yourself how the hell you got there, the question does linger for a while afterward. Especially while you're standing around waiting for a wheel ... or while you're on the rivet trying to catch the caravan. You can forget about catching the peloton after a crash like today. It's just one more thing to think about on your way to the finish line. God, I hate days like this.

Okay, enough complaining. I should count my blessings that my trusty helmet saw me through another crash, although I think I'm going to have to talk to my friends at Giro about some elbow pads. At first, it seemed that I had broken my right elbow today—which would have made for a perfect set, since I broke my left one at Liège-Bastogne-Liège two months ago. Luckily, x-rays revealed no fractures, but the swelling and pain are indicative of possible tendon damage.

The doctors back in Boston made a point of telling me last May to keep my elbow mobile to promote proper healing. Tomorrow will show how much I'm able to do of that and how much extension I have. It would be kind of hard to ride one-handed. But this is the Tour de France and stranger things have been done. Zülle screwed together a collarbone once, and I managed to ride with a concussion in '99.

The fans were out of control today. They were crowding the road as if we were on a mountain stage. This is kind of dangerous, considering 180 or so guys are barreling through the streets at 60 kilometers an hour. But the Tour de France is not a normal race, and its obstacles and challenges never cease to amaze me—probably because they never have anything to do with the racing itself. They usually come in the form of speed bumps and camera straps. Still, I have to say, the enthusiasm from the spectators never disappoints. Anyone who thinks cycling is dying on the vine should have been here today to witness the madness on the sidewalks. Even our group six minutes behind was bringing out the best in them.

Well, keep your fingers crossed that the swelling fates are kind and that I'm able to reach my rear brake lever by noon tomorrow. I'll be good to go if I have anything to say about it. And if you see a guy out on the course wearing football gear, don't laugh. Just think supportive thoughts.

men: Julich, O'Grady and Anthony Morin. It didn't do any harm that there were also two more Belgians in the mix, Lotto's Rik Verbrugghe and Lampre's Johan Verstrepen.

As this move was developing, there was a big pileup in the peloton, probably caused by one of those humongous speed bumps. This was the second crash of the race for Millar and Italian champion Daniele Nardello of Mapei. Others, including Postal's Hamilton and Jean Delatour's Laurent Roux, left the pileup with gashed elbows, blood on their faces and a time loss of six minutes or more.

As this drama was being played out, the front 16 riders came together, raced hard for the remaining 26km and took a maximum lead of 43 seconds 10km from the finish. Toward the end, O'Grady and his teammates did a four-man team time trial along the wide highway into Antwerp, in the belief that the Aussie would take the yellow jersey, or at least the green.

What they hadn't counted on was a shock attack in view of the 1km-to-go marker by a Belgian—Wauters—who was chased and caught by Pretot. Those two sprinted out the finish, and although they were almost caught on the line, Wauters took the win and its 20-second bonus, which gave him the overall lead by 12 seconds on the Aussie. O'Grady also came up short in the points contest, conceding the green jersey by just two points to Kirsipuu.

"It was devastating," claimed O'Grady. "I didn't know Wauters was so dangerous."

Dangerous? Maybe. Predictable? For sure. Give a Belgian a stage that ends near his hometown and he's certain to rise to the occasion. Wauters's win shocked the C.A. boys, but sent hundreds of thousands of Belgians home happy—and not at all surprised.

STAGE 3: STARTS AND FINISHES

A cursory reading of the results of this dramatic third stage from Antwerp to Seraing— from Flanders to the Walloon region of Belgium—could lead to two logical, but badly mistaken, conclusions: first, that Zabel had earned his 10th Tour de France victory in seven years by taking a 102-strong field sprint; and second, that Australia's gutsy O'Grady had taken over the yellow jersey thanks to his sprinting ability.

Wrong, and wrong.

Zabel did win thanks to his remarkable turn of speed, but he was only able to do that because of an impressive collective performance by his Telekom teammates—including Ullrich. Similarly, O'Grady owed his new conquest of the *maillot jaune*, three years after

Kevin's diary: Stage 3

July 10, 2001

SERAING: If I think about it, the racing so far has been about as I expected, although I forgot how hard the first week of the Tour is. You remember all of the mountain stages, but this first week comes as a shock every time—and it's not over yet.

The Giro d'Italia was hard the first week, too, and, like here, there were plenty of crashes. But there were always times on each stage where the riders would all relax, and you knew nobody was going to attack. It just had a natural rhythm to it, and you would get 30-50K that were easy. In the Tour, though, there is never an easy pace where guys are just talking in the pack. These stages are intense and nervous, guys are attacking nonstop, and the average speed is high every day. Some breaks with dangerous guys have gotten away, but so far it's been good that a few teams have cooperated to bring them back. Like today, we had Udo Bölts in the break, but Moreau was up there, so we and Postal worked together to bring it back.

We talked about winning the stage this morning. Our director knew that it could be a good one for us—with three short, hard hills near the end and an uphill finish. On the first two of those climbs, there was a rush of attacks, but by the third one, it was just us on the front. That one was no quick hill; it was 4K long, and we controlled it well.

For Erik Zabel and the team, two wins is a good start. Today, it worked out for us to work for Erik winning the stage, because it accomplished both of our objectives. By all of us staying at the front, we kept Jan protected, while at the same time giving Erik a leadout. It helped that all of us got up there. You get motivated off of your teammates all working hard for each other, and it carries through the team.

We've been lucky with the weather so far, but it's raining tonight and the forecast is for rain tomorrow (stage 4). Looks like another hard day, with several hard hills at the beginning and maybe bad weather. I will continue to stay near Jan and make sure we stay up front and out of trouble.

The next day is the team time trial, and we should do well. We haven't specifically practiced the team time trial, but we've done more than enough team chases and everyone on the team has quite a bit of experience. What's important is to find a speed where everyone can do their job. There will always be some guys who are stronger, but the way to go the fastest is to go a speed where everyone can pull—some shorter, some longer—and the team doesn't fall apart.... It's still the first week and we have all been recovering well, so even if it's hard tomorrow and we have to chase, we'll be okay in the team time trial.

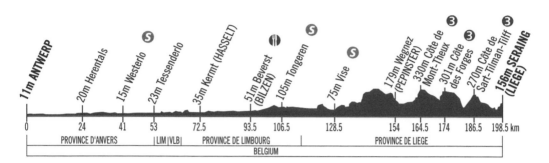

taking the Tour leadership with time bonuses, to another fine showing by Crédit Agricole. And then there was overnight leader Wauters....

In ways, this stage was like two races in one. The first was a three-hour victory parade for Wauters, who raced by fans wearing hastily produced yellow Marc Wauters T-shirts, and stopped in his hometown of Lummen to kiss his wife (who was wearing a festive orange wig to celebrate her husband's team colors) and be cheered by thousands of his supporters. The second race involved a debilitating series of attacks over the Mont Theux, Côte des Forges and Sart-Tilman, Cat. 3 climbs in the Ardennes that proved just too much to withstand for not only Wauters and rival sprinter Kirsipuu—who both finished more than six minutes back—but also for one of the top pre-race favorites, Casagrande.

The Fassa Bortolo leader was still feeling the effects of a pre-Tour stomach virus and his lack of racing since his Giro crash, and after getting dropped four times (even on the flats!) and fighting back each time, he was definitively left behind on Sart-Tilman with less than 15km to go. The Florentine limped home in a beaten group of 16, a disastrous 4:54 behind the peloton.

But along with these hard-luck stories, there was a positive outcome in store for many. Early in the day, the Telekom, Postal and ONCE teams (for Ullrich, Armstrong and Beloki) had

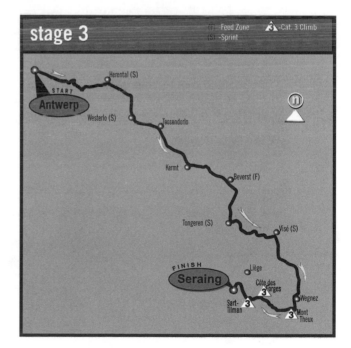

worked hard together to close down a dangerous 19-man break that contained Moreau, O'Grady and Laurent Jalabert. Then, after the last of the flatland attacks (by Frenchmen Frédéric Guesdon of La Française des Jeux and Nicolas Jalabert of CSC-Tiscali) was absorbed on the mythical Côte des Forges, a probable preview of climbs to come was given when 13 riders went away before the summit. The group was headed by Armstrong, Ullrich, Beloki, Moreau and Santiago Botero, as well as those just hoping for a good result on the day: Axel Merckx of Domo, Paolo Bettini and Michele Bartoli of Mapei, and Benoît Salmon of AG2R.

The hill proved too short for a clean break by these strongest riders, and the race was subsequently taken over by Telekom, which placed all nine of its riders at the head of the pack. They were still at the front starting the final, curving 2km uphill to the finish line, where Zabel needed all of his teammates' help to contain the last desperate attacks. Among the men contesting this last-gasp sprint were Armstrong (who was 10th), Mapei's Stefano Garzelli (third) and Bonjour's former French champion François Simon (fifth). But it was Zabel who managed to hang tough, and he was certainly relieved to see the line after the exuberant Frenchman Emmanuel Magnien of La Française des Jeux made a remarkable late surge to come within an ace of taking the win.

Then, in the fine spirit that this Tour was being fought, Magnien playfully tapped Zabel on the shoulder as he coasted by the German just beyond the line.

STAGE 4: BATTLE STATIONS

After the prologue and three demanding road stages, fast speeds and frequent crashes, this long, mostly hilly stage 4 through the Ardennes to the World War I battlefields of Verdun should have given everyone a brief, quiet respite before the next day's challenging team time trial. There's nothing worse than going into a race against the clock with heavy legs. But sometimes things don't work out as expected. And this was just such a case....

Despite a strong head-crosswind on the 215km journey from the lower to the upper valley of the Meuse, the first attacks from the 186-strong field began only 8km out of Huy—the town where April's Flèche Wallonne classic is based. And it was former two-time Flèche winner Laurent Jalabert of CSC-Tiscali who headed the first successful move. With him went another ex-winner of the Flèche, Michele Bartoli of Mapei-Quick Step, and eight others. To cover the attack, race leader O'Grady sent along teammate Sébastien Hinault, while Ullrich had his Kazakh teammate Alex Vinokourov along as his watchdog. That 10-man move gained only 20 seconds, but it forced a 15km-long chase out of Postal and ONCE, and set an aggressive tone for the day: As soon as one attack was contained, another began.

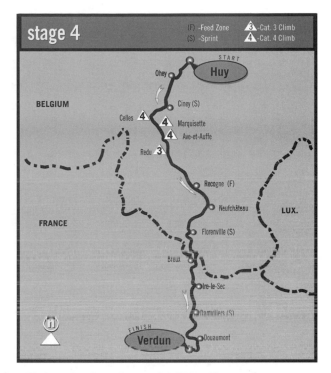

This blitz continued until the stage's defining breakaway group went clear around the 50km mark, just after two short, steep Cat. 4 climbs that left the field's appetite for chasing greatly reduced.

The attack was started by Jean Delatour's Patrice Halgand, who had taken the first two KoMs on his way to claiming the polka-dot jersey. Three other Frenchmen went with him: marathon break specialist Christophe Agnolutto of AG2R, Christophe Mengin of La Française des Jeux and Loïc Lamouller of BigMat-Auber 93. Also there were Spaniards Luis Perez of Festina and José Vidal of Kelme-Costa Blanca, and they were joined by the three who mattered most—Rabobank team leader Michael Boogerd, Crédit Agricole's rejuvenated leader Julich and Telekom team man Udo Bölts.

By now, the course had changed from southwest to southeast, putting a more favorable element in the cool, moist air as it gusted over the Ardennes' wheatfields and pastures, and through its forests of tall, dark pines. This gave an impetus to the leaders, and over the day's third Cat. 4 climb, at Ave-et-Auffe, their lead mushroomed from 0:40 to 2:40. And by the summit of the much longer, winding Cat. 3 Côte de Redu, 13km later, the gap was up to 9:25!

"I was a little excited … when the gap went to 10 minutes," Julich later said. "I was in the front because Jens [Voigt] and I were told to go with any breaks."

Voigt had already covered two earlier moves, so it was the tall American's turn. At first, Julich sat on the back of the break as a good teammate of the yellow jersey should, but "I soon started to roll through," he explained. This was just fine with O'Grady, who was quite happy to concede the lead role to his teammate if the break were successful.

Seeing the widening gap, Armstrong and Postal director Johan Bruyneel were clearly anxious. Both Boogerd and Julich finished top-five at the '98 Tour, and certainly couldn't be given a 10-minute gift. For that matter, neither could Telekom's Bölts. So there was no choice: Postal had to chase.

The effect was devastating. A sudden increase in speed, the powerful crosswind and the undulations of the Ardennes plateau all combined to split the peloton into three separate echelons.

Within moments, only 39 riders were left in the first chase group led by eight Postals (only the injured José Rubiera didn't make the cut), along with the complete ONCE team—which soon lent its support to the pursuit. Ullrich and five of his Telekom teammates gratefully followed, happy to have Bölts in the break.

The chasers thundered through the feed zone at kilometer 90 without grabbing their food bags, the gap already down from 10:15 to 9:30, and the chase continued for more than an hour at an average speed of 50 kph. It was an impressive display of strength by Armstrong's men, but not the sort of "practice" they needed 24 hours before the team time trial.

In closing down the Julich-Boogerd break, they left behind the next part of the peloton (36 riders) by 1:25, while the remaining 100-or-so men were scattered back down the rolling road and destined to finish 18 minutes behind the leaders. Among those who were in the back group were sprinters Zabel, Steels, Vainsteins and Kirsipuu, along with potential top-10 Tour finishers Haimar Zubeldia of Euskaltel-Euskadi and Andrei Kivilev of Cofidis. For these men, hopes of success in this Tour were now seriously compromised....

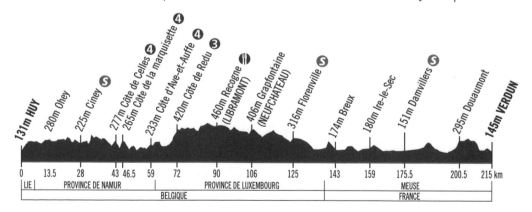

And for Italy's Francesco Casagrande, one of the prerace favorites, there was no hope left at all. Severely fatigued after coming into the race short of racing miles because of the wrist he broke at the Giro d'Italia, and weakened by a stomach virus he suffered in the week before the Tour, he had already abandoned.

Meanwhile, the speed at the head of the race was unrelenting. From the point where the Julich break was caught, just before the race returned from Belgium into France, 82km from the finish, it took the group of 36 chasers—pulled by the Domo, Kelme and CSC teams—another 43km of all-out effort to catch the leaders. In the process, several riders were spit out of the front group, including potential stage winner, La Française des Jeux sprinter Casper.

Once the chase was over, only 79 riders were left at the head of affairs, and the focus shifted from who would win the Tour to who would win the stage. The first to take out an option was Lampre-Daikin's Ludo Dierckxsens, who attacked over the top of a short hill with 30km to go. He was joined on the ensuing long descent by the day's original attacker, Jalabert, and the last Tour's top young rider Francisco Mancebo of iBanesto.com.

This trio took a maximum lead of 1:50 before the long stage's final climb, which curved up through the forest to the open hills surrounding Verdun's memorial to the 150,000 men killed here during the most infamous battle of World War I. It may seem irreverent to evoke such grim statistics in connection with a mere bike race, but the Tour de France was already a national passion when the Great War started, and the ghosts of those soldiers who died in the cause of peace almost certainly loved watching these modern warriors of the wheel race through their killing fields.

By the top of the Douaumont hill, alongside the war graves and with 15km to go, the three leaders were still 1:09 ahead. This gave Jalabert, only 0:39 behind O'Grady on G.C., the chance of taking the yellow jersey. With that in mind, Crédit Agricole team director asked Voigt and Julich (O'Grady's only teammates in the group) to add their support to a chase being conducted (remarkably!) by six riders from France's Division II Bonjour outfit, who realized that their Damien Nazon, who comes from this region, was one of the few sprinters still at the head of the race.

The following chase was enough to save the jersey for O'Grady, but not quite enough to give Bonjour its first Tour stage win. Instead, the wily Jalabert attacked in the final 2km and then outsped Dierckxsens to the line to give his new Danish team *its* first Tour success.

Tyler's diary: Stage 4

July 11, 2001

VERDUN: The television coverage of today's stage probably didn't do justice to the level of racing going on. It doesn't get much more difficult than a day like we had. Any way you slice it, working at the front all day at full speed is a hard day at the office.

An attack went at the 15km mark that included Vinokourov from Telekom, so we made a point of chasing it down. If we had let him get some time on the field, he would have become one more rider we'd be forced to keep track of—and we don't want to have to worry about him when the roads start slanting up. When the big break of the day reached the 10-minute point, we went to work along with ONCE and Telekom to reel it in.

My elbow hurt more today than yesterday, so I went back to the caravan to visit the medical car during the race. This is a vehicle that follows the peloton and treats riders while they're on their bikes. They do anything they can to help—including re-bandaging your road rash while hanging out their car window going 30 mph. You could say they're incredible. They also help respond to crashes. During my visit, the docs sprayed my arm down with something that was icy-cold and gave me a painkiller. The quick visit helped the aches go away, but gave me a stomachache.

Tomorrow is the much anticipated team time trial. Everyone gets a little nervous about an event like this, because so much is riding on the strength of your fifth guy and you never know what could happen. It's important to get a good night's sleep beforehand and not get too worked up about things. Nerves are your enemy in a TTT. We visited the course back in June, to practice riding together and to work on our team formation. Then, prior to the start in Dunkirk, we put a little bit more time in, finalizing the lineup. It's critical for the team to be as cohesive and prepared as possible for this event stage.

My roommate, Steffen Kjaergaard, will be ready, since he has just the trick for helping him sleep at night: He brought his own down comforter to the Tour. Of course I was immediately jealous, but I try not to let it show. It's okay that I'm sleeping under my germ-infested, dirt-covered, standard-issue, polyester-blend bedspread, while Steffen is all curled up in Norwegian goose feathers. His subtle psychological warfare isn't affecting me at all....

Actually, Steffen had kind of a close call yesterday after the stage. He was doing an interview with a Norwegian television station, when a race jury car started to drive over his foot. Steffen screamed at them and they stopped. He probably could have handled the pain, though—after all, his nickname is the "Viking."

Jalabert grabbed all the headlines in the morning newspapers, but the day's real story was how Postal was ready to control the race, that O'Grady was not just a lucky race leader, and that Julich was back. As for the next day's team time trial, Julich said, "It's a very hard course … but the yellow jersey can give you a lot of motivation."

Especially when everyone has heavy legs after a stage so hard that O'Grady called it "the day from hell."

STAGE 5: DRAMA IN THE RAIN

Right after finishing their team time trials in torrential rain at Bar-le-Duc, atop a stiff 1.8km switchback climb, the riders had to turn left up a steep alleyway to reach the place where their team buses were parked. This narrow, newly blacktopped path became a corridor of emotional highs and lows as the men from each succeeding team arrived. And by reading their body language, you could tell how each had performed.

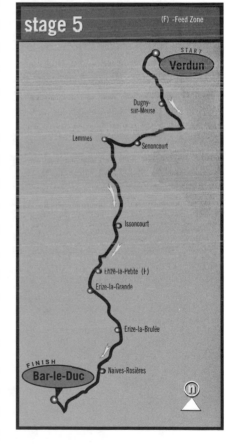

Ullrich, the first of the main contenders to finish, had a look on his broad, bronzed, unshaven face that was more stoic than usual. This wasn't surprising, as his Telekom squad was never in contention in the 67km TTT. One reason was the wet conditions: "Our guys had thick legs because of the rain," said team director Rudy Pevenage. Livingston was dropped, then Zabel flatted and Jens Heppner had to change bikes, leaving just six men for the last 20km.

As Telekom finished in a time of 1:23:22, 20 minutes back down the road was Ullrich's main rival, Armstrong, who appeared to be heading for some major time gains. His Postal team's time split 22km from the finish was a minute faster than Telekom's, and that looked like growing to at least 1:30 by the finish—especially since the American squad had adopted its usual policy of starting out conservatively (only sixth best at 19.5km), before stepping up the pace (for the middle 23km, Postal was only one second slower than the fastest team).

Then, with 14.5km still to ride, two men fell—a crash that was destined to be replayed endlessly on TV: Christian Vande Velde skidding sideways, Heras running into him, and their cumbersome TT bikes clattering down the highway. "A little bit of panic went through everybody," team member George Hincapie reported. But team director Bruyneel stayed calm and because co-leader Heras was one of the downed riders, Bruyneel immediately told the other seven to slow the tempo and wait.

It was a pre-agreed decision, but one that would cost Armstrong in his quest for a third Tour title. Time splits later showed that in the 15km stretch where the crash took place, Postal conceded 50 seconds to the fastest team, instead of being level or faster. There were also some hidden time losses, as Hincapie intimated: "Probably, we lost a lot of rhythm."

The nine Postals did fight back though, with Armstrong continuing to be the dynamo, making the longest, hardest pulls—just as he did when he was with the Motorola team in the early 1990s. And while the squad's Viatcheslav Ekimov and Steffen Kjaergaard dropped off before the final climb, Armstrong led his men to the line and came through the alleyway with a look of satisfaction. His words the next morning reflected that: "I think the team showed a lot of heart and a lot of guts to get back together quickly and come back strong."

The unfortunate Vande Velde was not as calm as his boss. He hadn't shifted his gears down after finishing and needed a strong push to make it up the steep path to the bus. When asked about the crash, his face tightened with frustration. "It was the white line," he said. "The rain made it slick—I was even slipping on the turns on this hill to the finish."

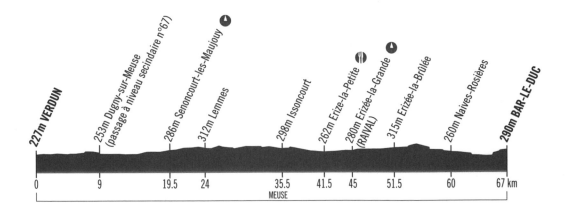

After a few moments to catch his breath, the 24-year-old Midwesterner added, "I'm so mad with myself. I had great legs...."

Despite the crash, Vande Velde played a big role in Postal recording 1:22:58, the fastest finish time yet posted. There were three teams remaining, however, and they all had faster times at the previous check. First of these to arrive was ONCE-Eroski of Spain, the winner of the 2000 Tour's TTT, but starting this time with only two of its 2000 Tour team. As a warm-up to the Tour, ONCE's new-look, Beloki-led lineup dominated a 24km TTT at the Tour of Catalonia. And here, they almost *sprinted* up the last climb, to stop the clock in 1:22:03—the time that U.S. Postal Service would probably have matched without its crash.

Beloki was clearly pleased. As he turned into the alleyway after the finish, shifted into a low gear and smoothly pedaled up toward his team bus, he looked like a man who had just completed a hard training ride, rather than one of the Tour's toughest stages. He was ready for the mountains.

The next team was Festina, led home and up the alley by a proud and confident-looking Moreau, with a time of 1:22:26. This French team consistently does well in team time trials, despite an unusual mix of talents: the pure power of Moreau and French TT champion Florent Brard; the smoothness of Spanish climber Angel Casero; and the speed of former Postal team sprinter Sven Teutenberg.

Like Festina and the new ONCE, Crédit Agricole is a team that makes the best use of its resources, which it did to finish fourth in the 2000 Tour TTT. If any confirmation were needed of its potential in *this* Tour, that was provided on stage 2, when Julich, O'Grady, Voigt and Anthony Morin headed the day's winning break, riding a mini-TTT on the run-in to Antwerp. At the time there was disappointment in their camp, because O'Grady just missed out on taking both the yellow and green jerseys. "All that for nothing," said a frustrated Julich in Antwerp.

His frustration disappeared when O'Grady *did* take the race lead at Seraing, and the next day Julich himself rode strongly in the stage-defining break through the Ardennes. As for this stage, the *real* TTT, the tall American said, "I was feeling nervous [in the opening kilometers] ... because I was feeling so good.... I knew we were going fast, but at the same time I was thinking, 'Man, we've got to pick the speed up here.' And when we came through the first time check and we had the best time it was like, 'Okay. Don't change anything, just stay like this.'"

Freddy's diary: Stage 5

Friday, July 11

BAR-LE-DUC: Whew, today was tough. After yesterday's fiasco, I was really hurting. It was not very sportsmanlike what ONCE and U.S. Postal did on stage 4. ONCE attacked as a full team at the feed zone on a windy day. Feed zones are already dangerous enough, and it's an unwritten rule not to attack there. Sometimes it might happen that a single guy might try to get away in a feed zone—but you don't expect an entire world-class team to do it. It's like attacking when the yellow jersey gets a flat. The move caught our team and other teams by surprise, and the fact that Postal and Telekom followed suit, well, we weren't happy about that. At the end, at least I got a fourth place out of it.

Today, I was a tired guy after a 100K "team time trial" yesterday. Our main goal in today's real team time trial was to keep Axel in G.C. contention. We started at a comfortable pace, but right from the gun, I couldn't go hard. My heart rate was depressed, and I was the weakest guy. It was the first team time trial we had all ridden together. Most teams were riding a tight two-person echelon and moving in a circle. We tried to go with longer pulls and a one-man echelon, but with that crosswind, it slowed us down. In looking back at it, we realized that Axel rode very strong for us, as did Museeuw and Wadecki.

* * *

It's fun and it gives me pride to wear the stars-and-stripes jersey. I worked hard for it—and the odds were against me in Philadelphia this year—and I pulled it off. It's the first time anyone has done two in a row. Eddy Merckx made a special bike for me, too, and the whole team is really psyched about it. The team surprised me with it in Dunkirk. They told me to come check right away on some luggage, and I was getting stressed out that something was missing, and they were all standing with it out in the hall, like "ta da!" I had asked the director a few weeks ago if there were any chance of them getting me a new bike, and he said they were really busy and probably not. But they were all just playing with me. It was fun.

The main feature of the bike is that it is oversized Easton aluminum and super light—and, of course, the special paint job with stars and stripes. I think Eddy is working on marketing it in the United States. The rumor I heard was that his wife and daughter were behind it. Anyway, it's pretty cool.

It probably helped Julich's Crédit Agricole team that there were few flat stretches on the course, because the American and his strongest teammates Vaughters, Voigt, Hushovd and O'Grady all prefer racing on rolling roads. In all, there were some 19 uphills of varying length and gradient, most of them after the 24km mark, where Crédit Agricole turned onto the historic *Voie Sacrée* (the Sacred Way) with a 10-second lead over second-fastest Festina. In World War I, this narrow, rolling highway was the only lifeline between Paris and French troops at the two-year-long Battle of Verdun. A constant slow-moving stream of army trucks carried reinforcements and supplies to the warfront, and returned with dead or injured soldiers. Now, it was a fast-moving steam of pro cycling teams racing down the Sacred Way from Verdun to Bar-le-Duc.

Symbolically, at every kilometer stone along the route, the teams passed a rifle-toting sentry, dressed in a somber ankle-length greatcoat and plumed helmet of the 1914–18 era. The soldiers not only provided an emotional link with the past, but also lent a mythical quality to this drama-filled stage.

Julich's own drama played out just after his team had swept through the second time check, at 45km, with a lead of 23 seconds over ONCE, which had displaced Festina from the runner-up spot. The final result remained uncertain, though, and seemed to go against Crédit Agricole when Julich's front tire went flat. A spare bike soon came from the following car, and the rest of the team waited ... but disrupting a team's rhythm like that can often be fatal.

Still, the American turned the negative into a positive.

"It couldn't have happened at a better place," Julich said, "because it happened right at the base of the climb that when we did the team time trial in training I was a little nervous about—because it was about a K-and-a-half, a long drag and towards the end. When I flatted ... I didn't realize that we were going up the hill, because I was so nervous trying to catch back up and get the team organized again. So when I started rotating again I'm waiting for the climb to come, and I knew when we came to 10K-to-go that we must've passed it already. But it gave everyone a little rest there ... and we were flying at the end."

Indeed. Despite the persistent rain, the hills, and the strong head and side winds, Crédit Agricole was averaging more than 49 kph. Even with Julich's flat, the team recorded the fastest time over the final 22km, with its former world under-23 time trial champion Thor Hushovd pulling all the way up the difficult climb to the finish.

Realizing they were going to win—and O'Grady was going to keep the yellow jersey—some of the riders began punching the air in celebration well before they crossed the line in a stunning 1:21:32. "It was a great feeling," Julich confirmed. "I haven't had that feeling of winning a race in three or four years. That's as good as it gets."

Rarely has any team, let alone an underdog, won a TTT in such thrilling circumstances. So stunned was Julich that, as he turned into and up the narrow alleyway, his emotions burst out of him in a series of ecstatic, high-pitched roars. Those whoops were more eloquent than any speech, but Julich's Colorado teammate Jonathan Vaughters supplied the words. "We may not have the best riders in the world," he said, "but we work really well together."

Vaughters sure is a master of understatement.

STAGE 6: DOWN TO THE WIRE

For riders on different teams, there's little time for conversations during the long, fast stages of the Tour's opening week, and they rarely stay at the same hotels. So every morning you see them chatting to each other before the stage start. That was the case with Postal's Vande Velde and Festina's German sprinter Sven Teutenberg on the morning after this transitionary stage between the team time trial and the first serious day of climbing.

The two riders had been teammates on Postal in 1998, which was Vande Velde's rookie year. Since then, the American had developed into one of the most valued members of Armstrong's Tour-winning entourage, while Teutenberg, still only 29, had had an anonymous two seasons with Division II Gerolsteiner. Now he was back on a Division I formation, a replacement for Festina's previous German sprinter, Marcel Wüst, who had become a consultant with the team after an eye injury ended his racing career.

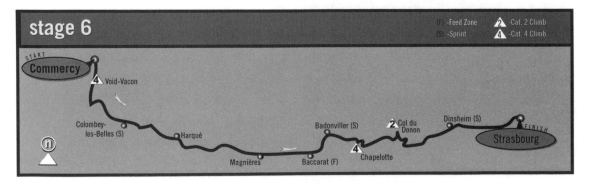

Vande Velde, showing his friend the bandaged arm that resulted from his TT crash, was commiserating with Teutenberg over the previous day's stage 6 finish into Strasbourg.

"You were in the ideal position," said the American. "I think you would have won."

As Vande Velde signed a fan's photo, a journalist joined the conversation, asking Teutenberg if he agreed with the Postal rider's assessment. "You can say afterward that you may have won," replied the tan, Roman-nosed sprinter, "but it wasn't normal what he did, to move so far across...."

Teutenberg was referring to the recently crowned Belgian champion Ludovic Capelle, who led out the sprint from 500 meters for his AG2R teammate Jaan Kirsipuu, and then, with 200 meters to go, swung far to his left and started coasting, blocking Teutenberg's path. Both the German and Kirsipuu had been drafting off Capelle, and when the Belgian peeled off, Kirsipuu sped straight for the line, while Teutenberg, who perhaps has a little better acceleration than the Estonian veteran, was forced to stop pedaling completely.

Kirsipuu won, Teutenberg crossed the line in 28th place ... and Capelle should have been penalized for a maneuver that prevented the German from contesting the win. Instead, the judges decided to penalize another Belgian, the resurgent Tom Steels of Mapei, who they accused of impeding the effort of double-stage winner Zabel when he was trying to challenge Kirsipuu in the final meters.

Zabel went for the same gap that was also being sought by Steels on his left and Nazon on his right. With about 100 meters left, Nazon and Zabel had already made contact, causing two spokes to snap in the Frenchman's front wheel. Then, as Bonjour's Nazon challenged on the right, he touched shoulders with Zabel just as Steels made his move and

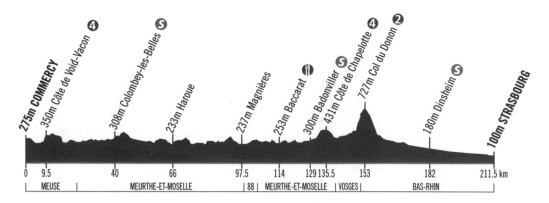

Tyler's diary: Stage 6

July 13, 2001

STRASBOURG: It's Friday the 13th at the Tour de France. Kind of a scary thought. This is, after all, the race in which grown men curse bad luck and pray that good karma is on their side. I don't know if the date was on most riders' minds today. But historically, I've always been somewhat fond of the number 13, and it's never frightened me too much. In fact, after finishing 13th in the Tour in '99, it became a lucky number of sorts.

Well, after today, I'm going to have to scrap all this 13 worship and join the ranks of the leery. I officially dislike Friday the 13th because today, as they say back home, rotted. Maybe I torched myself yesterday, stressing about the TTT and trying to ride like a man with a mission. Who can say? All I know is that I didn't feel so hot during today's stage. It was as if my stomach wasn't digesting food. Sometimes your body has to revolt a little. I guess it's nature's way of asking what the hell you think you are doing.

I battled hard to keep my position through most of the stage. I tried to stay at the front of the peloton and help my teammates as much as I could. But honestly, I fell short on the detail today. I made it over the Cat. 2 climb all right, which is reassuring, but toward the end I felt like I should relax a bit. Around 9km to go, we were battling crosswinds and the guy in front of me sat up. There's not much you can do in a situation like this. I lost contact with the field and wound up finishing a few minutes down. I can honestly say that I'm all set with riding in crosswinds.

The time deficit is not the issue, though. The bigger concern of the day was feeling a little off. It's stressful because you don't know if it's from eating something or if it's just a bad day in general. I'll keep my fingers crossed that it passes. As I've said before, my overall time is not important; what's important is being strong enough to help Lance in the mountains. That is my sole purpose in being here, and I don't want to let him down.

That said, I'll be the guy riding with the garlic around his neck tomorrow....

clipped Zabel's other shoulder. Steels was relegated to last place in the pack, but Zabel said he wouldn't have won anyway and that Kirsipuu was stronger.

Two things helped the Estonian sustain his long sprint and claim a second Tour stage win two years after winning stage 1 in 1999: the leadout by Capelle and the strong tail wind.

Earlier in the race, that 20-kph wind helped a marathon five-man break come very close to succeeding. After a flurry of breaks had been caught, Domo's Axel Merckx attacked on one of the many short hills, 45km into the stage from Commercy. He was quickly joined by three other stars of the sport: Michele Bartoli of Mapei, Laurent Brochard of Jean Delatour and Rik Verbrugghe of Lotto. And Crédit Agricole's Frédéric Bessy went along to ride shotgun for the yellow jersey.

These weren't riders whom Crédit Agricole (or any of the major contenders) could give any leeway to—especially Bartoli, who was the best placed of the leaders, 3:43 down on O'Grady. So by riding a strong tempo, the French team kept the gap at between 2:50 and 3.40 for most of the 160km span of the breakaway. Yet despite a flurry of attacks over the Cat. 2 Col du Donon, the five leaders were still three minutes up on reaching the flat roads of the Rhine Valley, 30km from Strasbourg.

As it turned out, though, it wasn't quite enough for the break to stay away. The last man standing was Verbrugghe, who tried to use his time-trial strength on a solo move with 7km left—the same distance of the Giro prologue he won at almost 59 kph. But even that speed wasn't fast enough to hold off a peloton driven by the sprinters' teams at more than 60 kph, and Verbrugghe was caught 3km from the line.

It was a line that AG2R's Kirsipuu reached first ... while it could have been Vande Velde's pal, Teutenberg, had he not been blocked. But as the German told his buddy the next morning, as they lined up for stage 7, "There's still 14 days to go." And 14 more chances to win a stage....

STAGE 7: A DAY FOR THE FRENCH

This unusual first week of the Tour had seen four leaders in seven days; no conventional field sprints; and a mixture of time trials, flat days and hilly stages—none of them easy. Now it was time for a mountain stage ... not high mountains, but five climbs that promised a total of 8000 feet of climbing and descending on this 162.5km stage through the Vosges. They also promised an aggressive race, particularly from the

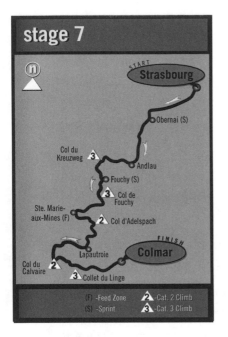

French, as this was their national holiday of July 14, Bastille Day.

That promise was quickly met when French riders began the opening moves. First, AG2R's Agnolutto attacked only 9km out of Strasbourg, as the race headed west between wide fields of corn and pastureland. Next, Jean Delatour's Laurent Brochard counterattacked with Fassa Bortolo's Sergei Ivanov and Cofidis's *lanterne rouge* David Millar, as they rode up through the sloping vineyards of Alsace and dropped into the painfully pretty village of Andlau. Over chocolate-brown cobblestones, the trio raced between black-and-white half-timbered cottages adorned with boxes of red geraniums and French tricolors waving from the windows, 50 seconds ahead of the pack.

They then headed into the mountains, via a steady 3.8-percent climb that curved its way alongside the bubbling Andlau creek up to the Cat. 3 Col de Kreuzweg. Even though it was a gentle, if 14km-long, introduction to the day's climbing, it was enough to see the break absorbed and for 20 riders to be dropped—and destined to finish 24 minutes down.

Up at the front, the attacks continued on the steep descent that twisted through a forest of dark pine trees. Looking across a deep valley, a clinging mist could be seen lifting from the wooded ridges, like a theater curtain rising before a play.

Enter Laurent Jalabert.

The French hero's acceleration on this first downhill was impressive. It clearly confirmed that three days after his stage win at Verdun and four-and-a-half months after falling from a ladder and cracking three vertebrae, he was finally back to his aggressive self.

This first attack didn't go anywhere, but when seven men went clear on the next climb—the shorter, steeper Col de Fouchy—Jalabert chased and caught them with King of the Mountains leader Halgand of Jean Delatour and Crédit Agricole's Voigt.

Again, the move didn't last.

All these attacks kept the pace high, though, and the peloton was flying along when it reached a narrow, bucolic valley after the Fouchy descent. Right then, another exploratory move was made by Fassa Bortolo's talented Italian Ivan Basso and Jean Delatour's enigmatic Roux—a 28-year-old Frenchman who was trying to return to an elite level after three years of up-and-down results that included a drug-control positive for amphetamines.

It was while this chase was at its height through the little village of Lièpvre that Postal's Vande Velde overshot a turn and collided with a steel post, breaking his left forearm and sustaining heavy bruises and abrasions to his left shoulder and neck. The severity of his injuries wasn't immediately obvious, and within five minutes he was on his bike and chasing—only to stop within a quarter-hour and climb into the ambulance.

Vande Velde's elimination was a blow to Postal, which values the young American's speed and strength on the flats and in the mountains. It would certainly add to the workload of men like Hincapie, Hamilton, Kjaergaard, Rubiera and Victor Hugo Peña, the other all-around team riders. In fact, on the final two climbs of this stage, the only teammates remaining in the front group with Postal leaders Armstrong and Heras were Hincapie and Rubiera.

While the Vande Velde drama was being played out, a furious chase after Basso and Roux was undertaken by Jalabert, second-placed Voigt and Cofidis's Spanish climber Iñigo Cuesta. This trio had the two leaders in sight for 13km before they managed to bridge, 3km from the summit of the Cat. 2 Col d'Adelspach. The intensity of the pursuit had taken the five leaders 2:40 ahead of the pack—which was being pulled by Postal at a steady tempo.

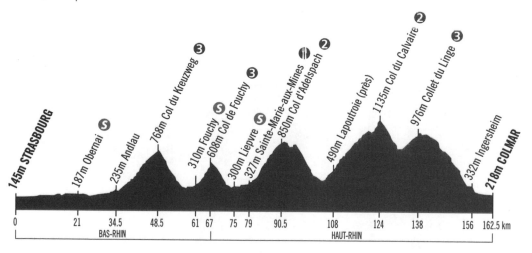

Freddy's diary: Stage 7

July 15, 2001

COLMAR: *Going into today's stage to Colmar, I didn't know how I was feeling after so many hard stages. I stayed at the front not because I was trying to attack, but as a tactic for survival. Again, guys were attacking from the gun. Finally, on the first climb, it was at full speed and we were flying up. After a while, I was feeling comfortable enough at the front. When I saw the 1K to go, I shut it down a fraction, allowed several guys to go by, and rolled down the descent back to the front. This was generally how I was on all of the climbs. Romans (Vainsteins) tried letting the guys go a bit on the climbs and let a gap open up by the top. He thought he could catch back on the descents, but he was wrong. Today, there was no letup. You'd go straight down and then straight back up again—there was no chance to catch back up.*

I survived until the second-to-last climb, when Telekom put the hammer down. Why they did that, I don't know. I talked to Kevin and even he didn't know why they were hammering. I stayed with Zabel thinking that if I were with him, maybe we would get back up, since Telekom might try to set something up for him. But they didn't. We ended up 11 minutes down.

The good news is that I was feeling safe on the descents today. The roads were rough, so you didn't tend to slide out, but if you crashed, it would hurt bad on that surface. I didn't see any corners that were too difficult. The only problem was if you misjudged a corner and went straight off the road. That's what I think happened with Christian (Vande Velde), who crashed right in front of me. This isn't like a criterium where you see the course over and over. In the Tour de France, we're always going into these corners blind. We don't know if there's a cliff on the other side or what. If you're in a breakaway or trying to catch back on, you might take more of a chance.

The crowds were incredible today, especially for not being a big mountain stage. This is my second Tour, and it was like this when we went into Germany last year. Whenever the Tour comes close to Germany, the crowds are huge. Today reminded me of Belgium, too, where there were also giant crowds.

Later, I was surprised at how good I felt when I was down on the massage table. Yesterday, I was saying, "Ow, that hurts," all of the time; but today I was comfortable on the table. You'd think it would be worse after another day of suffering, but somehow your body recovers.

Four of Ullrich's Telekom riders then took over, setting a cracking pace up the difficult final part of the Col du Calvaire. Only 72 riders were left in the group by the 3723-foot summit, where massive holiday crowds were thrilled to see riding on the wheels of the dark-pink Telekom train the very men who'd likely be fighting out the Tour in a few days' time: Ullrich, Moreau, Armstrong, Beloki and Julich.

For now, though, the focus was on the five men racing for the stage win some five minutes ahead. Jalabert went on a probing solo on the descent before the last little climb, the Collet de Linge; but the leaders were back together as they went under the 25km-to-go banner. Soon, Jalabert was at the front again, and in a light rain, he forced the pace on the long, long descent toward Colmar.

The former world No. 1 was favored to win his second stage of the week, but both the impressive Voigt, who was heading for his first yellow jersey, and Basso looked likely to challenge the veteran French rider. That speculation suddenly meant nothing when on a fast right turn, with Jalabert ahead, Basso skidded out on a slick white line. Voigt just avoided the fallen Italian (who would finish the stage before discovering that he had broken a clavicle), and by the time Roux, Cuesta and the tall German had regrouped, Jalabert had bolted.

So for the second time in his career, six years after his memorable solo victory at Mende, Jalabert won a Tour stage on Bastille Day. And in the process, CSC-Tiscali's French leader had jumped to second on G.C., 2:34 down on Voigt—the fifth race leader in a week.

The French were jubilant, while the rest of the world could only wonder, What did this crazy Tour have in store for us next?

STAGE 8: TURNING BACK TIME

Nothing had gone right for Cofidis in the Tour's first week. First, the French team's main hope, Millar, crashed in the prologue when on target for a top finish. The result? A bandaged left leg that caused the tall Brit to be dropped on every stage, unable to follow the peloton's accelerations. Next, on stage 4 to Verdun, the entire team was caught in the back part of the pack when it split in three during the crazy pursuit of the Julich break, putting all the Cofidis riders at least 18 minutes behind the main contenders. Then, on stage 7 in the Vosges, the team's former Tour King of the Mountains, Christophe Rinero, had to quit with an injured left knee.

The one relatively bright spot was the squad's eighth place in the team time trial, when it finished slightly faster than Jalabert's CSC-Tiscali squad and Stefano Garzelli's Mapei-Quick Step team. After that stage, all the Cofidis riders agreed that from then on they would try to have a representative in every break that mattered.

Their new attitude paid off the very next day, only 8km into stage 6, when three Cofidis men led the pack up the day's first KoM climb, the wall-like Cat. 4 hill at Void-Vacon, to lead out its Kazakh climber, Kivilev, who took the second-place points.

True, Cofidis failed to put a rider in the elite five-man break that led that stage for 160km, but the next day's stage 7 went better. Millar, although by now last on G.C., inspired his colleagues by jumping into the first serious move with Brochard and Ivanov. Then little Cuesta triggered the counterattack that took him, Jalabert and Voigt up to the day's winning break. Cuesta finished fourth.

With their morale restored, the Cofidis men were again ready to go into action on this 222.5km transitional stage 8 from Colmar to Pontarlier. So were several other teams....

Rolling out through the narrow medieval streets of Colmar in light rain, the 176-strong peloton knew it was going to be a long day, especially if the rain and wind persisted. Some riders were wearing calf-length tights, most had arm warmers, and a few had already donned rain jackets. And with the midday temperatures hovering around 15 degrees Celsius (59 degrees Fahrenheit), this blustery July day had the feel of March in Belgium. In fact, in terms of the weather, the terrain and the roll call of major players, this could have been a stage of the gritty Three Days of De Panne.

There was a strong sidewind blowing from the left in the opening 20km, which headed southeast on the straight and narrow D13 back road past fields of tall corn and low wheat. The first attack, after only 5km, was started by two Belgians: Domo's Ludo Dierckxsens, who played such a strong role in the 2001 Paris-Roubaix, and Rabobank's Marc Wauters, a former Paris-Tours winner who had worn the yellow jersey five days earlier. With them were two other willing workers, Italian Nicola Loda of Fassa Bortolo and Spaniard Aitor Gonzalez of Kelme-Costa Blanca.

Just as this move began, there was a pileup in the peloton, which left five men with a medley of elbow, knee and shoulder injuries. It also left a split in the pack, with Armstrong one of those behind. "[But] I had a couple of guys waiting for him," reported Postal director Bruyneel.

By the time the peloton regrouped, another 11 riders had set off in pursuit and joined the four leaders. This new wave included some more classics' specialists: Paris-Roubaix winner Servais Knaven of Domo, Amstel Gold Race winner Erik Dekker of Rabobank and former Tour of Flanders winner Jacky Durand of La Française des Jeux.

In the context of the Tour, though, the names that mattered in the break were Telekom lieutenant Vinokourov (a former Dauphiné Libéré champion and recent winner of the Tour of Germany), the high-flying O'Grady ... and Cofidis's Kivilev (who won the first race of his four-year pro career just before the Tour, a mountain stage of the Dauphiné). Vinokourov, only 56 seconds behind Armstrong on G.C., was the biggest danger, of course, while Kivilev still had that deficit of more than 20 minutes on the Tour's defending champion.

By the time Armstrong's Postal team had organized its forces and begun the chase, the 15 leaders had a 22-second gap. That increased to 35 seconds before

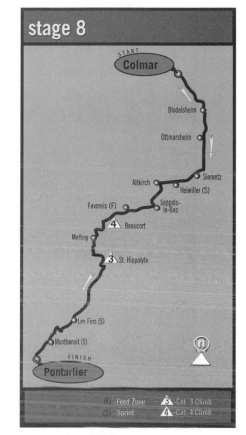

the course turned right at 21km, giving the leaders a strong north wind at their backs. Beloki's ONCE riders had joined Postal in the pursuit, but the gap was still growing. It was up to 40 seconds when Vinokourov raised his hand to signal he had flatted. Not benefiting from a line of follow cars to bridge back (none are allowed when the gap is this small, except for a neutral support vehicle), the Telekom man waited for the pack after getting a replacement wheel.

So, with the danger passed, Bruyneel ordered his men to cease the chase. They didn't slow down in front though. All 14 riders were contributing to the paceline, especially the three Rabobank men: Dekker, Wauters and Bram De Groot. After an hour of riding on the flat valley roads at 49 kph, they were four minutes ahead ... and the gap widened to 25 minutes (!) in the second hour, as they headed west through the steady rain toward the rolling hills of the Franche-Comté region.

The bad weather was one reason for the peloton's malaise. Another was later expressed by Dekker: "It's the result of a very fast race in the first week ... everyone is too tired to chase." It was also a calculated gamble by the major teams to ignore the potential danger of the break and not even increase the tempo.

Rarely in the Tour had a big group like this been given such leeway. In fact, you'd have to go back a few decades to find something similar.

In 1956, also on the eighth stage, Frenchman Roger Walkowiak finished in a 31-man break that gained almost 19 minutes on a flat 244km stage from Lorient in Brittany to Angers in the Loire Valley. Walkowiak took the yellow jersey, and although he lost it three days later, he hung tough in the Pyrénées and reclaimed the overall lead in the Alps. The major contenders neglected the threat of Walkowiak because he was on a minor team; but he was a useful climber and had finished second the previous year in the mountainous Dauphiné Libéré stage race. Walkowiak remains the Tour's most unlikely winner, especially as he didn't finish top three in any of the stages at that '56 Tour.

Forty-five years later, his name was on the lips of many race followers and fans alike, as this year's stage 8 break continued to power its way forward.

As the French say, this was racing à l'ancienne. Old-style racing. And there was an old-time feel in the village of Faverois, where the day's feed zone was stationed 101.5km into the stage: spectators standing under umbrellas, rain dripping from overhanging trees, shop signs of faded paint dating from the '50s, and a narrow, gravel-tarred road dipping into town, crossing a small bridge, making some tight turns and then climbing back out into the countryside of small meadows and woods.

Just after 2 p.m. the break swept though town, riders grabbed their canvas satchels of food and straight away buckled down to their pacemaking. Dekker again: "It was cold and

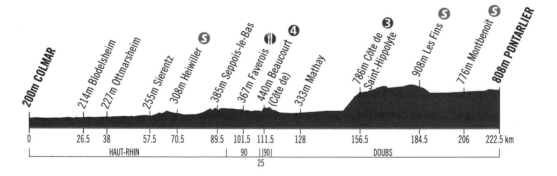

raining, but when you are in a breakaway it is better, as you're going to finish a half-hour shorter and the motivation for the stage win takes over."

Almost half-an-hour later, the bedraggled, leaderless bunch rolled through Faverois. Many of the 160 riders were nursing wounds, fighting stomach problems or suffering from pure fatigue. Postal's Hamilton was one of the first week's victims, as he said before the start: "This fricking arm [injured in his stage 2 crash] has been a little bit of a pain for me … and the medication has kind of messed up my stomach. I've definitely been empty the past couple of days…. I just need to tough through it."

The poor conditions accentuated the riders' pain, and heavier rain was falling from black clouds swirling around limestone crags when the race crossed the rushing, greenish waters of the Doubs River at Pont-de-Roide. The gap was 32:50 and wasn't going to get any smaller.

Soon the unsmiling peloton climbed out of the Doubs gorge up to a high plateau, where the temperature was even colder, dipping to 50 degrees or less. "It was very cold the last 50 kilometers," confirmed Frenchman François Simon of Bonjour, who was the best placed of the 14 leaders after O'Grady, and a former teammate of the Crédit Agricole rider.

That damp frigidity had the least effect on the Belgians and Dutchmen in the group, and with just over 20km to go, Knaven and Dekker escaped from the group along a fast, smooth road curving through the small upper valley of the Doubs. The chase was taken up, remarkably, by Kelme's 25-year-old Gonzales, the only Spanish rider in the break, who was racing like a classics veteran. Gonzales was shadowed by Wauters, but he still managed to catch the two leaders with 6km remaining, the Spaniard then pluckily led out the final sprint … but it was Dekker who came through at the last second to snatch the win.

A frozen O'Grady led the other 10 men in two-and-a half minutes later, and just as the aggressive Aussie was being presented with his fourth yellow jersey (and first green jersey) of the Tour, the peloton reached 20km to go. O'Grady and Dekker were the big names in the break, but Kivilev of Cofidis—who now moved into fourth place overall—was the only name that concerned the Tour's main contenders.

A few days later, Armstrong said, "Kivilev is a damn good rider. He can climb, he's got form —he just won the Route du Sud before this race. We might have made a very big mistake."

Cofidis had finally placed a man in a break that mattered. The days ahead would tell whether he could become a real contender, maybe another Walkowiak.

Tyler's diary: Stage 8

July 15, 2001

PONTARLIER: What do you get when you mix rain, freezing-cold temperatures and the Tour de France? One long day and a backache. I don't know what we did to deserve it, but Mother Nature is sure letting us have it. If I could have a conversation with this woman, I'd beg for mercy. Enough with the wind and the rain and the unseasonable temps already. This race is enough of a challenge all by itself.

The early part of the day was a bit hectic, given that Telekom's Vinokourov was part of the epic break that went up the road at 5km. Perhaps the cycling fates were on our side and didn't want us to chase like maniacs for the entire day. When Vinokourov flatted and lost contact with the other escapees, the peloton breathed a collective sigh of relief. It's hard going full tilt with rain pelting your face—and the number of crashes today proved that. Needless to say, things would have been sketchier if he didn't come back to the group. Anyone who doesn't believe that luck is a factor in bicycle racing doesn't need to look any further than this for an example to prove them wrong. Vinokourov's bad luck was our good luck, plain and simple.

It doesn't take much for a guy like me to get seriously cold on a day like today. Even though I was wearing multiple layers of clothing, what can you do when you're soaked to the bone—especially when there's no end to the rain pouring down on you? Luckily, there weren't any huge descents. When you're as cold as I was today, a downhill section can do you in. In the past, I've been so cold that my hands were too numb to change gears. And after a stage like we endured today, you can also look forward to duking it out with your roommate for rights to the bathtub. That is, if you're lucky enough to have one in your room. Plenty of European hotels only have shower stalls. But tonight I was able to cop a little spa time to warm up. Now, if only there were room service....

It's unbelievably hectic after the race. Usually we have to drive a ways to get to our hotel. Upon arrival, everyone showers, gets a massage, grabs a quick snack, sees the chiropractor and phones home to confirm that they've made it through another day. When we're done with all that, we head to dinner. And sometimes, there are team meetings scheduled before bed. There really is no such thing as downtime here at the Tour. Mornings are equally busy. We eat three hours before the start, visit the chiropractor again, pack up our suitcases so they can be loaded onto the team truck, meet to discuss the day ahead ... and then we depart. Now you know why bike racers don't like to leave their house between races.

STAGE 9: AIX AND PAINS

Since World War II, the lakeside city of Aix-les-Bains had witnessed a wide variety of alpine stage finishes. The most dramatic were those in 1948, when Italian legend Gino Bartali scored a solo win almost six minutes ahead of the next rider, to take the yellow jersey from French hero Louison Bobet; and in 1958, when Luxembourg's Charly Gaul made a phenomenal Tour-winning attack through the mountains in torrential rainstorms.

More recently, Greg LeMond outsprinted Laurent Fignon for a stage victory here in 1989, two days before his epic Tour-winning time trial in Paris; and in 1996 Michael Boogerd held off the peloton by one second, to win and make his international breakthrough on a day of apocalyptic weather. This was also the stage on which Armstrong abandoned the Tour in a thunderstorm, complaining of fatigue he couldn't explain. His cancer diagnosis came some 10 weeks later.

Despite the renown of these anecdotes from the past, Aix-les-Bains is known by most current race followers as the place where the Tour almost died on July 29, 1998. That was the year of the Festina doping scandal, which triggered the investigations of other teams, specifically TVM; and after the police raided the Dutch squad's hotel the night before the Albertville to Aix-les-Bains stage, the Tour riders rebelled.

First, they staged two sit-down strikes along the course; then the Spanish teams, led by ONCE, decided to quit the race; and after the stage was officially canceled, the riders continued riding at a slow pace. That sunny evening in Aix, a couple of hours behind the race schedule, the TVM squad symbolically led them across the finish line in a seeming requiem for the Tour.

The Tour *did* continue, but cycling was still recovering. Coincidentally, three years on, the charges against three officials from the now defunct TVM team were being heard on the same day that this Tour's stage 9 took place. (Ex-team director Cees Priem, along with the doctor and soigneur, were all handed down suspended jail sentences and substantial fines.)

As for the TVM riders who went through that ordeal in '98,

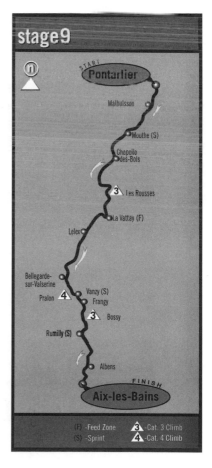

89

one was Sergei Ivanov, whose tainted reputation worsened at the start of the 2000 Tour, when his blood hematocrit tested above 50 percent and kept him from starting the race. Disgraced, the Russian was given a second chance in 2001 by Fassa Bortolo, whose Svengali-like team director Giancarlo Ferretti had restored Ivanov's confidence. By March, his form was such that he was leading the Tirreno-Adriatico stage race in Italy, when he crashed in a sprint finish, fracturing his skull. A month off the bike followed by rehabilitation left him short on fitness. "I felt very bad, had headaches, stopped every race … and then I was sick before the Giro," he said.

The fighting Russian made it through the Giro d'Italia, and he came into the Tour with the job of helping team leader Casagrande mount a challenge for the yellow jersey. That goal changed when Casagrande dropped out on stage 4, and stage wins became Fassa's main objective.

Ivanov led the way by making an early attack on stage 7, and teammate Basso then got into that day's winning move—and may have pulled out the win if he hadn't crashed and broken his collarbone. Then, on stage 8, Fassa Bortolo's Loda was in the break to Pontarlier that turned the Tour upside down, finishing 10th.

That break's success seemed to uncork every team's ambitions, and leaving Pontarlier the next morning, the attacks began cascading as soon as the flag was dropped. More than 50km were covered in the first hour. Fassa Bortolo's Matteo Tosatto figured in two of the attacks, but the successful one was made by Brad McGee of La Française des Jeux—after some advice from fellow Aussie, O'Grady of Crédit Agricole.

"I told Brad to wait," O'Grady said later, "that there was a false flat about an hour into the race where he could attack."

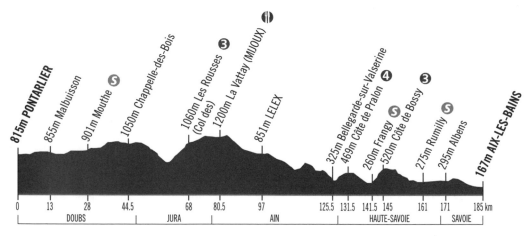

This came at 35km, just after the course turned left onto an old back road and curved up 300 feet through a pine forest to a plateau of small meadows, where wild parsley and gentian grew along the roadside. The lean McGee, a former world junior pursuit champion, was joined by Euskaltel-Euskadi team leader David Etxebarria, and these two established a 30-second lead before a solo rider jumped away from the pack: Ivanov.

It was perfect timing, because the pace then slowed behind, and by the time the Fassa Bortolo rider caught McGee and Etxebarria in the dark valley town of Morez, they were 2:25 clear. All three men worked hard on the ensuing Cat. 3 climb to Les Rousses, then along the crest of the Jura mountains and down almost 40km of descending roads. Their lead grew to nine minutes.

That gap was down to 2:30 after cresting the surprisingly steep Côte de Bossy 40km from the line—where most of the sprinters were dropped and O'Grady hung tough ("It was the yellow jersey that got me through," he said). And only 58 seconds of their lead was left at the 10km-to-go sign, after Telekom and Bonjour led the chase for Zabel and Nazon, the only sprinters left in the group besides O'Grady.

The smooth-pedaling McGee looked the best of the leaders, until the wily Ivanov, after missing a few pulls, suddenly bolted clear. McGee (with Etxebarria on his wheel) did his best to pull back the Russian, pegging the gap at six seconds until 4km to go. But that was it.

So three years after that infamous stage ending with TVM, Ivanov crossed the same finish line, alone. A winner this time, he was probably hoping that another page had been turned—for him, at least, if not for the Tour.

Tyler's diary: Stage 9

July 16, 2001

AIX-LES-BAINS: I was having flashbacks today. It felt like 1998 all over again. That year I had been fighting an intestinal bacteria throughout the season and the battle came to a head during stage 8 of the Tour. It was unbelievably warm, over 100 degrees, and I lost 18 minutes that day. Our team doctor was asking me every so often if I wanted to stop. But it was the Tour de France and quitting was out of the question.

In a word, today was grim. My stomach was giving me trouble from the start. Things began getting hairy on Friday. I've tried to convince myself it will all pass, but today was by far the worst—and the mind-over-matter thing wasn't working anymore. When I started throwing up, I knew it was going to be a hard day. I kept trying to eat because I knew I had to finish, but nothing would settle in my stomach. And so, I rode most of the day in no-man's land. All by myself. And I finished well behind the peloton. Just like '98.

Upon arriving in my hotel room I was immediately surrounded by 15 concerned staff members, each suggesting a culprit and a cure. The truth is we don't really know what's causing the indigestion, although the primary suspect is the dosage of anti-inflammatories I was given to treat my elbow injury. Those things can wreak havoc on a stomach.

Kevin's diary: Stage 9

July 16, 2001

AIX-LES-BAINS: Today's was another hard stage. They attacked from the start. There was a tail wind and a lot of up in the beginning. We kept on hammering until the feed zone (at La Vattay, after the second climb), and it was then when the leaders suddenly gained five minutes. Bonjour and some other teams took up the chase. The last climb (the Côte de Bossy) was particularly challenging. Some of our guys had to chase back on.

At the end, our team rode strong for the last 20km or so to get Zabel up for the sprint. Too bad we didn't make it, but we're not that disappointed. We tried, and tomorrow's L'Alpe d'Huez stage is the big day for us. It's difficult to say how we're all feeling. Jan is feeling very good, I think. As for me, I'm kind of nervous about how I'm climbing, but I think it should come around okay. Otherwise, it will start just like any other day on the Tour. But then it will get very, very hard....

Results: Dunkirk to Aix-les-Bains

WEEK 1

Prologue: Dunkirk TT. July 7.

1. Christophe Moreau (F), Festina, 8.2km in 9:20.58 (52.714 kph); 2. Igor Gonzalez de Galdeano (Sp), ONCE-Eroski, 9:23; **3. Lance Armstrong (USA), U.S. Postal Service, 9:24;** 4. Jan Ullrich (G), Telekom, 9:27; 5. Florent Brard (F), Festina, s.t.; 6. Santiago Botero (Col), Kelme-Costa Blanca, 9:30; 7. Joseba Beloki (Sp), ONCE-Eroski, 9:33; 8. Carlos Sastre (Sp), ONCE-Eroski, 9:34; 10. Toni Tauler (Sp), Kelme-Costa Blanca, s.t.; 11. Jaan Kirsipuu (Est), AG2R, 9:35; 12. Brad McGee (Aus), La Française des Jeux; 13. Marc Wauters (B), Rabobank, both s.t.; 14. José Gutierrez (Sp), Kelme-Costa Blanca, 9:36; 15. Didier Rous (F), Bonjour, s.t.

Others: 23. George Hincapie (USA), U.S. Postal Service, 9:39; 36. Jonathan Vaughters (USA), 9:44; 43. Bobby Julich (USA), Crédit Agricole, 9:46; 45. Tyler Hamilton (USA), U.S. Postal Service, 9:48; 61. Christian Vande Velde, 9:51; 109. Fred Rodriguez (USA), Domo-Farm Frites, 10:02.

Stage 1: St. Omer-Boulogne-sur-Mer. July 8.

1. Erik Zabel (G), Telekom, 194.5km in 4:55:15 (39.526 kph); 2. Romans Vainsteins (Lat), Domo-Farm Frites; 3. Jimmy Casper (F), La Française des Jeux; 4. Thor Hushovd (N), Crédit Agricole; 5. Kirsipuu; 6. Damien Nazon (F), Bonjour; 7. Steven De Jongh (Nl), Rabobank; 8. Christophe Capelle (F), BigMat-Auber 93; 9. Sven Teutenberg (G), Festina; 10. Nico Mattan (B), Cofidis, all s.t.

Others: 21. Julich; 22. Ullrich; 31. Moreau; 49. Armstrong; 50. Hincapie; 55. Hamilton; 57. I. Gonzales de Galdeano; 75. Beloki; 104. Francesco Casagrande (I), Fassa Bortolo; 110. Livingston; 117. Vande Velde, all s.t.; 166. Millar, at 5:45; 173. Vaughters; 179. Rodriguez, all s.t.

Overall: 1. Moreau, 5:04:35; 2. Gonzalez de Galdeano, at 0:03; 3. Armstrong, at 0:04; 4. Kirsipuu, at 0:07; 5. Ullrich, s.t.

Stage 2: Calais-Antwerp. July 9.

1. Marc Wauters (B), Rabobank, 220.5km in 4:35:47 (47.972 kph); 2. Arnaud Pretot (F), Festina; 3. Robert Hunter (SA), Lampre-Daikin; 4. Servais Knaven (Nl), Domo-Farm Frites; 5. O'Grady; 6. Davide Bramati (I), Mapei-Quick Step; 7. Rik Verbrugghe (B), Lotto-Adecco; 8. Ivan Basso (I), Fassa Bortolo; 9. Marco Milesi (I), Domo-Farm Frites; 10. Erik Dekker (Nl), Rabobank; 11. Pol Van Hyfte (B), Lotto-Adecco; **12. Julich;** 13. Johan Verstrepen (B), Lampre-Daikin, all s.t.; 14. Anthony Morin (F), Crédit Agricole, at 0:03; 15. Matteo Frutti (I), Lampre-Daikin; 16. Jens Voigt (G), Crédit Agricole, both s.t.; 17. Kirsipuu, at 0:22 (155 riders in main peloton).

Others: 177. Hamilton, at 6:45.

Overall: 1. Wauters, 9:40:17; 2. O'Grady, at 0:12; 3. Knaven, at 0:27; 4. Moreau, s.t.; 5. Kirsipuu, at 0:28.

Stage 3: Antwerp-Seraing. July 10.

1. Zabel, 198.5km in 4:34:32 (43.383 kph); 2. Emmanuel Magnien (F), La Française des Jeux; 3. Garzelli; 4. Fabio Baldato (I), Fassa Bortolo; 5. François Simon (F), Bonjour; 6. Guennadi Mikhailov (Rus), Lotto-Adecco; 7. Christophe Capelle (F), BigMat-Auber 93; 8. Franck Bouyer (F), Bonjour; 9. Serge Baguet (B), Lotto-Adecco; **10. Armstrong.** (102 riders in main peloton)

Others: 111. Hincapie, at 2:49; 119. Casagrande, at 4:54; **126. Vande Velde, s.t.; 147. Rodriguez, at 6:36;** 152. Wauters, s.t.; 154. Millar, at 10:58.

Overall: 1. O'Grady, 14:14:59; 2. Moreau, at 0:17; 3. Verbrugghe, at 0:18; 4. Voigt, at 0:20; 5. I. Gonzalez de Galdeano, s.t.

Stage 4: Huy-Verdun. July 11.

1. Laurent Jalabert (F), CSC-Tiscali, 215km in 5:17:49 (40.589 kph); 2. Ludo Dierckxsens (B), Lampre-Daikin, s.t.; 3. Damien Nazon (F), Bonjour, at 0:07; **4. Fred Rodriguez (USA), Domo-Farm Frites;** 5. Alessandro Petacchi (I), Fassa Bortolo; 6. Sven Teutenberg (G), Festina; 7. Robert Hunter (SA), Lampre-Daikin; 8. Stuart O'Grady (Aus), Crédit Agricole; 9. Pol Van Hyfte (B), Lotto-Adecco; 10. Sébastien Talabardon, all s.t.

Others: 18. Christophe Moreau (F), Festina; 22. Joseba Beloki (Sp), ONCE-Eroski; 24. Wladimir Belli (I), Fassa Bortolo; 27. Michael Boogerd (Nl), Rabobank; 29. Santiago Botero (Sp), Kelme-Costa Blanca; **30. Lance Armstrong (USA), U.S. Postal Service;** 33. Jan Ullrich (G), Telekom; 34. Igor Gonzalez de Galdeano (Sp), ONCE-Eroski; **35. Bobby Julich (USA), Crédit Agricole;** 38. Francisco Mancebo (Sp), iBanesto.com; 46. Roberto Heras (Sp), U.S. Postal Service; **47. George Hincapie (USA), U.S. Postal Service;** 48. Stefano Garzelli (I), Mapei-Quick Step; **49. Tyler Hamilton (USA), U.S. Postal Service;** 50. Victor Hugo Peña (Col), U.S. Postal Service; 61. Andreas Klöden (G), Telekom; **66. Christian Vande Velde (USA), U.S. Postal Service; 67. Kevin Livingston (USA), Telekom, all s.t.** (NOTE: Main peloton finished at 18:33)

Overall: 1. O'Grady, 19:32:49; 2. L. Jalabert, at 0:18; 3. Moreau, at 0:23; 4. Jens Voigt (G), Crédit Agricole, at 0:26; 5. I. Gonzalez de Galdeano, s.t.; **6. Julich, at 0:27; 7. Armstrong, s.t.;** 8. Ullrich, at 0:30; 9. Florent Brard (F), Festina, s.t.; 10. Botero, at 0:33.

Stage 5: Verdun-Bar-le-Duc TTT. July 12.

1. Crédit Agricole (F), 67km in 1:21:32 (49.305 kph); 2. ONCE-Eroski (Sp), 1:22:03; 3. Festina (F), 1:22:26; **4. U.S. Postal Service (USA), 1:22:58;** 5. Kelme-Costa Blanca (Sp), 1:23:10; 6. Rabobank (Nl), 1:23:19; 7. Deutsche Telekom (G), 1:23:22; 8. Cofidis (F), 1:24:27; 9. BigMat-Auber 93 (F), 1:24:28; 10. Mapei-Quick Step, 1:24:30.

Overall: 1. O'Grady, 20:54:21; 2. Voigt, at 0:26; **3. Julich, at 0:27;** 4. Gonzales de Galdeano, at 0:57; 5. Beloki, at 1:07; 6. Carlos Sastre (Sp), ONCE-Eroski, at 1:08; 7. Jörg Jaksche (G), ONCE-Eroski, at 1:12; 8. Moreau, at 1:17; 9. Ivan Gutierrez (Sp), ONCE-Eroski, at 1:20; 10. Marcos Serrano (Sp), ONCE-Eroski, at 1:23.

Others: 12. Angel Casero (Sp), Festina, at 1:33, **15. Armstrong, at 1:53;** 17. Botero, at 2:11; 19. Ullrich, at 2:20; 21. Horas, at 2:34; 24. Boogerd, at 2:47; 25. L. Jalabert, at 3:19; 29. Garzelli, at 3:44; 36. Mancebo, at 4:40; 45. Belli, at 5:00.

Stage 6: Commercy-Strasbourg. July 13.

1. Jaan Kirsipuu (F), 211.5km in 4:50:39 (43.661 kph); 2. D. Nazon; 3. Jan Svorada (Cz), Lampre-Daikin; 4. Erik Zabel (G), Telekom; 5. O'Grady; 6. Jimmy Casper (F), La Française des Jeux; 7. Nico Mattan (B), Cofidis; 8. Christophe Capelle (F), BigMat-Auber 93; 9. Alexei Sivakov (Rus), BigMat-Auber 93; 10. Vainsteins, all s.t.

Others: (163 riders in main peloton); **165. Hamilton, at 4:45;** 183. Millar, at 16:35.

Overall: 1. O'Grady, 25:45:00; 2. Voigt, at 0:26; **3. Julich, at 0:27;** 4. Gonzales de Galdeano, at 0:57; 5. Beloki, at 1:07; 6. Sastre, at 1:08; 7. Jaksche at 1:12; 8. Moreau, at 1:17; 9. Gutierrez, at 1:20; 10. Serrano, at 1:23.

Stage 7: Strasbourg-Colmar. July 14.

1. L. Jalabert, 162.5km in 4:06:04 (39.623 kph); 2. Voigt, at 0:11; 3.

Laurent Roux (F), Jean Delatour, s.t.; 4. Iñigo Cuesta (Sp), Cofidis, at 0:13; 5. Ivan Basso (I), Fassa Bortolo, at 1:36; 6. David Etxebarria (Sp), Euskaltel-Euskadi, at 4:28; 7. Alex Vinokourov (Kaz), Telekom; 8. Laurent Brochard (F), Jean Delatour; 9. Matteo Tosatto (I), Fassa Bortolo; 10. Franck Bouyer (F), Bonjour, all s.t.

Others: (71 riders in main peloton); **90. Hamilton, at 10:50; 108. Livingston, s.t.;** 165. Millar, at 24:50.

Overall: 1. Voigt, 29:51:29; 2. Jalabert, at 2:34; 3. O'Grady, at 4:03; **4. Julich, at 4:26;** 5. Gonzales de Galdeano, at 5:00; 6. Beloki, at 5:10; 7. Sastre, at 5:11; 8. Jaksche at 5:15; 9. Moreau, at 5:20; 10. Gutierrez, at 5:23.

Stage 8: Colmar-Pontarlier. July 15.

1. Erik Dekker (NI), Rabobank, 222.5km in 4:59:18 (44.604 kph); 2. Aitor Gonzalez (Sp), Kelme-Costa Blanca; 3. Servais Knaven (NI), Domo-Farm Frites, both s.t.; 4. Marc Wauters (B), Rabobank, at 0:04; 5. O'Grady, at 2:32; 6. Sven Teutenberg (G), Festina; 7. Jacky Durand (F), La Française des Jeux; 8. Bram De Groot (NI), Rabobank; 9. Ludo Dierckxsens (B), Lampre-Daikin; 10. Nicola Loda (I), Fassa Bortolo; 11. Ludovic Turpin (F), AG2R, all s.t.; 12. François Simon (F), Bonjour, at 2:36; 13. Andrei Kivilev (Kaz), Cofidis, at 2:40; 14. Pascal Chanteur (F), Festina, at 9:23; 15. Robert Hunter (SA),

Lampre-Daikin, at 35:54. (160 riders in main peloton.)

Overall: 1. O'Grady, 34:51:29; 2. Simon, at 4:32; 3. De Groot, at 21:16; 4. Kivilev, at 22:07; 5. Teutenberg, at 27:15; 6. Voigt, at 29:23; 7. Diercksens, at 29:49; 8. Wauters, at 30:12; 9. Turpin, at 30:35; 10. Gonzalez, at 31:56.

Others: 11. Jalabert, at 31:57; **12. Julich, at 33:49;** 14. Beloki, at 34:33; 17. Moreau, at 34:43; **24. Armstrong, at 35:19;** 27. Ullrich, at 35:46.

Stage 9: Pontarlier-Aix-les-Bains. July 16.

1. Sergei Ivanov (Rus), Fassa Bortolo, 185km in 3:57:48 (46.678 kph); 2. David Etxebarria (Sp), Euskaltel-Euskadi, at 0:16; 3. Brad McGee (Aus), La Française des Jeux, at 0:17; 4. Zabel, at 0:24; 5. Nazon; 6. O'Grady; 7. Paolo Bettini (I), Mapei-Quick Step; 8. José Gutierrez (Sp), Kelme-Costa Blanca; 9. Petacchi; 10. Teutenberg, all s.t.. (111 riders in main peloton.)

Others: 150. Millar, at 8:35; **168. Rodriguez, at 10:56; 171. Hamilton, at 13:25.**

Overall: 1. O'Grady, 1685.2km in 38:55:30 (43.293 kph); 2. Simon, at 4:32; 3. De Groot, at 21:16; 4. Kivilev, at 22:07; 5. Teutenberg, at 27:15.

WEEK 2
Climbing Ahead

F inally, the race was at the foot of the mountains. It was time for the "real" Tour to begin, and yet no one had imagined that this 88th Tour de France would be heading into the Alps with all the main favorites a half-hour or more behind the leaders. The long stages through Belgium and northeastern France, often in cold, wet or windy weather, had produced a bizarre-looking leader board.

In the yellow jersey was one of two Australians in the race, Stuart O'Grady, whose spiky, punk-style bleach-blond hair seemed as incongruous as his position at the top of the standings. Not that he didn't deserve his elevated position. O'Grady rode a strong prologue; battled for sprint bonus seconds in the opening road stages; bridged to the break into Antwerp; took the race lead by out-climbing the other sprinters in the Ardennes; defended his yellow jersey by leading his Crédit Agricole formation to victory in the team time trial; and, after ceding the overall lead to teammate Jens Voigt for a day, took it back spectacularly in the famous half-hour breakaway to Pontarlier.

In other words, O'Grady had raced hard—every day. So much so that he was almost on the point of collapse by Pontarlier, and he admitted that it was only the power derived from wearing the yellow jersey that helped him stay with the pack on the last climb into Aix-les-

Bains. The battling Aussie knew that his sturdy, fast-twitch calf and thigh muscles weren't compatible with the hour-long mountain climbs that lay ahead, and that his adventure in yellow would almost certainly come to an end at L'Alpe d'Huez: the first of five summit finishes that made this second week the toughest tier of the Tour. It was only a matter of time....

While O'Grady was ready to go into survival mode for a week, others were ready to challenge for the yellow jersey. First in line were the two other principals from the Pontarlier break: François Simon and Andrei Kivilev. Simon, the gritty French veteran, was lying in second place overall, at 4:23—a time he was capable of taking back from O'Grady on a single mountain climb. And Kivilev, the pale-faced newcomer from Kazakhstan, potentially was even more dangerous in the final reckoning. He *was* 22:07 behind O'Grady; but a possibly more important number was 13:12, the lead he held over Lance Armstrong. Whether that would be enough for Kivilev, a promising climber, to *remain* a major threat would be revealed in the long days of climbing that would unfold in the Alps and Pyrénées.

These upcoming stages also would reveal whether the 2001 Tour de France was going to turn into a repeat of 2000: a two-man contest between defending champion Armstrong and Jan Ullrich. After 10 days of racing, the two super-favorites were separated by just 27 seconds. On those opening stages, Armstrong's Postal teammates and Ullrich's Telekom troops had been waging a war of one-upmanship that saw Telekom taking the upper hand with two stage wins for Erik Zabel, and Postal replying with a superior performance in the team time trial. On a personal level, Ullrich had enjoyed a calm, out-of-the-public-eye opening week, while Armstrong had been on the defensive with the media, answering drug-related questions concerning his association with the controversial Italian sports doctor, Michele Ferrari, an association that was made public in newspaper articles during the Tour's first weekend.

Armstrong had avoided having a news conference on the subject, which though now dormant looked likely to flare up should he re-enter the spotlight by winning stages in the mountains. Despite the potential distraction, the defending champion was ready to do battle on his bike. And if Ullrich didn't emerge as Armstrong's biggest opponent, then Spanish climbers Joseba Beloki, Igor Gonzalez de Galdeano and Oscar Sevilla were all waiting to challenge the Texan.

A first verdict would come at L'Alpe d'Huez....

STAGE 10: REALITY ON THE ALPE

It was just after 6 p.m. at L'Alpe d'Huez. The last of the 166 finishers of the Tour's 10th stage, French sprinter Jimmy Casper, had crossed the line a few minutes earlier. Thin clouds covered the evening's wan sunshine, and with temperatures dropping into the 50s, it was starting to feel cold up here at 6000 feet above sea level. Television crews had wrapped up their live broadcasts and were sitting around their compounds, talking about the day's momentous events, sipping drinks and planning where to have dinner. Up and down the mountainside the crowds were dispersing, folding up picnic chairs, rolling up flags and banners, and trekking back to their buses, cars, tents or camper vans. One of the greatest spectacles in sport was over for another year.

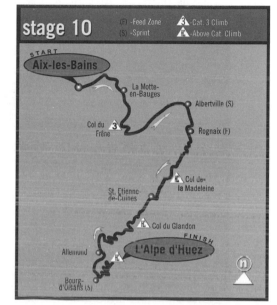

Just then, deftly weaving down between departing fans and past three lines of accredited Tour vehicles, came a figure on a blue-and-gray bicycle. Wearing dark tights and a long-sleeve top over his team uniform, he smiled and called out a friendly greeting to a friend on foot, and continued on down the hill toward his hotel for the night, a multistory Club Med, as happy as any five-year-old on his first two-wheeler.

Some fans spotted the departing rider. *"C'est Aarm-struung!?"* they shouted in part-disbelief, not quite sure that this was cycling's miracle man cruising past. It was indeed the man who, just one hour before, they had watched in true disbelief as he tore apart his opposition in a dazzling display of athleticism.

Lance the cyclist lives for moments like this. Moments when the years of meticulous preparation, tough training camps, long gym workouts, daily diet sacrifices, technical planning and plain old hard work come to fruition. His best-selling book was called *It's Not About the Bike*. But right then, after racing up the Alpe's 14km, 8-percent grade at a near-record speed, his existence was *all* about the bike.

"It's a very special stage," Armstrong said at his stage winner's press conference. "It's a stage that means a lot to everyone in cycling, probably the most famous climb in all of cycling. And that motivated me today. I wanted to win Alpe d'Huez, something that not many people have done."

This was the 22nd time that a Tour stage had finished on the Alpe, the first being in 1952 with a solo victory by the legendary Fausto Coppi, when the road of 21 switchbacks was still unpaved. And the mythical locale had seen five repeat winners: the Dutchmen Joop Zoetemelk (1977 and '79), Hennie Kuiper (1977 and '78) and Peter Winnen (1983 and '85), and the Italians Gianni Bugno (1990 and '91) and Marco Pantani (1995 and '97).

So Armstrong was now one of 17 riders to have won this prestigious Tour stage; the second American, after Andy Hampsten in 1985; and, if he were to go on to win this Tour, he'd be only the second man to take Alpe d'Huez and the Tour in the same year. The first was Coppi.

"It's an honor to win today," Armstrong emphasized. "If I won in a sprint between three guys, I would be just as happy. It wasn't a question of trying to take time out of the rivals; that was just a decision I made on the road. But it was our plan to win today. In the team meeting this morning, Johan [Bruyneel] and myself said that the team should ride to win the stage."

Armstrong felt that his Postal team needed a lift after a tough nine stages in which most of the team had either crashed, been sick or had to cope with injuries. Their bad luck continued 70km into this opening stage in the Alps when Postal's Norwegian, Steffen Kjaergaard, was involved in a pileup. The road rash and bruises on his left thigh and head added to the team's woes, and meant that Armstrong would have one less mate to make tempo on the approach to the three giant climbs that lay ahead: the Col de la Madeleine, Col du Glandon and L'Alpe d'Huez.

A team medical report would have revealed the following: Armstrong okay; Heras recovering from a crash (in the team time trial) and a sore knee; Ekimov okay; Hamilton, stomach bug and recovering from two crashes; Hincapie okay; Kjaergaard just crashed; Peña okay; Rubiera recovering from a sore knee; Vande Velde out.

This left only Ekimov, Hincapie and Peña to protect their leaders in the valleys. Ekimov would stay with Hamilton as soon as the climbing began, while the other two would give what help they could to Armstrong and his lieutenants on the early slopes of the Madeleine.

Rising 5000 feet in 25km, with constantly changing grades, the Madeleine is not the sort of climb where you can find a steady rhythm and hang in. So, with Hamilton in survival mode, Postal knew that Armstrong could rely on only Heras and Rubiera for the difficult second half of the day. And with neither of the Spanish riders at 100 percent, the team was somewhat relieved when Ullrich's squad decided to play a stronger-than-usual role.

"We did not know that Telekom was going to start riding tempo from the beginning of the Madeleine, which is 130 kilometers from the finish," said Armstrong. "It worked perfectly for us that they could control the race, the breakaway didn't get too much time, and we could sit back."

The breakaway in question was not particularly dangerous. It consisted of Kelme's Toni Tauler, who was the best placed of the three, 18:51 behind Armstrong; Jean Delatour's Roux, who featured in the winning break in the Vosges; and iBanesto.com's Eladio Jimenez, a winner of a Vuelta stage in 2000, but already 32 minutes behind Armstrong in this race.

The three riders had attacked on an uphill valley road that opened the 209km stage from Aix-les-Bains, and after an initial chase by the peloton, their lead grew to 13.35 as they started the hour-long ascent of the Madeleine. By its 6560-foot summit, Tauler had been dropped and the gap was down to 8:30.

Behind them, five Telekom men set the tempo, and even though it was not a particularly hard pace, two thirds of the field dropped back. Already, race leader O'Grady and third-placed De Groot had gone; but there were also some more surprising names among those who fell off the pace, including Julich.

Riding with the American just before he was dropped was his teammate Vaughters, who later related a radio conversation he had with his team director Roger Legeay: "I said to

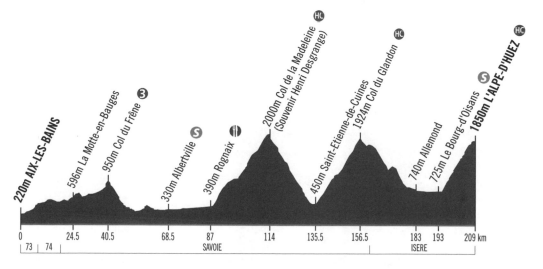

Tyler's diary: Stage 10

July 17, 2001

L'ALPE d'HUEZ: Well, I made it. Historically speaking, it's been a long time since I found satisfaction in merely finishing a race. But today, finishing within the time limit was my sole objective. Once underway, I mentioned to Lance that I'd help as much as I could, but he said, "I'd prefer that you concentrate on finishing." I took his orders to heart—although I was able to show my face at the front of the peloton for a little while at the base of the Madeleine. After that, it was all about getting through. The stomach fates are being somewhat more cooperative. I was still quite sick with nausea today, but it seems to be subsiding.

I tried to eat as much as possible this morning, since I was worried about not getting enough calories last night. I had rice for dinner and that's not going to fuel you for a stage like today. Our chiropractor is a bit of a jack-of-all trades and he has helped me a ton with homeopathic stomach remedies. He even made me a protein shake with rice blended in it this morning to get me going. I'm definitely going to be indebted to this guy after all is said and done.

It was decided in our team meeting that Lance was going to go for the win on L'Alpe d'Huez. This approach is a departure from our team's traditional tactics. Normally, we'd just concentrate on putting time into the competition and hope that a guy low on G.C. would go for the breakaway. Things went as planned, with Lance playing it calm all the way to the base of the Alpe. This worked out perfectly from a tactical standpoint. Telekom spent all day at the front burning matches, while Lance, Roberto and Chechu cooled their heels in the peloton. Little did anyone know that Lance was crouching like a panther ready to pounce. This guy is special—and I hear he's in the running for an academy award.....

Having made it through today, I will focus on resting and recovering as much as possible on Wednesday and Thursday. My parents and my wife are scheduled to visit on the rest day, which is something good to look forward to—especially since I had my wife call home last night and tell them to sit tight before closing their suitcases. Luckily, my parents are understanding and flexible, and with three hours to spare before catching their plane, they were officially green-lighted.

Roger I'd gladly wait for him [Julich] ... I had no problems. But Roger just said, 'Well, what can you do at this point?' I mean, the group wasn't even going hard yet on the first climb...."

Julich did catch back with others on the long, fast descent, but he was dropped again on the 20km-long Glandon and finished the day in a 12-strong group that lost more than 23 minutes.

While Julich was being dropped from the group, two of his former Motorola teammates, Livingston and Armstrong, were playing very different roles at its head. Livingston was finally showing why Ullrich signed him as a team rider, by setting a strong climbing tempo for his new leader with Telekom teammate Andreas Klöden.

And Armstrong? Well, he was showing off a new skill: acting.

Already content with Telekom setting the pace, he decided to give the German squad added confidence (over-confidence?) by riding near the back of the group ... and feigning fatigue. A grimace or two, and dropping his shoulders when the TV cameras were on him, may not have had Shakespearean subtlety, but his gestures were enough to make his rivals believe that he might be having a bad day.

Armstrong added to the illusion by crossing the top of the Glandon in an unaccustomed 12th place, right behind the anonymous Spanish rider Iñigo Chaurreau of Euskaltel. Besides Chaurreau, there were several other unexpected characters in the 30-rider group that began the last descent 5:46 behind Roux, who had dropped Jimenez with an acceleration on one of the Glandon's 10-percent pitches.

Several riders—including Telekom's Livingston and Vinokourov—rejoined the Armstrong-Ullrich group on the early part of the 27km downhill. Also catching back was virtual race leader Simon and the other danger man from the Pontarlier break, Kivilev. It would be instructive to see how these two fared on the upcoming Alpe.

Telekom's Livingston, Vinokourov and Klöden continued to pull the lead group along the 10km of flat valley roads that precede the famous ascent.

Roux, who by now had been in the front of the race for almost five-and-a-half hours, took a six-minute cushion into these final 14km. It seemed like a big gap; but when he was told by his Delatour team director Michel Gros that there were some attacks near the start of the climb, Roux said he knew his chances were slim.

What happened behind Roux was this: Livingston led the group onto the Alpe's walllike opening, preparing for an attack by Ullrich, perhaps like the one he made in the 1997

101

Tour to take the yellow jersey at Arcalis in Andorra. But then, after playing his possum act, Armstrong suddenly showed his true colors. He sent Rubiera to the front, and the 28-year-old Spaniard put in a staggering burst of speed, out of the saddle, throwing his bars from side to side and flaying his pedals in a fury.

Suddenly, there was no group. Only Armstrong, Ullrich and the ambitious Kivilev could follow. Then, just after turn No. 21, the one named for Fausto Coppi, Rubiera sat up and his boss—after turning to witness the shock in Ullrich's face—sprinted away to destiny.

After the first minute of his attack, and his first 100 pedal revs, Armstrong looked back to see the damage: There was no one in sight. Ullrich looked devastated. The German knew that he was riding strongly, because only Beloki, Botero and Moreau had managed to stay with him, but he also knew right then that his best might not be good enough.

While Armstrong passed Roux with 6km to go, and went on to his historic victory, Ullrich held up to take second place two minutes back, after dropping Beloki and Moreau in the last 3km. Kivilev fought hard to take 12th on the stage and move from fourth to second overall—but still conceded 4:37 to Armstrong. As for Simon, he came in with Vaughters, 10:20 back, which was good enough for him to take the yellow jersey from a distant O'Grady.

Strangely, Armstrong had some doubts about his performance. When asked about the next day's vital time trial, the Texan said, "The scary thing is that an effort like ... I have to tell you guys, that was everything that I had there. I couldn't have gone any harder. And that's the bad news. It's tough to recover from an effort like that ... and I imagine—I've never done it before—I imagine it's very tough to do ... an individual time trial up a difficult climb like Chamrousse ... the day after a stage like this. The answer is, I might pay for that effort. I could lose two minutes tomorrow. I hope not."

For the moment, though, Armstrong was floating in the Alpe's thin air, as he gleefully got back on his bike to slalom his way down to the Club Med. "Aarm-struung" was up and running.

STAGE 11: CHAMROUSSE SHOWDOWN

If Ullrich was going to challenge Armstrong's supremacy in this Tour, then the Chamrousse mountain time trial was the stage in which he would have the best chance. The German likes time trials that allow him to focus purely on power output without having to constantly brake and accelerate, and this was just such a course. After 5km of straight, flat roads through the suburbs of Grenoble, the course climbed into the countryside on a steady 5km-long hill to a long ridge, before taking a short downhill to reach the start of the true climb after 13.5km. From here to the finish, a further 18.5km, it was all uphill on a well-paved mountain road that curved gently through a thick forest of tall pines at an almost con-

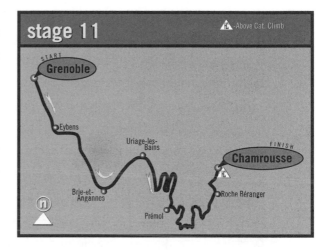

stant grade of 7 percent. It was a tough climb, but one on which Ullrich would be able to pedal a big gear at a steady 80-rpm tempo without having to get out of the saddle— except for a 9-percent pitch in the eighth kilometer.

Even the weather was tailor-made for Ullrich. He hates racing in cold, wet conditions. But heavy morning rain and thick mist on the mountain gave way to afternoon sunshine and just the hint of a breeze by the time the second half of the 166 riders started. Working against Ullrich, however, was the length of the climb. While his power output was similar to or slightly better than Armstrong's, he *did* weigh more than the Texan, and a few extra kilos make a big difference in power-to-weight ratio, which takes on more importance on longer climbs.

For the tens of thousands of fans along the 32km course, the big interest would be the day's keynote battle between Ullrich and Armstrong. They were also keeping an eye on race leader Simon and second-placed Kivilev, who had respective leads of 20:07 and 8:13 over the defending champion. Others being closely watched were those riders within a couple of minutes of Armstrong: Beloki and Moreau. And there was still the possibility of an "unknown" coming through with a strong stage showing.

After such a tough opening week, followed by one of the toughest mountain stages, many men who had hoped to be challenging for a top-10 position were buried deep in the overall classification. Those totally out of contention started with Julich in 29th over- all, 22 minutes behind Armstrong.

Of the early starters, the first to put in a significant ride was stage 8 hero McGee, who'd gagged at the Dunkirk prologue and needed to confirm his aptitude for time trials. The young Aussie didn't disappoint, and although he wasn't racing to his limit, he put in a great opening 13.5km. His split of 20:26 would remain the fastest for more than three hours, until the first of the top 10 on G.C. arrived. McGee claimed that he didn't push himself on the climb itself, and he ended with a solid time of 1:12:36.

Sixteen riders after McGee came the Colombian climber Felix Cardenas of Kelme, who had turned pro only one year before at age 27, yet had scored a mountain stage win at the Vuelta a España. His job at this, his first Tour, was to ride for team leaders Botero and Sevilla, which explained his finishing in a group 32 minutes back at L'Alpe d'Huez. In this stage, though, Cardenas needed to make a strong effort to help Kelme challenge for the overall team prize (after 10 stages, Rabobank led second-place Kelme by 37:30). Cardenas came through, and his time of 1:11:36 stood as the fastest until, 50 riders later, Spanish climber Cuesta of Cofidis went seven seconds faster.

The two other early starters with ambitions for the day were Vaughters and Euskaltel's Roberto Laiseka. Vaughters started fast, only 19 seconds behind McGee at 13.5km, but the tall American said that he didn't have his best legs for the climb and he ended up with a 1:11:58.

As for Laiseka, who came in ninth at L'Alpe d'Huez four minutes behind Armstrong, he was relatively slow to start (equal with Cardenas's 21:23 at the 13.5km split), but then the 32-year-old Basque climber took off. There were three time checks on the final mountain: after 8km and 14.8km, and at the finish (18.5km). Laiseka's climbing splits were phenomenal: 22:58 for the first 8km, 13:35 for the next 6.8km and 9:34 for the closing 3.7km,

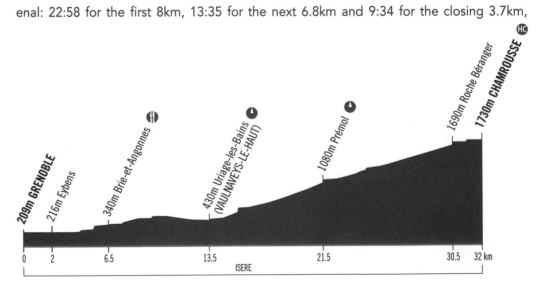

which gave him an overall time of 1:09:30. Fastest until then by two whole minutes.

Only Sevilla of Kelme (1:09:51) and ONCE's Igor Gonzalez de Galdeano (1:09:58) came close to matching Laiseka's time before Ullrich, seven riders from the end, set off from outside Grenoble's Palais des Sports (where the city's annual six-day track race takes place each November). Wearing a long-sleeve skinsuit, the Telekom leader rode a strong opening 13.5km, but although his time split of 19:52 was the fastest yet, it was only a single second better than Galdeano's and six seconds ahead of Kelme's Colombian climber, Botero. Starting six minutes after Ullrich, Armstrong claimed that he took it easy in the flat opening kilometers, but by the time he reached the first split he was already 11 seconds ahead of his main rival!

Once on the main climb, Armstrong showed the full benefit of his meticulous preparations: fitting special clip-on bars; adding a 22-tooth sprocket; and remembering what he had learned about the course in a May training camp based in Grenoble that saw him make four complete climbs to Chamrousse and a couple of partial ascents. He knew exactly when he could use the clip-ons to cut a few seconds here and there, and where he could efficiently stand on the pedals to overcome the steepest sections.

Armstrong was quickly into the fast-pedaling form that he showed the previous day on the Alpe, and he flew up the first 8km of the climb: His split of 22:41 was 36 seconds faster than Ullrich's, or the equivalent of 4.5 seconds per kilometer! Ullrich wasn't even second fastest on this climb's tough opening, as Laiseka's split was 19 seconds better.

Hearing of his deficit on Armstrong (47 seconds), Ullrich fought back over the next less-steep section, an expression of anger (or was it frustration?) on his face and renewed energy in his pedal strokes. It was a huge effort, and did bring a small turn-around—five seconds faster than the Texan on this 6.8km split, while only three seconds better than Laiseka.

Ullrich loves the heat, but he looked too hot by this point, perhaps because of the long sleeves and the undervest he revealed on pulling down the zipper on his skinsuit. Armstrong, too, had exposed his chest to get the full effect of the cooler air as he climbed. But there was no letup in the Postal star's remorseless cadence, with the silver cross dangling from his long neck chain swinging in time to the rocking of his shoulders.

Ullrich clearly faded at the end, despite using the big ring on some of the easier grades near the top, and he looked totally fried as he sprinted for the line. His 1:08:27 cut 63 seconds

Freddy's diary: Stage 11

July 18, 2001

GRENOBLE: Today's uphill time trial was just a day for me to get to the finish fast enough to secure a spot in the remaining stages of the Tour. You never know when you're going to have tired legs, and after yesterday's stage up L'Alpe d'Huez, I wasn't too excited about the time trial. The course was somewhat rolling before the above-category climb. My plan was to arrive at the climb fresh and ride steady, but quickly, to the top of the mountain. You don't want to miss the time cut.

That was also my goal yesterday, which was really grueling for everyone, especially those looking for a G.C. placing. It didn't look like Lance was too tired … but everyone else was.

Race fans pay a lot of attention to the front of the peloton, but there's action at the back, too. There was a group of 70 to 80 riders yesterday—the gruppetto—that finished together. The gruppetto formed on the first climb and rolled together for the rest of the day, toward the finish with a goal of making the time cut. Stuart (O'Grady) was with us for a bit, but then attacked us. I guess he was seeing if he could make up some time to keep the yellow jersey.

There's a temperature gauge in the gruppetto: When it's quiet, it's a comfortable pace. When the Italian riders start yelling "piano, piano," then it's going too fast. Sometimes, I don't know where guys get the energy to yell. I just keep quiet and ride. But yesterday, I did find the energy to speak up.

Jacky Durand is known by fans for his constant breakaways. With riders, he's also known for grabbing onto cars in the caravan after he's been dropped when the course goes uphill. I don't understand why he never gets caught. He'll hang on to a vehicle, then let go as soon as a race official rolls through. He's dropped before the gruppetto is even made, and yet he always gets back on.

Yesterday, guys (mostly from Italian squads) were yelling at him, "You get dropped on every climb, then you're always attacking us." Jacky didn't take it for long before he shouted back, "In the Giro, everyone grabs the motos." Then a little later I looked up and saw that he had grabbed onto a caravan car moving past the gruppetto. I had to give him a piece of my mind.

Armstrong Matches Bahamontes!

On the rest day after the Chamrousse time trial, there was much talk regarding the dominance Armstrong had shown on the two summit finishes in the Alps. Was his performance, well, unusual? Asked about this, Ireland's former world No. 1 Sean Kelly—working as a color TV commentator for Eurosport during the Tour—said, "It's nothing new. Others have done what Lance is doing. Fignon in '84 probably put two minutes into Hinault on Alpe d'Huez."

Looking at actual records, in time trials with mountaintop finishes, Armstrong compared well with some of the greatest climbers in Tour history. On Alpe d'Huez, for example, the American averaged 22.095 kph for the 14km climb, second only to Marco Pantani, who raced up the Alpe at 22.350 kph in 1997.

No two climbs are identical of course, but there's one climb that was used in past Tour time trials that is very similar to the one used in the Chamrousse TT. It is a climb in the Pyrénées from Luchon to Superbagnères. While Chamrousse, at 18.5km, is 300 meters longer, the height difference is similar (1300 meters or 4265 feet for Chamrousse, and 1171 meters or 3841 feet for Superbagnères). Almost 40 years ago, Spanish climbing legend Federico Bahamontes averaged 23.235 kph on Superbagnères, which compares with the 23.237 kph by Armstrong on that last 18.5km to Chamrousse!

Armstrong's overall speed for the Chamrousse time trial also compares favorably with those at four similar time trials held at the Tour de France over the past 36 years. The Texan's 28.466 kph was significantly faster than the efforts of Felice Gimondi in 1965 (on a course that had 7km of flat roads before the Revard climb), Bernard Hinault in 1989 (5.6km flat before Superbagnères) and Jean-François Bernard in 1987 (14km flat before Mont Ventoux); but slower than Piotr Ugrumov's performance in 1994 (on a course that featured two Cat. 4 hills and two fast descents before the 14km climb to Avoriaz).

PURE MOUNTAIN TTs AT TOUR

1958: Bedoin-Mont Ventoux (21.5km)
1. Gaul (20.756 kph); 2. Bahamontes, at 0:31; 3. Dotto, at 4:35.

1959: Clermont Ferrand-Puy de Dôme (12.5km)
1. Bahamontes (20.689 kph); 2. Gaul, at 1:26; 3. Anglade, at 3:00.

1962: Luchon-Superbagnères (18.2km)
1. Bahamontes (23.235 kph); 2. Planckaert, at 1:25; 3. Anquetil, at 1:28.

1977: Morzine-Avoriaz (14km)
1. Van Impe (24.839 kph); 2. Thévenet, at 0:20.

1983: Clermont Ferrand-Puy de Dôme (15.6km)
1. Arroyo (22.978 kph); 2. Delgado, at 0:13; 3. Jimenez, at 0:29.

1983: Morzine-Avoriaz (15km)
1. Van Impe (25.603 kph); 2. Roche, at 0:36; 3. Winnen, at 0:49.

2001: Chamrousse (^last 18.5km)
1. Armstrong (23.237 kph); 2. Laiseka, at 0:21; 3. Ullrich, at 0:49.

OTHER TOUR TTs WITH SUMMIT FINISHES

1965: Aix-les-Bains-Le Revard (26.9km)
1. Gimondi (26.774 kph); 2. Poulidor, at 0:23; 3. Pingeon, at 1:40.

1979: Luchon-Superbagnères (23.8km)
1. Hinault (26.530 kph); 2. Agostinho, at 0:11; 3. Zoetemelk, at 0:53.

1987: Carpentras-Mont Ventoux (35.5km)
1. Bernard (27.239 kph); 2. Herrera, at 1:39; 3. Delgado, at 1:51.

1994: Cluses-Avoriaz (47.5km)
1. Ugrumov (34.338 kph); 2. Pantani, at 1:38; 3. Induráin, at 3:16.

2001: Grenoble-Chamrousse (32km)
1. Armstrong (28.466 kph); 2. Ullrich, at 1:00; 3. Beloki, at 1:35.

Tyler's diary: Rest Day

July 19, 2001

PERPIGNAN: As I've mentioned in previous years, rest days at the Tour de France are kind of a misnomer. You might think we get to sleep in, drag ourselves to breakfast and then hang out for the day. But truth is, we do just about everything but rest.

For starters, we usually have to make a transfer—which we did today by plane from the Alps. This meant that we got up at the crack of dawn so we could eat breakfast and have our bags packed well before departure time. The flight was an hour long and we arrived in Perpignan in the pouring rain. I don't know if the storm clouds are following us or if the Tour itself is channeling the unseasonable stuff. But it's starting to get ridiculous!

Luckily, the wet stuff subsided so we could get a ride in. The alternative was slugging it out on the trainers under the mechanic's truck's canopy. As soon as we finished with training, it was back to the similar drill we face after a stage: massage, chiropractor's adjustment and the usual bombing around and checking in with all the appropriate parties.

Rest days are also jam-packed with interview requests. We have a media coordinator who works with the team at the Tour and who schedules requests. Just her luck, today, the first rest day, is her birthday. I doubt she had much time to celebrate. I spoke with reporters running the gamut from my hometown newspaper to national news outlets from countries I've never even visited. It's been crazy.

The best part of the day was a long-awaited visit from my wife and parents. They drove up from Spain today to meet me. We were able to spend some time together while I was on the massage table. It was good to catch up with them. They will be along the route throughout the Pyrénées, and their presence is a huge morale boost.

The next three days are critical for the team. We've been preparing for this section of the race since May, and for the last few days, we've been concentrating on getting everyone back on track.

Hopefully, our hard work and extra effort will pay off. There's still plenty of work to be done if we want to get Lance to Paris in yellow. I think the group weathered some tough challenges in the first half of the race, and several guys are eager to show what they are truly capable of. The order of the day from here on out is making those intentions a reality.

off Laiseka's previous best, but he knew that Armstrong would be faster. The American was just over 2km from the finish when Ullrich crossed, and Armstrong rode most of that distance out of the saddle. He came within 25 seconds of catching his two-minute man, Beloki (whose 1:09:02 gave him third on the stage), as he completed his time trial in 1:07:27, exactly one minute faster than Ullrich.

So Armstrong won his second stage in succession, and he was now only 13:07 behind the elusive Simon, and just 2:06 behind Kivilev. "Kivilev finishing six minutes back surprised me," Armstrong claimed. "I thought it [the gap] would be three or four minutes."

Then, asked about the deficit he was taking into the next stages, in the Pyrénées, Armstrong answered with confidence and clarity: "The objective now is the yellow jersey."

STAGE 12: HEROES AND VICTIMS

François Simon is a down-home pro cyclist from the Champagne region to the east of Paris, one of four brothers who have all raced bikes for cash. He's a short man with a round face, small gray eyes, cropped graying hair and a hesitant smile of uneven teeth. When he and Kivilev gained more than 33 minutes in the famous 14-man break to Pontarlier on July 15, few people believed in their chances of holding off the inevitable charge by Armstrong, Ullrich and company. Yet here we were five days later, sitting on a mountainside in the Pyrénées at the end of another very tough stage, and Simon and Kivilev were still sitting atop the overall classification.

Simon, 32, had been a team worker for most of his 11-year career, first with Castorama, then with GAN and Crédit Agricole. But after taking a shock victory at the French national championship in 1999, he signed a contract with Bonjour, the low-budget French team launched in 2000 by Jean-René Bernaudeau. Along with Didier Rous and Jean-Cyril Robin, Simon became one of the

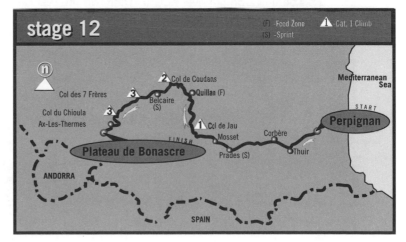

109

team leaders—by virtue of his experience rather than his potential. He did win a stage of the Giro d'Italia back in 1992, and lost the overall title at the Tour de l'Avenir by less than a second in '93, but he was best known as a gritty rider with a useful sprint, particularly at the end of a tough race.

In 2000, Simon rewarded Bonjour with a stage win and fourth overall at Paris-Nice in March; and he came close to pulling off a stage win in his hometown of Troyes at that year's Tour. His oldest brother Pascal nearly won the Tour itself in 1983: He took the yellow jersey in the Pyrénées, crashed the next day and suffered a hairline fracture of the shoulder blade, and then defended the lead for another six days. The pain finally became too much for him and he quit the race on the stage to L'Alpe d'Huez.

On the morning of this year's stage to the Alpe, Pascal Simon called his youngest brother to wish him luck in trying to take the yellow jersey—18 years after he had conceded it at the same place. François duly obliged by staying with the lead group that dropped overnight leader O'Grady over the Madeleine; hanging tough until 4km from the top of the Glandon; chasing back on the descent; and finally taking 29th place—and the yellow jersey—on the Alpe. Simon then finished 46th in the Chamrousse time trial, and packed a new yellow jersey in his suitcase for the rest-day journey to Perpignan.

Meanwhile, the other French rider who wore the jersey in this Tour, prologue winner Moreau, flew to Perpignan with his spirits low. After finishing fourth on the Alpe, the 30-year-old with the trendy goatee was talking about a place on the podium in Paris. That talk was put on hold when he took a dismal eighth place in the time trial, dropping two minutes behind podium rival Beloki. Then, on the rest day, a planned Moreau press con-

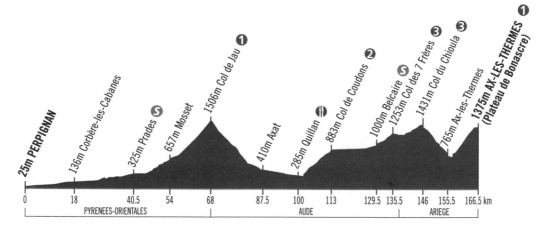

ference was canceled ... and the rumor mill started turning: Was he sick? Or was he the subject of another positive drug test, after the one for steroids in 1998 and his subsequent suspension for admitting he had used EPO on the old Festina team?

Whatever the reason, Moreau didn't look too happy as he sat alone in the *village du départ* at Perpignan before stage 12. He later said that he had caught a cold on the wet Pontarlier stage and been treated with antibiotics. Now he was worried that he hadn't recovered from the efforts he made in the Alps and was in no shape to take on the three giant stages that awaited him in the Pyrénées.

Usually, this mountain chain that separates France from Spain is shrouded in clouds, but not on this crystal-clear day. Still, it wasn't hot. A ferocious wind was blowing from the northwest, slowing the peloton to only 28km in the first hour. It was a wind that became Moreau's enemy when the attacks started, and he found himself at the wrong end of the peloton as it turned off the highway into very narrow back roads leading to the day's first climb, the Cat. 1 Col de Jau. Things got worse for Moreau when he was involved in a small pileup and then got dropped. Some Festina teammates went back for him, but as the grade steepened, the speed was still high in front, making it hard to organize a chase. "My legs were empty ... I didn't feel well," Moreau told *L'Équipe* the next day. "I was in 39x21, while my guys were riding in the big ring."

Even though they could see their leader's morale was low, his teammates were shocked when Moreau told them he couldn't go any farther. The French hope for the podium climbed off his bike and into his team car. After Casagrande in the first week, another contender had left the Tour.

At the same time, Simon was faring much better. His Bonjour teammates were keeping the race leader near the front of the pack as a 12-man break formed on the Jau's upper slopes. That group was caught soon after starting the plunge into the limestone canyons of the Aude River on a tight, twisting downhill. Green-jersey leader O'Grady and Italian Paolo Bettini then made a spectacular break, and they garnered a 3:40 lead before Quillan and the start of the Cat. 2 Col de Coudons. Here, a six-man chase formed, and two of these riders, David Etxebarria of Euskaltel and Cardenas of Kelme, jumped away before the 2900-foot summit. They caught O'Grady, who had been dropped on the climb, and set off into a strong head wind blowing across the wide fields of a flat plateau.

Bettini, in search of his Mapei team's elusive first stage win, was 1:50 ahead at the

Kevin's diary: Stage 12

July 20, 2001

AX-LES-THERMES: *It was windy today right from the start in Perpignan, on the southeastern coast. A head-crosswind made things tough, even on the opening flats. The attacks then started just before the first climb, and U.S. Postal and even some Bonjour riders took control of the race for a while. Because of the wind, groups went away but kept coming back.*

We rode this stage once during training, so I knew that the first climb wasn't very steep and I could kind of picture happening what did. Despite the course profile, it was an uneventful stage. The climbs were short and not steep enough to break the group up. Given the wind and the style of the climbs, it just came down to the final 8Ks, and I had no chance there once the attacks went.

It's funny sometimes how you can be moving around with no idea of where you are. I was thinking about that tonight after the race. We came by helicopter from the finish (at the ski area of Ax-les-Thermes), then we drove about 8km to the hotel. We just drive through towns and arrive at a hotel somewhere. I couldn't even tell you if there's a supermarket next to the hotel or what. It's very strange.

Once we arrive at the hotel, the team personnel stays out cleaning our bikes and clothes. We always have a new set of clothes for a big race like the Giro or the Tour. At the beginning of the year, we all got a net laundry bag with a number on it. You put everything in there, and they take care of it. The truck has a washer and dryer in it. Most every team has the same kind of arrangement.

The morale on the team is good. At the dinner table and hanging out, everybody is cheerful. I'm happy with how I'm riding and I hope tomorrow—to St. Lary Soulan over five passes—that I can do again what I did on L'Alpe d'Huez. I didn't know what to expect that day. All of us had gotten so beaten up in those winds and the other challenges of the first week. I had felt so bad on this little climb into Aix-les-Bains the day before that I was worried—motivated, but worried before Alpe d'Huez. There's not much you can do when your form's not there. But I just pushed it and did my job for the team on the climbs, and I'm happy with how I rode in the Alps. Now I hope I can do it again in the Pyrénées.

day's second intermediate sprint, where O'Grady took the second-place points and promptly sat up. The Aussie knew there was no sense in him wasting energy on the three climbs still ahead.

Cardenas and Etxebarria had no such thoughts. They started to close on Bettini and were just half-a-minute behind him on starting the 9.5km climb from the medieval streets of Ax-les-Thermes up to the finish in the small, modern ski station at Plateau de Bonascre.

It wasn't a long climb, but it was deceptively difficult, with pitches of 9 and 10.7 percent in the first 5km, as it zigzagged out of the narrow Ariège valley above the pink-tiled roofs of Ax.

After the two chasers caught Bettini on the first steep section, Etxebarria was the first to counterattack. Cardenas—a second-year Colombian pro with Kelme—went after him, joined the Spaniard and immediately went away himself. There were just over 5km left.

Back down the wooded mountainside, after starting the climb three minutes back, Ullrich attacked from the main group and only Armstrong and Kivilev could follow. Ullrich was ready for a scrap, and his second acceleration was too much for the brave Kivilev. So by the time Cardenas made his move in front, Armstrong and Ullrich were just one minute behind.

That wasn't the end of the story, though. Just as Ullrich and Armstrong caught and passed Bettini with 4.5km to go, the hidden hero of the Chamrousse time trial, Laiseka, managed to catch them. Knowing that his teammate Etxebarria had been dropped by Cardenas, the Euskaltel veteran caught his breath behind the Ullrich-Armstrong tandem for a few minutes, before he audaciously sprinted away from them with 3.5km remaining.

Ullrich continued his steady progress, but 2km from the top he stopped pedaling for a moment, forcing Armstrong to lead. The Texan gladly took over, and a half-kilometer later he attacked hard, leaving Ullrich in his dust. For a few moments it looked as if Armstrong would charge straight through to win his third consecutive stage ... but his rapid progress wasn't favored by the final kilometer: It started out flat, then went downhill before a last kick to the finish.

That respite was all the front two riders needed to stay away, with Colombia's Cardenas having 15 seconds in hand as he celebrated the stage win, on his country's independence day, by standing up on his pedals, high above his saddle with his arms straight up. Laiseka hung on for second, 15 seconds back, with Armstrong taking third *and* another 20 seconds out of Ullrich

As for the Pontarlier pair, Kivilev paid for his attempt at staying with the big two, coming in 18th just behind a group of nine, 1:32 behind Armstrong; and race leader Simon, who had been dropped on the preceding climb, came home with another small group, four minutes back. But with 9:10 still in hand, there'd be at least one more day in yellow for the tenacious Simon.

STAGE 13: RIDING FOR FABIO

After a 23-year-old Lance Armstrong audaciously raced away from a breakaway group of seasoned riders on a hot, sunny day in July 1995, soloed for 20km and won the Tour stage into Limoges, he said, "I had the strength of two today." He was alluding to his Motorola teammate Fabio Casartelli, who had died three days earlier in a numbing crash when descending the Portet d'Aspet pass in the Pyrénées. Armstrong dedicated that victory in Limoges to his departed friend, and he still referred to it as the win that was most meaningful to him.

Memories of Casartelli came pouring back on this 13th stage when, for the first time since the tragedy, the Tour descended the road where he died. Those who had been there couldn't help but see images from that time: The young Italian racing down the steep, narrow mountain road at 80 kph; another rider overshooting a left turn and somersaulting into a ravine, causing Casartelli to swerve, skid and then collide with a low concrete block, cracking his head open on the granite-chip pavement; and his body lying inert in the center of the road.

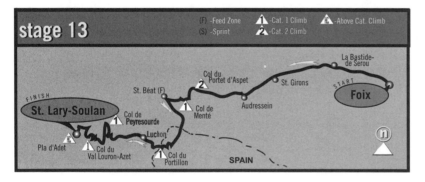

"I have to admit that I was crying like a baby six weeks ago," Armstrong said at this year's stage finish in Pla d'Adet, referring to a late May training-ride visit to the beautiful, white-marble memorial that has been created for Casartelli near the crash site. "And when we passed today, I decided then and there that I was going to win today."

The calm authority with which Armstrong spoke those words was indicative of the manner in which he was controlling this Tour de France. No doubts, no reservations.

When this stage did pass the memorial, one turn before the foot of the 15-percent descent, Armstrong was near the head of the peloton, six minutes behind a nine-rider break that had formed 50km earlier. In the break was Laurent Jalabert, who, with two stage wins already in his pocket, now used the Portet d'Aspet descent to make an audacious solo attack. Was he thinking of a third stage victory? If so, it was a daunting challenge, with 120km remaining and the bulk of the day's 16,000 feet of climbing ahead: four Cat. 1 climbs (the Menté, Portillon, Peyresourde and Val Louron) and the above-category climb to the finish at Pla d'Adet.

In his fearless descending style, Jalabert took 35 seconds on the pursuing Vinokourov of Telekom and held that margin over the Menté, which climbs in a series of switchbacks up a steep mountainside. Then the Frenchman opened it up: He added a minute to his lead on the equally steep descent, and after a short loop into Spain, he reached the top of the zigzagging Portillon with a 3:20 margin over Vinokourov.

Almost nine minutes behind Jalabert on this 8km climb, the field was breaking apart, and a fatigued Fred Rodriguez was one of those who had already abandoned. A giant stage like this one would seek out the slightest weakness.

It was also a stage that offered strategic opportunities to the strong. That's why Ullrich, who had never felt stronger, had already sent Vinokourov ahead as a possible springboard to a winning move. The best scenario would have had Vino' staying with Jalabert. Instead, as the runaway Frenchman continued his solo charge, the blond rider from Kazakhstan was joined over the Portillon by another who had been in the original nine-man break, Belgian Stive Vermaut

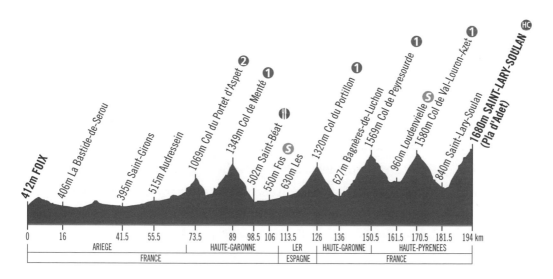

of Lotto. After linking up in the crowd-lined streets of Luchon, Vino' and Vermaut set off 3:55 behind Jalabert on the 13km haul up the Col de Peyresourde. In turn, a chase group headed by 2000 Giro winner Stefano Garzelli of Mapei was at 6:20, while the pack was at 10:20.

With Telekom's Guerini and Livingston working for Ullrich, and Postal's Heras and Rubiera for Armstrong, the peloton's pace picked up on the Peyresourde. Race leader Simon was dropped with 9km of climbing still to go, and the fast-moving Ullrich-Armstrong group mopped up most of the riders from earlier moves.

Approaching the Peyresourde's 5147-foot summit, Jalabert was still four minutes ahead of Vinokourov. By now, the Telekom rider had dropped Vermaut, was only a half-minute ahead of Garzelli and had 1:30 on the Armstrong group.

Ullrich was ready to play his next two cards. First, he told Livingston to jump ahead before the top, and then he made a sharp attack himself. Armstrong was the only one who could reply, while Beloki (still above Ullrich on G.C.) fell back.

Discussing the move, Livingston later remarked, "At first I didn't know why [Jan told me to go]. But when I thought about it and saw him at the top coming up ... I think it was a good tactic—that I go and then Jan come up—because it gave me a little motivation that I got away, and this helps...."

Ullrich was not only thinking about putting time on Beloki. He was also hoping to link up with teammates Livingston and Vinokourov, and perhaps isolate Armstrong before the final two climbs. Taking up the story, Ullrich said, "I jumped after [Kevin], thinking, 'Okay, we might as well risk something on the descent to stop the others coming back to us.' I was chasing hard on the descent, but then my brakes didn't work right."

Ullrich, with Armstrong on his wheel, had just caught Livingston, who had a front-row seat of what happened coming into a tight left turn. "We knew the turn from training," said Armstrong's former teammate. "But you misjudge it and this happens ... I saw it coming, I saw him [Ullrich] braking, and whatever ... He did the right thing, because he went off on the side and he braked as hard as he could and he went over."

Ullrich avoided catastrophe by steering into a meadow, and, as he said, "Yeah, I landed right in this river [actually a small mountain stream]. I was rather wet, but I was okay."

He may have been okay, and Livingston soon paced him back to Armstrong, who waited, but the crash clearly took the momentum out of the Telekom move. The Ullrich-Livingston-Armstrong trio did link up with Vinokourov, but before they reached the second-to-last climb—the nasty Val Louron, with its frequent 9- and 10-percent pitches—Beloki and Kivilev had caught them, while Heras would catch back on the climb.

Beloki twice attacked on Val Louron, while Ullrich made another surge, but the small group stayed together. And by the high summit, from where the modern ski buildings at the Pla d'Adet finish could be seen across the deep valley, the situation was this: Jalabert in the lead; Garzelli at 1:50; then Ullrich-Beloki-Botero-Kivilev-Heras-Armstrong at 2:45.

Jalabert was still racing hard, but there were signs that fatigue was finally hitting him. First, he misjudged his speed coming into a sharp left switchback on the fast descent to St. Lary-Soulan and almost skidded. Then, making the right turn into town he *did* slide out, fell on his right elbow and needed a replacement bike. Lesser riders would have thrown in the towel right then. Not Jalabert. He was quickly back into his stride and began the 10km climb to the finish 1:30 ahead of Garzelli and 2:50 ahead of the Armstrong-Ullrich group—which a few riders had rejoined, including Postal's Rubiera.

Having his two Spanish teammates with him was a huge boost for Armstrong, who first told Heras to accelerate, then Rubiera. Their efforts thinned out the group, with the brave Kivilev being one of those unable to hang on. Then Heras put in an even fiercer surge on Pla d'Adet's steepest section, 2km into the climb.

Only Armstrong and Ullrich could follow the little Spaniard, with Beloki the last one to lose contact. Heras, still with a bandage on his left knee from his crash in the first week, kept up the pressure until Garzelli was caught. Ullrich then made an immediate attack, and once again he and Armstrong were side by side: the American often out of the saddle, spinning his 39x23, Ullrich sitting down, climbing hard.

They raced together for a kilometer. But both knew that Armstrong was about to repeat the acceleration he had made at Ax-les-Thermes 24 hours earlier.

The acceleration was the same, while the motivation was different, more powerful. Not only did the Texan know that the yellow jersey was awaiting him, Lance was again riding with the strength of two.

Armstrong soon rode past Jalabert—who had earned the KoM jersey with his long solo raid—before he sprinted up the last steep pitch. And then he was crossing the line, pointing to the sky, just as he did at Limoges in 1995, remembering Fabio.

Tyler's diary: Stage 13

July 21, 2001

ST. LARY-SOULAN: I don't know if I've ridden many stages more difficult than today's. When we came to preview this course in May, we realized that today was probably going to be one of the most critical of the Tour de France. It was a course with no mercy—just up and down and back up again.

Good bike karma has not been on my side too often at this edition of the Tour. For the third time in this year's race, my bike had mechanical issues. For the second time, the derailleur on my climbing bike broke. There's nothing you can do in a situation like that except stop. It's not like having a flat, where you can keep rolling. The team car was nowhere near, so I had to wait a while to make the change out to my standard road bike. Unfortunately, this happened at the base of a climb, so I had to chase hard to get back to the group.

The race passed by the Fabio Casartelli monument today. There was some talk in the peloton about stopping like we did a few years back; but with attacks going from the gun, we weren't able to. Our team, however, paid its respects during our training camp in the Pyrénées back in May. The monument is so breathtaking that every time I see it, I'm humbled by it. Lance dedicated his stage win to Fabio in much the same style he did the year he lost his teammate, pointing to the sky as he crossed the finish line. Although I never knew Fabio, I like to think that he was smiling somewhere today, seeing his old friend succeed.

Phil Knight, the CEO of Nike, was on hand today to view the race from the passenger seat of the first team car. If Lance were trying to impress his guest, I'd say he did so and then some. It's not every day that you get to see the guy you're rooting for win a stage and take over the yellow jersey at the Tour de France.

My family was at the finish in Pla d'Adet. They braved the crowds and decided to head to the mountaintop for a bird's-eye view of the final kilometers. I don't think they were disappointed to see Lance come charging up the mountain all alone. And with their collection of American flags and Postal regalia, I'm sure they managed to irritate more than one Frenchman! But knowing my family, they probably gave Jaja equal time.

STAGE 14: BASQUE FEVER

The fever-like passion the Basque people have for cycling is nothing new. Hemingway wrote about it in his novel *The Sun Also Rises*, after he bumped into a pro bike race on a 1930s road trip to the Running of the Bulls in Pamplona. There were no bulls in Tarbes for the start of this Tour's stage 14, but there were plenty of Basques. A trio of them, decked out in the orange T-shirts of their region's team, Euskaltel-Euskadi, had a nice surprise as they stood outside a café, beer glasses in hand, hoping to catch a glimpse of their heroes. About an hour before the start, the big Euskaltel team bus chugged into the start area and stopped right in front of them.

If they'd been French fans, they would probably have politely applauded; Germans would have blown air horns or chanted their heroes' names. But these were Basques. They put down their beers and went down on their knees, as if to worship the ground on which the Basque bus was standing.

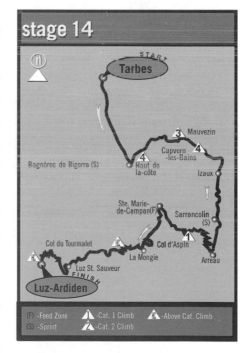

Roberto Laiseka, the Euskaltel rider who challenged Armstrong and Ullrich at the Chamrousse time trial, used to be one of these cycling-mad supporters of Basque cycling. "I often came with my family to see the Tour," Laiseka remembered. "We would come by bus and watch the Tour in the Pyrénées. I remember seeing LeMond when he was the world champion, and taking a photo of Induráin when he won the stage at Luz-Ardiden [in 1990]."

Laiseka was already an amateur cyclist back then, and when the Euskadi region (the locals' name for the Basque Country) established its own pro cycling team in 1984, Laiseka, then 24, was signed up. It was a low-budget squad financed by donations from the Basque fans, and Laiseka was a low rider on the totem poll. The better racers, such as David Etxebarria or Joseba Beloki, got snapped up by bigger formations, like ONCE or Festina. Laiseka remained.

He didn't win any races in his first five seasons with the squad, but in his sixth year, 1999, when Euskaltel (the Basque telephone utility) became the title sponsor, Laiseka made a breakthrough at age 30. He won a semi-mountain stage of the Vuelta a España. A lucky break? No. He took a more prestigious stage of the Vuelta in 2000, the one finishing on the mountaintop of Arcalis in Andorra, and he finished sixth overall.

Laiseka's Basque team was never good enough to receive an invitation to the Tour de France, but the team's elevation to Division I status in 2001, along with some excellent results in early-season events, earned Euskaltel a wild-card slot for the Tour. Things didn't start too well, though. Euskaltel placed 17th in the team time trial, and by the time the race reached the Alps, the squad was lying last on team classification; and Laiseka, suffering with persistent knee pain, was in 86th overall, 57 minutes down.

Once the climbing started, Laiseka showed his worth: ninth on Alpe d'Huez, fourth in the Chamrousse mountain time trial, second at Plateau de Bonascre ... and he was up to 26th overall, at 37:30. Then came the big stage to Pla d'Adet, in which Laiseka had his hardest day yet of the Tour: He finished in 78th place, almost a half-hour down on Armstrong. He couldn't explain his poor performance, just saying that he needed all the vocal support he received from the Basque fans.

Now came this final mountain stage that would climb the famous passes of the Aspin and Tourmalet before the uphill finish to Luz-Ardiden. It was Euskaltel's last realistic chance to win a piece of Tour glory. And with tens of thousands of those orange-shirted fans lining every climb, the team would have plenty of inspiration.

Ideally, Euskaltel would put one of its riders in an early breakaway, which is a classic tactic for reducing the pressure on the rest of the team until one of them is ready to make a

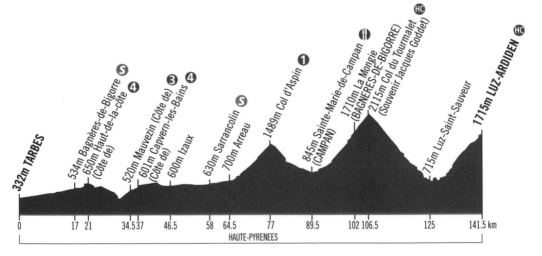

move. But when the key move was started by La Française des Jeux's Montgomery on the third of three short hills, 37km into the stage, no Euskaltel men were among the nine riders who joined the young Swiss-American. Still, the Basques revealed their ambitions by setting the peloton's tempo with Postal when the break quickly took a four-minute lead.

The leaders stayed together, and the gap remained the same over the Aspin. But once the first slopes of the mighty Tourmalet were reached, with 50km left in the 144.5km stage, the race exploded. The highest mountain pass of this Tour, at 2115 meters (6939 feet), the Col du Tourmalet measures 17km long on the eastern approach, averaging 7.6 percent. The final 6km is the most difficult section, with an average grade of 9.3 percent.

The remarkable Montgomery was first over the summit, taking the 20,000-franc (almost $3000) Souvenir Jacques Goddet prime, in memory of the long-time Tour director who died in 2000. If he had looked to his right, Montgomery would have seen the recently unveiled Goddet memorial statue, as he crossed the *hors-categorie* peak ahead of the other remaining members of the initial break: Belli of Fassa Bortolo, Moncoutié of Cofidis and Mario Aerts of Lotto.

Next, 40 seconds back, came Julich, who had also been in the early move, while a further 30 seconds behind him came the 10-man group that formed after accelerations by first Ullrich ... then Laiseka. Also in the group were Armstrong, Garzelli, Cardenas, Beloki, Kivilev, Sastre, Menchov and Pozzi. Others would rejoin on the super-fast descent, notably Postal's Heras and Rubiera, and Bonjour's Rous—who promptly went off in pursuit of the four riders ahead.

Already, Montgomery had been dropped on the descent; and as soon as the final, 13km climb began, Belli rode away from Aerts and Moncoutié. At the same time, 1:18 back, Laiseka made a sizzling attack to leave behind the Armstrong-Ullrich group.

The battle for the stage win soon became a pursuit between the Italian Belli, who said that he was hoping to dedicate the stage win to his late friend Casartelli, and Laiseka. It proved an uneven contest. The Italian was moving well, but the slim Basque with the haunting, deep-set eyes was remorseless. Every few meters, fans were waving Basque flags and banners in his face to urge him on, while others ran alongside, shouting words of support. Laiseka's response was to catch and pass Belli before halfway, and then ride the remaining 7km in a triumphal orange-lined blur.

He won the stage by 54 seconds over Belli, while Ullrich attacked the chase group

121

Tyler's diary: Rest day

July 23, 2001

PAU: This is the first rest day I can remember in a long time where we actually got to rest. Our team has been at the same hotel for the past two nights, and the start is right downtown from us tomorrow. Believe me, a few nights stay in one spot is a rarity at the Tour. I practically feel like I live here in Pau.

We went for a training ride at about 10:30 this morning, to preview a bit of tomorrow's course. The profile is grim. Don't believe people when they say the hardest stages are behind us, because the next two days are going to be tough. There are no mountaintop finishes, but the profiles are unrelenting: rolling and then rolling some more, with no breaks in between.

We set out for a two-hour ride, but somehow wound up diverted and spent almost three hours on our bikes. So I was looking forward to an afternoon nap. With over 200km in each of the next two stages, we're going to be put to the test—and I need all the rest I can get.

The region we'll be passing through is called the Massif Central. A couple years back, one of my teammates renamed the area "Massive $^ $#!@#" during a pass through here. That should give you an idea of how grueling the terrain is. I don't think there is one solitary flat section. The stage profile looks like back-to-back humpback camels.

My parents and my wife departed from the Tour today. They all had hoarse voices and looked a little haggard from driving over 1800km through the Pyrénées. But while they were with us, the weather was good and Lance assumed the lead in the race—so naturally, they feel like they were part of the good-luck streak while being here. They're even taking credit for curing the mishaps with my derailleur. I guess it is a good thing they showed up.

On a random note, if you think being at the Tour de France is an incredible opportunity, consider this: While my family was on the final climb yesterday, they found themselves positioned in no-man's land—meaning, they had no idea what was going on in the race since they weren't at the top of the climb where the television and radio broadcasts keep everyone posted. To stay informed, they were calling home to Massachusetts on their cell phones to find out what was going on and who won. So those of you who think you're missing out on the action back at home, rest assured. You're one step ahead of some of the fans on the roadside.

inside the final 2km, with just Armstrong on his wheel. This time, the Texan gestured to his German rival to cross the line in front of him. Ullrich gladly did so, then reached across to shake Armstrong's hand. It was an acknowledgment of both thanks and respect. The Tour's last mountain had been climbed. Armstrong was in yellow. Laiseka was in heaven. And the Basques could start celebrating the victory of one of their own. By nightfall, the last of their buses had departed Luz-Ardiden for the long journey to the Basque homeland. Even Hemingway couldn't have created a better ending to three tough days in the Pyrénées.

Results: Aix-les-Bains to Luz-Ardiden

WEEK 2

Stage 10: Aix-les-Bains-L'Alpe d'Huez. July 17.

1. Armstrong, 209km in 6:23:47 (32.675 kph); 2. Ullrich, at 1:59; 3. Beloki, at 2:09; 4. Moreau, at 2:30; 5. Oscar Sevilla (Sp), Kelme-Costa Blanca, at 2:54; 6. Mancebo, at 4:01; 7. Roux, at 4:03; 8. I. Gonzalez de Galdeano; 9. Roberto Laiseka (Sp), Euskaltel-Euskadi, both s.t.; 10. Leonardo Piepoli (I), iBanesto.com, at 4:07; 11. Boogerd, at 4:37; 12. Kivilev, at 4:39; 13. Botero, at 5:07; 14. Sven Montgomery (Swi), La Française des Jeux, at 5:09; 15. Didier Rous (F), Bonjour, at 6:18; 16. Axel Merckx (B), Domo-Farm Frites; 17. Marcos Serrano (Sp), ONCE-Eroski; 18. Belli, all s.t.; 19. Mikhailov, at 7:05; 20. Garzelli, at 7:54.

Others: 27. Vaughters, at 10:20; 29. Simon, s.t.; **43. Livingston, at 17:29; 48. Julich, at 23:10; 79. Hincapie, at 32:05;** 87. O'Grady, at 33:02; **109. Hamilton, at 40:20; 110. Rodriguez, s.t.**

Overall: 1. Simon, 45:34:09; 2. Kivilev, at 11:54; 3. O'Grady, at 18:10; 4. Armstrong, at 20:07; 5. Beloki, at 21:42; 6. Moreau, at 22:21; 7. Ullrich, at 22:41; 8. Gonzalez de Galdeano, at 23:34; 9. Sevilla, at 24:07; 10. Botero, at 25:52.

Stage 11: Grenoble-Chamrousse TT. July 18.

1. Armstrong, 32km in 1:07:27 (28.466 kph); 2. Ullrich, 1:08:27; 3. Beloki, 1:09:02; 4. Laiseka, 1:09:30; 5. Sevilla. 1:09:51; 6. I. Gonzales de Galdeano, 1:09:58; 7. Botero, 1:10:10; 8. Moreau, 1:10:27; 9. Montgomery, 1:10:34; 10. Garzelli, 1:10:35.

Others: 21. Vaughters, 1:11:58; 32. Kivilev, 1:13:34; 45. Julich, 1:14:20; 46. Simon, 1:14:27; 112. O'Grady 1:18:05; **115. Livingston, 1:18:09; 118. Rodriguez, 1:18:20; 119. Hincapie, 1:18:21; 128. Hamilton, 1:18:49.**

Overall: 1. Simon, 46:48:36; 2. Kivilev, at 11:01; **3. Armstrong, at 13:07;** 4. Beloki, at 16:17; 5. Ullrich, at 16:41; 6. Moreau, at 18:21; 7. Gonzales de Galdeano, at 19:05; 8. Sevilla, at 19:31; 9. Botero, at 21:35; 10. O'Grady, at 21:48.

Stage 12: Perpignan-Ax-les-Thermes (Plateau de Bonascre). July 20.

1. Felix Cardenas (Col), Kelme-Costa Blanca, 166.5km in 5:03:34 (32.909 kph); 2. Laiseka, at 0:13; 3. Armstrong, at 0:15; 4. Ullrich, at 0:38; 5. Etxebarria, at 0:59; 6. Sevilla, at 1:01; 7. Beloki, s.t.; 8. Botero, at 1:35; 9. Boogerd; 10. Vinokourov; 11. Garzelli; 12. Chaurreau; 13. Serrano; 14. Rous; 15. Mancebo, all s.t..

Others: 18. Kivilev, at 1:45; **21. Vaughters, 1:11:58; 40. Julich, at 4:04;** 41. Simon, s.t.; **59. Livingston, at 5:36; 91. Hamilton, at 12:08; 103. Hincapie, s.t.;** 124. O'Grady, at 14:38; **160. Rodriguez, at 29:23.**

Overall: 1. Simon, 51:56:14; 2. Kivilev, at 8:42; **3. Armstrong, at 9:10;** 4. Beloki, at 13:14; 5. Ullrich, at 13:15; 6. Sevilla, at 16:28; 7. Gonzalez de Galdeano, at 16:40; 8. Botero, at 19:06; 9. Rous, at 22:55; 10. Serrano, at 22:58.

Stage 13: Foix - St. Lary-Soulan (Pla d'Adet). July 21.

1. Armstrong, 194km in 5:44:22 (33.801 kph); 2. Ullrich, at 1:00; 3. Beloki, at 1:46; 4. Heras, s.t.; 5. Garzelli, at 2:29; 6. I. Gonzalez de Galdeano, at 2:52; 7. L. Jalabert, at 3:12; 8. Serrano, at 3:15; 9. Chaurreau, at 3:25; 10. Kivilev, at 4:02; 11. Botero, at 4:46; 12. Sevilla, at 5:46; 13. Mancebo, at 6:03; 14. Alexander Botcharov (Rus), AG2R, s.t.; 15. Rous, at 6:59.

Others: 21. Vaughters, 1:11:58; 28. Livingston, at 12:42; 31. Simon, at 13:21; **44. Julich, at 20:09; 64. Hamilton, at 28:47; 70. Hincapie, s.t.;** 142. O'Grady, at 35:12.

Overall: **1. Armstrong, 57:49:26;** 2. Kivilev, at 3:54; 3. Simon, at 4:31; 4. Ullrich, at 5:13; 5. Beloki, at 6:02; 6. Gonzalez de Galdeano, at 10:42; Sevilla, at 13:24; 8. Botero, at 15:00; 9. Serrano, at 17:23; 10. Garzelli, at 17:26.

Stage 14: Tarbes - Luz-Ardiden. July 22.

1. Laiseka. 144.5km in 4:24:30 (32.779 kph); 2. Belli, at 0:54; 3. Ullrich, at 1:08; **4. Armstrong, s.t.;** 5. Heras, at 1:29; 6. Beloki, at 1:39; 7. Sevilla, s.t.; 8. Rous, at 2:01; 9. Kivilev, at 2:27; 10. Gonzalez de Galdeano, at 2:30; 11. Cardenas, at 2:42; 12. Serrano, at 3:05; 13. Garzelli, at 3:27; 14. Chaurreau, s.t.; 15. Moncoutié, at 3:49.

Others: 31. Simon, at 7:31; **32. Julich, at 7:34; 52. Livingston, at 14:40; 63. Hamilton, at 19:43; 98. Hincapie, at 27:31; 114. Vaughters, s.t.;** 132. O'Grady, at 30:34.

WEEK 3

The Long Road to Paris

s they say in general election parlance, most of the results were in and the projected winner was Lance Armstrong. That was the verdict on the Tour's second rest day, in Pau, following the last of the mountain stages. As befits a "winner," Armstrong gave a press conference in Pau to talk about his campaign, which had been headlined by stunning performances in the five summit finishes: first, first, third, first and fourth. Those results—which had put the Texan into the yellow jersey with a comfortable five-minute lead over Jan Ullrich—earned Armstrong the admiration of most race followers. But for others, such dominance gave rise to further skepticism, and voices from all parts of the race entourage were saying that no one could maintain top form every day without using drugs. Given that environment, many of the questions the race leader fielded at the Pau press conference were related to doping and Armstrong's continued working relationship with Dr. Michele Ferrari. Armstrong knew there would be such questions, and he answered them, it was unanimously agreed, with the same strengths and skills he had displayed in handling the opposition on his bike: confidence and swift maneuvering. And when he *did* talk about the race, the American was the ultimate politician in emphasizing that the Tour de France wasn't over, that there was still a week to go, and that, as always, anything could happen.

Armstrong was right, of course, especially when looking ahead to the hilly (and probably hot) stages that would take the peloton through the Massif Central. With riders tired from racing in the sun for hours on end, crashes were one potential danger. Another was the likelihood of long breakaways, perhaps one like the 14-man move on the road to Pontarlier in week one. Reminders of that stage 8 break were constant, because its main beneficiaries were still riding high on G.C. Andrei Kivilev had emerged from the mountains in third place (just eight seconds behind Ullrich), while François Simon was in fifth overall. But both men knew that their positions were threatened by ONCE teammates Joseba Beloki (1:20 behind Kivilev) and Igor Gonzalez de Galdeano (1:10 behind Simon). Those time gaps could seem fragile in stage 18's time trial, a discipline in which the two Spanish riders excelled.

That upcoming time trial also seemed to offer Armstrong the best chance of consolidating his yellow jersey. Of the other contests, Laurent Jalabert had just about wrapped up the climbers' polka-dot jersey competition; and Kelme's Oscar Sevilla seemed to have a stranglehold on the white jersey as top rider aged 25 or under. Less clear were the outcomes in the sprinters' green jersey match-up between leader Stuart O'Grady and defending champion Erik Zabel; and the team prize, in which Kelme and ONCE were the protagonists. In other words, besides the daily quest for stage wins, there was plenty to race for on the still-long road to Paris.

STAGE 15: DIFFERENT DIRECTIONS

In the 70 years that Tour de France stages have been starting in Pau, the race has either headed south to the mountain roads of the nearby Pyrénées, or north across the billiard-flat plains to Bordeaux. Two stages in the 1970s did head northeast to Fleurance, but not until this July 24 in 2001 did a stage head due east. Although the mountains were behind the 152 survivors of the Tour's first two weeks, they would face plenty of climbing on this 232.5km course, the longest of the Tour. Besides four official climbs, one Cat. 3 and three Cat. 4s, there were some 20 other substantial hills that would make this a far from easy transition from small-ring to big-ring racing.

The first of those hills saw another premature Tour ending for the fated Vaughters, who

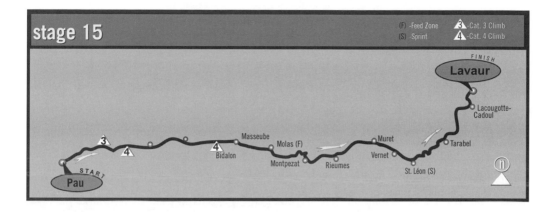

had an allergic reaction to a wasp bite on a rest-day training ride and, under UCI anti-doping regulations, wasn't allowed to have a cortisone shot; and the day's first unsuccessful attack by Rabobank's Dekker. The Dutchman finally got clear when a 16-strong group formed at the 30km mark, following the first two official climbs. One of the leaders, however, was Kelme's eighth-placed Botero, so a strong chase was initiated by ONCE, protecting the sixth place of its Igor Gonzalez de Galdeano, and the move was allowed no more than 30 seconds.

Then, just after the Tour passed its first field of sunflowers, on the seventh actual hill, 60km out of Pau, Frenchman Laurent Brochard of Jean Delatour set in motion a break that brought together 25 riders from 17 teams. The one potential danger man in the group was Rabobank's Boogerd. But starting the stage in 16th place, 31:18 behind Armstrong, the Dutch rider represented only a minor threat. Even so, for 50km the tempo set by Postal then ONCE kept the gap pegged to between two and three minutes. Then, after a cool misty opening, the sun finally broke through as the peloton turned onto a narrow back road replete with more nasty uphills. The combination of climbs and sudden heat reduced the ardor of the chase, and over the next 50km the 25-man break opened its lead to 13 minutes.

Kelme—defending the seventh and eighth places of Sevilla and Botero—didn't allow that gap to grow any bigger, even when the leaders started attacking each other in the final hour.

Remarkably, it was a solo rider, Lampre's third-year pro Marco Pinotti, who eventually got away with 31km to go. One of Italy's best time trialists, Pinotti was soon storming along the narrow roads of the Tarn region, reveling in the fast curving downhills, short climbs and tricky passages through small ocher-tiled towns.

Another fine time trialist, Giro prologue winner Verbrugghe, took up the chase. The tall Belgian from Lotto was showing himself at the front for the first time since he was caught on a late solo break into Strasbourg 11 days earlier, when he was pursued by the whole peloton. This time, the group behind was in temporary disarray, and Verbrugghe managed to bridge the 30-second gap to Pinotti with 13km left to race.

The seasoned Belgian and still-learning Italian worked beautifully together to keep the reorganized group at bay on the fast, descending road to the finish in Lavaur. It was Pinotti who led out the sprint. But it was Verbrugghe, despite having his sunglasses slipping down his nose, who proved faster, giving Lotto its first Tour stage win since Peter De Clercq took stage 20 at Nanterre in 1992.

The small town of Lavaur, population 9100, was welcoming the Tour for the first time in its history, and it comfortably coped with this 21st century invasion of giant TV trucks, satellite dishes and the media's myriad requirements. But the locals would soon be back to their quiet daily regimen, with time to show visitors their 13th century cathedral that was rebuilt in brick after it was destroyed in a two-month siege and subsequent massacre of the townspeople by the Crusaders of Simon de Montfort.

Now, they would have something new to talk about. When people gather each Saturday for Lavaur's renowned market in its narrow, shady medieval streets, they can chat about the day the Tour came to town. And how a man from Flanders named Verbrugghe was the first to arrive at the Place du Forail.

Those among the Tour's entourage also had some new images to recall. It's great, they agreed, when the Tour heads in a different direction.

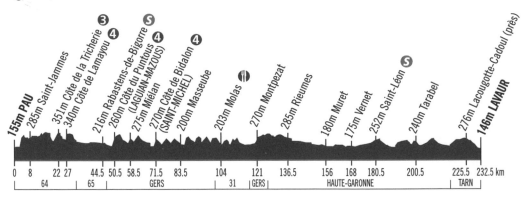

STAGE 16: SURVIVAL

For many, this Tour de France was already over. Barring accidents, Armstrong had his third title wrapped up; Ullrich was on his way to his fourth runner-up spot in five starts (he won the other one); and the rank-and-file were busy talking about the finish in Paris. Others, though, still had a lot to race for.

Take the French squad La Française des Jeux. Its team director, two-time Paris-Roubaix winner Marc Madiot, was an advocate of aggressive racing, and few breaks had gone away without one of his men in it—be it Durand, McGee, Magnien or Montgomery. The team's highlights had been McGee almost pulling off a stage win at Aix-les-Bains, and Montgomery leading the race over the Tourmalet. But there was still no jackpot for the riders who sported a four-leaf clover on their white team jerseys.

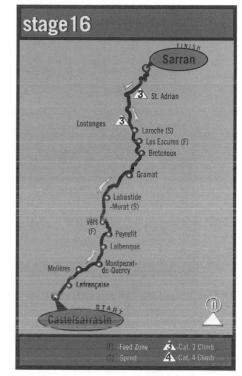

Perhaps this hot, hilly stage 16 would produce something different.

At 229.5km it was only 3km shorter than stage 15, but with more serious climbing. It started in the valley of the Garonne, crossed the Tarn River, and then headed northeast across mountain ranges separating the valleys of the Lot, Dordogne and Corrèze.

As on the previous days, there was a bewildering series of attacks in the opening hour, raced at 46 kph, with LFDJ riders in all but one of them. When the field regrouped, it was still moving fast, in one long line on a one-lane back road, through villages of dry-wall cottages, past fields of sunflowers and rolled-up hay bales, and into a forest of low oak trees on the Causse de Limogne.

This was where the day's key break finally extricated itself from the pack. Six men went clear: Luis Perez of Festina, Voigt of Crédit Agricole, Botcharov of AG2R, Nicki Sørensen of CSC, Eddy Seigneur of Jean Delatour and Stéphane Heulot of BigMat. Postal was setting the tempo as the gap stretched out to 27 seconds in 7km.

There was no one in the break from LFDJ, but the ambitious McGee was having a conversation with team boss Madiot. "Marc told me there was a hill coming up, so I elbowed

Kevin's diary: Stage 16

July 25, 2001

SARRAN: Both yesterday's stage and today's were hard from the start, because they were both just up and down the whole way. Yesterday, there were only three or four climbs that were categorized, but there were at least 10 or 12 climbs that should have been. I got away in one group, but Botero was in there, so ONCE chased it down. Another group we were in included Gonzalez de Galdeano, so that one got chased down, too. You have to watch out with these breaks, because guys high on G.C. try to slip in unnoticed. We can't afford to relax, in case a high-up guy is in it and they get 25 minutes, and you can only give them 20 minutes, and then you have to chase like crazy later on.

Finally, 25 guys got away, and we were riding tempo the rest of the stage. Still, things got out of hand, because Boogerd, who was in the break, got all the way up to eighth on G.C.. Can a team really control it? It's too hard to calculate where everybody is. I mean, is a whole team watching out for their guy in 10th place? I guess it's up to the directeurs sportifs to calculate all of that.

The peloton is out of control. It's crazy. There are just so many attacks! Everyone says they're tired, but if that's true, how can there be so many attacks, so much aggression? And then Kelme, I don't know what they were doing. They attacked with a couple of guys at the end yesterday—I think it was for team G.C., but everybody gets so excited. Nobody knows what's going on, so everyone jumps just in case.

The whole time, it never relaxes, and it's like that for the whole Tour. You've got the guys in the top 15 trying to stay up there, plus all of their teammates trying to be up there with them, plus all of the guys trying to attack. You can imagine the start: It's one big battle.

As for today, I'll only mention the crash. I was on the outside, and they crashed in front of me. There was wave after wave of guys falling toward me and across in front of me. There was a house there on the outside of the turn with a gravel parking area in front. I slammed on the brakes and slid along in the gravel in front of the house. I came to a stop in front of a pile of guys, and then somebody ran into me from behind, but I was stopped by then. I had skidded so far that there was no tread left on my tire—it was burned down to the tube. I mean, we were going 70-80 kph when it happened! It was just so scary.

One of the guys in the crash, Sven Montgomery, was hurt bad. I couldn't see him down off the road, but I heard the Kelme mechanic go over there and then start yelling for a medic. My teammate, Heppner, broke his collarbone. It's just the worst thing, to crash at that speed with so many riders.

my way to the front, turned the corner, and there was the hill," McGee reported. "I put everything into the effort to get across."

Using the speed that had won him Olympic and world pursuit championship medals on the track, the stylish Aussie sped across the gap to join the six leaders on a fast, swishing descent to the Lot River. It was a perfectly timed move as the pack now eased its pace, and by the feed zone 50km later, the break had a lead of 19:30.

So the stage win would be fought out between the seven leaders on the toughest part of the course: the last 40km, which included a plunging descent into the deep valley of the Corrèze at Tulle, an immediate 2km Cat. 4 climb back out of town, another short downhill, then a long gradual uphill toward a high plateau of woods, lakes and meadows 1500 feet above Tulle.

On the Cat. 4 hill, Magnien tried an attack, which Voigt immediately jumped on. Then, 5km later and with 22km to the finish at Sarran, Voigt launched his own attack. Only McGee had the strength to go with the German, who had worn the yellow jersey a couple of weeks earlier, but wanted to win a stage as much as McGee.

Just as McGee was heading toward the likely sprint finish, his friend Montgomery was in the pack, riding down the steep, 10-percent grade into Tulle. U.S. Postal was in the front, descending at a relaxed, but still very fast pace, when they came to a sharp left turn.

Julich was riding just behind them and described what happened next. "They were going just normal, but then there was a turn that came up that maybe caught them off guard a little bit, because everyone was so relaxed. They slammed on their brakes ... and, about 20 riders back, a bunch of guys started panicking, and with the carbon rims now

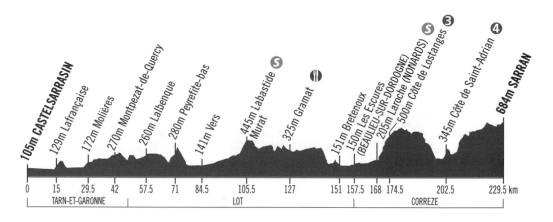

Tyler's diary: Stage 16

July 25, 2001

SARRAN: A funny thing happens on your way through the Tour de France: You get tired of eating. I'm thinking this is the ultimate sign of fatigue, because, generally, I like to eat. And considering that the team has its own chef, it's not about the quality of our daily cuisine. Rather, it's the mass quantities of calories we have to put down each day that gets tiring. It's ironic, actually, because throughout the season we have to be so maniacal about what we do and don't put into our bodies. And here, by the third week, it's kind of an anything-goes atmosphere.

We spent the day in the cockpit of the peloton: riding up front setting tempo, distracting breakaways, and keeping the lead group in check. This will continue to be our mode of operation until the end of the race. Being up front has its advantages. We missed out on the horrendous crash that took down 20 or so riders and forced five guys to abandon.

Crashing is such a huge part of this race, more than anything else. It's because every team and every rider is willing to risk it all at every moment. And with that attitude, you are bound to find trouble. Still, I can honestly say that although I've had at least one crash in every Tour de France I've ridden, hitting the pavement is not as common during the rest of the season.

Most times, the pileups have nothing to do with you. You just happen to be in the wrong place at the wrong time. And when you are moving at the warp speeds of the Tour de France, there's almost no amount of bike-handling skill that can help you when a guy goes down in front of you. Before you know it, you're five-deep in a mound of men and metal. So anyone who thinks bike racers crash a lot is misinformed. It's certainly an on-the-job hazard, but if you add up all the days a rider trains and races, you'd be hard-pressed to find a guy who pulls a yard sale more than 1 or 2 percent of the time.

That said, today's pileup was horrific. It's rare to see such a huge number of guys out of the race after one incident. But broken bones aren't very forgiving, and a rider losing consciousness is nothing to take lightly. And I'm sure there are a number of other guys who were involved and limped to the finish and will wake up feeling pretty bad in the morning.

Considering the risks, you might wonder if we sign disclaimers when we agree to participate in the Tour de France. Ha—now that's funny. Actually, the Tour is the sole reason many of us spend big money insuring our bodies. And mishaps like today's are the sole reason why the Tour is not over until you cross the finish line in Paris.

they don't brake so easily. Then, for no reason, two guys crashed right in the middle of the road. I was almost getting around them when a guy fell right into my front wheel. I did like a shoulder spin off the road. Behind me there were guys that just piled into the guardrail. There was nowhere to go, you're going so fast...."

Some skidded to a halt on the roadside gravel, but a dozen riders slid onto the grass on the outside of the bend and collided into a guardrail several meters back. The worst trajectory was taken by the blond Montgomery, who went headfirst under the rail. At first he wasn't spotted, hidden by the bushes. He was then taken to the local hospital and later transferred by helicopter to a better-equipped facility in Limoges, where he underwent surgery for a fractured skull, multiple fractures of his face, a broken clavicle and serious shoulder injuries.

Four others went to the hospital, three with broken clavicles, the other with a broken wrist; and a sixth man abandoned overnight after undergoing surgery to repair deep cuts on his leg and elbow.

While all these riders were in the ambulance, the stage finish was being fought out between Voigt and McGee. In a perfect world, perhaps, the Aussie would have taken the stage and sent the winner's bouquet to his friend Montgomery in the hospital. But this was the unforgiving world of bike racing. Tour rookie McGee had neglected to eat enough on this marathon stage, raced at an intense pace from the start, and when Voigt accelerated on a short climb with 500 meters to go, McGee could do nothing about it.

As the tall German celebrated, the Aussie snaked down the finish straightaway in a daze. "Everything was black the last five kilometers," McGee said a little later, after guzzling two Cokes in five seconds and getting a whiff of oxygen. "I was frightened. I almost fell at the end."

No, the Tour wasn't over. Only the dreams of some of its riders.

STAGE 17: MEN AT WORK

Sometimes, characters and stories from different eras come together in unexpected ways. That happened at Montluçon at the end of this delightful stage 17, when a sharp 74-year-old Frenchman in a crisp, short-sleeved cotton shirt and pressed pants shook hands with a solid 31-year-old Belgian in a sweat-streaked red Lotto-Adecco uniform.

The Frenchman was Roger Walkowiak, the total outsider who won the 1956 Tour de France, and who as Montluçon's most famed athlete was the day's honored guest. The Belgian was Serge Baguet, a total outsider who had just won this Brive-Montluçon stage in dramatic fashion. And if there had been time for more than a perfunctory greeting between these two men, they would have discovered that they had a lot in common.

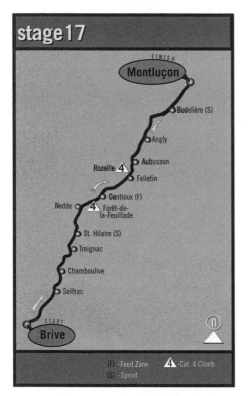

Back in the racing days of Walko'—as they affectionately call him in his hometown—bike racing was a low-paying profession. His Tour victory was built on hard labor in no-hope breakaways (such as this Tour's 14-man break on the stage to Pontarlier), followed by unexpected tenacity in the mountain stages. It was a time when using performance-enhancing drugs like amphetamines was the norm (anti-drug regulations and doping controls didn't exist until the late-1960s), yet Walko' distanced himself from such practices. He still believes that the Tour can be won, figuratively speaking, on mineral water.

Only four years after his Tour win, at age 32, Walko' retired from cycling with just enough cash to buy a small café-gas station in Montluçon, where he worked all hours to make a living. He didn't even have time for his favorite pastime: fishing on the local trout streams and lakes. So the former Tour winner eventually sold his small business and reverted to his original profession as a lathe operator in an auto-parts factory. At least he had time to fish....

As for Baguet, he grew up in Flanders where bike racing is *the* sport, and that's what he always loved doing. At age 15, he was winning every race he entered, became a successful junior and then a good enough senior amateur to earn a pro contract with Lotto at age 21. Before Baguet became a full-time bike racer, his parents made him learn a regular profession, like all "good" Flemish sons. He chose to work in the building trade.

Baguet raced with Lotto for five seasons, winning at least one important victory in each of the first four years. His fifth year, 1995, didn't go as well, and he spent the following season with the low-budget Vlaanderen 2002 squad. "After six years, I couldn't take it anymore," he recalled, "so I quit [cycling]."

With no real savings, Baguet went back to his first profession, and for three years worked full-time repairing roofs for his father-in-law's construction business. He worked hard, went to the pub most evenings and put on more than 20 pounds. But he did miss the bike. So Baguet started riding a little on the weekends, and one day in 1999 he went training with two former Lotto teammates, Mario De Clercq and Aussie Scott Sunderland. They told him that he still had it, and after some hesitation he decided to go back to racing with Lotto.

"When I returned to racing last year, I decided to give it 200 percent," said Baguet. "I suffered a lot … only my wife knows what sacrifices I made to come back."

Returning to the sport at age 29 wasn't easy. Still, Baguet had a reasonable 2000 season: He placed 24th at Ghent-Wevelgem and 51st at Liège-Bastogne-Liège in the spring classics; finished the Tour de France in 121st, but found better form to take 10th at the GP Ouest France at Plouay; and he finally won his first race in six years, the Belgian semi-classic GP of Geraardsbergen. Then, in 2001, Baguet scored a breakthrough with a late counterattack at the Dutch World Cup classic, the Amstel Gold Race, to finish third behind breakaways Dekker and Armstrong.

At the Tour, before this stage 17, he was lying 87th overall, more than two hours behind Armstrong; but as in 2000, he was coming through the final week in good form. And when teammate Verbrugghe gave Lotto its first Tour stage win in nine years at Lavaur, Baguet saw a possibility for himself. He was in one of the early breaks on stage 16, and at this stage's start in Brive-la-Gaillarde, he was ready to try again.

With temperatures in the 80s and high humidity to match, not everyone was ready to tackle another long, hilly stage on roads where melting tar and flying grit would make life miserable. What made the stage even tougher was an unclassified hill right at the start. The climb out of the Corrèze valley was almost 6km long, much to the liking of Fassa Bortolo's Belli, who attacked just two minutes into the stage. He was soon neutralized, but then a dozen other men, including KoM leader Jalabert, went off the front. Again, the move was closed down.

Immediately, Telekom's Vinokourov counterattacked and was joined by nine others, including stage 12 winner Cardenas, Danish champion Jakob Piil, Italians Lelli and Tosatto, and Lotto's Vermaut. This 10-strong group had an eight seconds' lead a kilometer from

Tyler's diary: Stage 17

July 26, 2001

MONTLUÇON: The U.S. Postal Service has transformed itself from a cycling team into a circus act. I'm not talking about any new-found juggling skills or amazing death-defying feats here. No, I'm speaking of our new status of freak side-show. Last night, our hotel's dining room had giant windows facing the street. As we were eating dinner, a massive crowd formed outside and soon, the gazes of men, women and children were fixed on our every move. You could almost imagine the commentary being whispered in hushed tones as if these folks were on the sidelines at the Masters: "Psst. Didja catch that? George just ate some pasta.... Hold on, I think Eki's taking a sip of water.... Wow, Roberto hasn't touched his bread.... Wait a second, Vic's reaching for the fruit salad...."

Call me crazy for asking, but is any of this stuff interesting? We had an audience at breakfast this morning as well. As I sat there, trying to wake up while drinking my coffee, people were staring.

Tonight we ate outside on the patio since it's so hot. To provide a little privacy, the staff moved our team bus and the mechanic's truck to form walls around our table. Even so, there were still a few folks peering around the corners. Some of my teammates are finding the humor in our situation and are starting to make animal noises as they eat. If you feel like a caged zoo animal, you might as well have a little fun and act like one, I guess.

You have to love the support, though. Without the interest of these folks, we wouldn't have this great sport of ours. But the intrigue can provide a little stress sometimes. Take for instance an interview Lance was trying to give earlier tonight. It was fed into ABC's "Nightly News with Peter Jennings." Since Mr. Jennings is back in New York, Lance was answering canned questions, while speaking directly into a stationary camera. It's a difficult thing, pretending to be conversing with another human being when all you are staring at is a mechanical object. But Lance is used to this kind of challenge and pulled it off, I'm certain—even though he had to do so with over 200 curious French folks looking on.

Today was hot like you read about, and my allergies are making me crazy. They've been in full swing since we arrived here in the South. Nothing like adding a little lung butter to the mix, I always say. I'm getting laser treatments to break up the congestion in my sinuses and chest. I have no idea if they're helping, but it makes me feel like I'm getting ready to do battle with intergalactic space enemies. Hey, whatever keeps you going.

It's so hot here in our hotel room that I'm sitting with my feet hanging out the window ... and I know someone down there is staring at them.

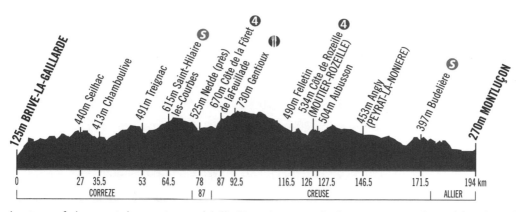

the top of the straight, main-road hill. Six others—including Baguet—chased hard and latched on by the summit.

It was a move that had great potential. None of the riders was dangerous on G.C., 13 teams had men up front, and the presence of a Telekom man in the break meant that Ullrich and Zabel would not be ordering a chase. Despite that, the eight unrepresented teams didn't give up in a hurry, particularly the Bonjour team of sprinter Nazon, who still felt he had a stage win in his legs.

With Bonjour taking over the tempo-making from Postal, the gap hovered between 50 seconds and a minute for the best part of an hour. Then, with 150km left to race, the sprinters' teams decided that keeping the break on a tight leash rather than pulling it in made more sense.

The gap opened up to four minutes by the time the course turned off a wide high-way at 74km and headed into the first of a series of narrow back roads that would take the stage all the way to Montluçon. Despite the often bumpy surface, the break averaged almost 48 kph for the final 100km!

At that speed it was tough for the peloton to chip more than 30 seconds from the deficit every 10km. And the 16 leaders were still 1:25 ahead when Lelli made what proved to be the key move with 36km remaining. The veteran Italian's all-out effort came just after a similar attack by his French Cofidis teammate Moncoutié.

The first to respond was an alert Piil—the winner of Philadelphia's USPRO Championship in 1999—who bridged on a slight rise before the course momentarily flattened out. This was where Baguet decided his time had come, and he made a strong chase to catch the two leaders before they headed into a long swerving down-hill that paralleled a small creek.

137

It was the perfect place for an attack, and as the three sped between a row of old stone houses and a lake at Chambon 5km later, the gap was already 30 seconds. Six were chasing, while the rest of the original 16 would soon be caught by the pack.

With Baguet and Piil doing most of the work on a winding uphill out of Chambon, their lead increased to 44 seconds at the 20km-to-go mark, with the peloton at 1:10. The six in between were soon reeled in, leaving Baguet, Lelli and Piil with a 52-second gap as they headed down toward Montluçon with 10km left. It was a tenuous situation for the break, especially as Lelli was claiming fatigue and not pulling through. Festina (for Teutenberg), Telekom (for Zabel) and Fassa Bortolo (for Petacchi) were all riding hard at the head of the pack. Even Ullrich made a long effort. But the gap was still 35 seconds as they reached the 5km marker.

When Baguet took the Geraardsbergen race in 2000, he made a late escape from a nine-man group to win by seven seconds. Here in Montluçon he tried to get clear with 1000 meters left, when the pack was still 25 seconds behind. That's when Lelli suddenly found his legs, chased the Belgian down, and eventually launched the sprint. Piil then sprinted strongly on the right, and as Lelli faded, Baguet made use of a short uphill 100 meters from the line to accelerate, overhaul the Dane, and win the greatest victory of his life.

Up in the stands, Walkowiak was standing up and applauding the courageous victor. Two workers. Two winners.

STAGE 18: LIKE A WHIRLWIND

Armstrong said it himself: "I have never felt so good in a time trial." And he never looked so good, or won by such a wide margin. Armstrong again: "I'm racing at the highest level in my career." What more can be said about a race leader who rides a faultless time trial, averages almost 50 kph on a challenging 61km course against an unfavorable wind, and rides 1.6 seconds per kilometer faster than his chief opponent?

What *can* be said is that Armstrong's victory in this 18th stage (1:39 ahead of Ullrich) was close to the best of five-time Tour winners Miguel Induráin, Bernard Hinault, Eddy Merckx and Jacques Anquetil. Induráin's most dominating performance was in the 65km time trial at Luxembourg in 1992 (3:41 ahead of main rival Gianni Bugno). Hinault's came in the 75km test from Sarrebourg to Strasbourg in 1985 (2:20 ahead of Stephen Roche); Merckx's in the 53.8km TT from Versailles to Paris in 1971 (2:36 faster than Joaquim

Agostinho); and Anquetil's in the 74.5km test from Bergerac to Perigueux in 1961 (2:59 ahead of Charly Gaul). Going further back, the widest winning margin in Tour time trial history was achieved by Fausto Coppi who, in 1949, beat Italian rival Gino Bartali by 7:02 on the 137km (!) stage from Colmar to Nancy.

For each of those past champions and for Armstrong, different factors helped them become dominant riding against the clock. Coppi and Anquetil were the most natural time trialists in terms of their position on the bike and their physical potential. Hinault was the first to use a wind tunnel to perfect his time-trial style and his bike's aerodynamic qualities, while he assiduously prepared for each time trial by reconnoitering courses and totally focusing his mind.

As for Merckx and Induráin, they were most similar to Armstrong in terms of fully developing their skills over the years. Armstrong will never forget the long time trial in the 1994 Tour, when Induráin started two minutes behind the American and came blasting by him well before halfway into the 64km stage from Perigueux to Bergerac (the American took 13th on the stage, 6:23 back). Since that time, Armstrong first improved his aero' positioning, and within two years he was beating riders like Tony Rominger at time trials in the Tour DuPont. Then came cancer.

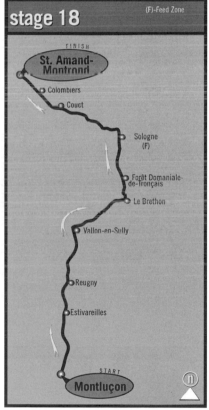

On his return to competition in 1998, Armstrong was soon at a high level, as he showed by placing fourth at the world time trial championship that October. That was the start of his first campaign to win the Tour de France, and he continued to perfect his aero' positioning, pedal stroke and cadence, while scouting the courses and mentally preparing. Everything came together with his prologue wins at the 1999 Dauphiné Libéré and the Tour ... followed by his breakout win in that year's Tour in the long time trial at Metz.

Two years later, at the stage 18 time-trial start in Montluçon, the Texan had further benefited from continuing technical developments and total confidence in his physical and mental preparations. Nothing had been forgotten, and like Hinault before him, Armstrong examined every detail of each course. It sounds like an obvious thing to do, yet not all con-tenders do it. In fact, after this stage, when asked about his loss to Armstrong, Ullrich said, "Perhaps one thing that made a difference is that I didn't look over the whole course. That would certainly have allowed me to approach it differently."

The course was a complex one. After the intimate downtown start on newly surfaced streets, there were four substantial hills and two shorter ones in the first 10km, as the course headed due north into the wind on a wide, mostly flat, sometimes rolling main road. At 23km, the course made a sharp right turn and climbed steeply for more than a kilometer, before turning left on a one-lane country road that gradually climbed to the highest point of the course around 32km. The next 10km were through a forest of tall beech trees on a straight narrow road, before turning left and taking a series of sharp turns past a lake and then into the fastest section, heading northwest past fields of sunflowers and harvested wheat. The finale included four more sharp turns, a narrow bridge into St. Amand-Montrond, and a last kilometer on the widest, flattest roads of the stage.

Armstrong had the fastest splits for each of the four timed sectors: 25:01 for the first 21.3km (51.085 kph); 28:39 for the next 21.9km (45.863 kph); 13:47 for the next 11.9km (51.801 kph); and 6:49 for the last 5.9km (51.931 kph). Significantly, the rider in the yellow jer-sey made his biggest time gains on the second, most difficult split, where he put 36 seconds on runner-up Igor Gonzales de Galdeano (out of a 1:24 gain) and 49 seconds on Ullrich.

Gonzales de Galdeano's second place was not a huge surprise. He had already finished second in the Dunkirk prologue, a second ahead of Armstrong, and was sixth on the mountain time trial at Chamrousse. Here, on roads more suited to his power-based style, the ONCE rider quickly overcame the 70-second overall deficit he had on fifth-placed Simon, and finally defeated the Frenchman by five minutes. The other G.C. match,

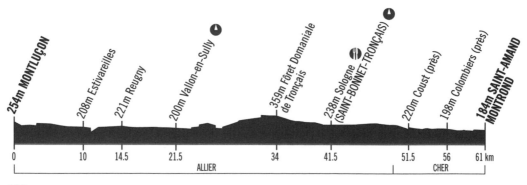

between Kivilev and Beloki for third place, was also an uneven contest, with the Basque rider eliminating his 80-second deficit by halfway.

It was logical that Beloki would grab third place overall, the position he finished in at the 2000 Tour, but it was somewhat of a surprise that he took only sixth place on this stage. The time trial's fourth place was fought out between him and three other men who had ridden strong Tours: Julich, Bonjour's French champion Rous and ONCE's Serrano. There were never more than 12 seconds between these four riders the whole way, and Julich got the short end of the draw.

"It was a perfect course for me, rolling hills the whole time," said the American, who did his best time trial since placing second to Ullrich in the '98 Tour's final TT. "I just wish I could have gone 12 seconds faster and gotten fourth place ... but I was happy with seventh."

Julich lost his 12 seconds in the final 18km, which he hadn't seen beforehand. "In truth, I was saving something for the end because it looked like, when I was watching the guys finish on TV, it was on a climb. They were out of the saddle.... So I was kinda bummed when I got to the last 2K and it was so flat."

The fully prepared Armstrong knew it

Lance Chasing Miguel

I n his five winning Tours, Miguel Induráin raced in nine so-called "long" time trials. He won eight of them, three by two minutes or more. His one loss, to Tony Rominger in 1983, was partly explained by his being out of sorts on the day. Now the winner of three Tours, Armstrong won all four of the long time trials included in those Tours, but has yet to win one by more than two minutes.

THE INDURÁIN YEARS
1991: Argentan-Alençon (73km)
1. Induráin (45.752 kph); 2. LeMond, at 0:08.
1991: Lugny-Macon (57km)
1. Induráin (47.665 kph); 2. Bugno, at 0:27.
1992: Luxembourg TT (65km)
1. Induráin (49.038 kph); 2. De las Cuevas, at 3:00; 3. Bugno, at 3:41.
1992: Tours-Blois (64km)
1. Induráin (52.349 kph); 2. Bugno, at 0:40.
1993: Lac de Madine (59km)
1. Induráin (48.603 kph); 2. Bugno, at 2:11.
1993: Bretigny-Montlhéry (48km)
1. Rominger (50.495 kph); 2. Induráin, at 0:42.
1994: Perigueux-Bergerac (64km)
1. Induráin (50.539 kph); 2. Rominger, at 2:00.
1995: Huy-Seraing (54km)
1. Induráin (50.409 kph); 2. Riis, at 0:12.
1995: Lac de Vassivière (46.5km)
1. Induráin (48.461 kph); 2. Riis, at 0:48.

THE ARMSTRONG YEARS
1999: Metz (56.5km)
1. Armstrong (49.416 kph); 2. Zülle, at 0:58.
1999: Futuroscope (57km)
1. Armstrong (50.085 kph); 2. Zülle, at 0:09.
2000: Freiburg-Mulhouse (58.5km)
1. Armstrong (53.986 kph); 2. Ullrich, at 0:25
2001: Montluçon-St. Amand-Montrond (61km)
1. Armstrong (49.282 kph); 2. Gonzalez de Galdeano, at 1:24; 3. Ullrich, at 1:39.

Tyler's diary: Stage 18

July 27, 2001

ST. AMAND-MONTROND: If things went according to plan, I would have ridden the first half of today's time trial hard, to set splits for Lance. But at about 5.2 seconds into the race, it was apparent that my body was still crying "Uncle." Knowing that I wouldn't be setting any land-speed records this afternoon, I opted for plan B, which was to ride steady while conserving a few matches for the next two days. This race won't be finished until Lance crosses the line in Paris, and we'll be on guard until that very moment.

It's safe to say, Lance is the only member of the team who put the pedal to the metal today. And fly he did. Because we're friends and have been teammates for so long, I view my comrade as more than merely a great cyclist. But on days like today, I'm reminded of just how incredibly talented he is. Racing alongside him is surely frustrating for his main competitors, but it's an honor and a rare opportunity for any rider to support this guy, who is so clearly in his own league.

We raced point to point in today's time trial, so there were only team cars at the finish. This meant there was no bus to hide in after we were done racing. The Postal team cars were standing amid a log jam of fans and press. Every rider had to wade through the throng signing autographs, answering questions and posing for pictures. All great fun— after you've had something to drink and changed out of your soggy skinsuit. Before then, however, it's trying on your patience.

You know everyone means well, but when you feel like your head is about to explode from the heat and the effort you just put out, it's hard to concentrate on the story Mary from Kansas is telling you about her son Jebb who is sure to be the next American Tour de France winner. Somewhere along the line, usually about the point where Mary recites how Jebb rides 80 miles one way to school each morning, things start getting blurry and you kind of lose track of where the story is actually going. All you can think about is how to make the quickest getaway to the car for that sip of Xtran you so badly desire.

When your bodily needs begin taking precedence over your ability to be polite, and you suddenly find yourself thrashing Mary to the ground so you can get to what you are sure by now is life-saving replenishment, all you can hear in your wake is chatter and huffing about how Mary has never met anyone so rude in her entire life. But after taking that sip from the water bottle you were finally able to reach, you rest assured that Jebb will make things right with his Mom when he gets to the Tour de France and explains how wasted everyone is two seconds after they cross the finish line.

was a flat finish. Even so, he was out of the saddle, sprinting for the line as if his life depended on it. Perhaps it did.

STAGE 19: A TALE OF THREE SPRINTS

It has been a postwar tradition of the Tour to have a time trial near the end of the race: sometimes on the last day (as when LeMond came from behind to defeat Fignon in 1989), but normally a day or two before reaching Paris. And, for some time, it had also been a tradition to follow that time trial with long stages: In 1961, after a final TT at Perigueux, the Tour reached Paris with stages of 309km and 252km. That tradition died in 1994, when the final two legs measured 208km and 175km. But there was an attempt in 2000 to return to that formula, when the last two days saw stages of 254km and 138km. However, that marathon penultimate stage wasn't well received by a tired peloton that was anxious to be in Paris already. So the Tour organizers listened, and in 2001, after finishing the stage 18 TT in the center of France, the teams climbed into their buses and headed north on the autoroute for 150km to Orléans.

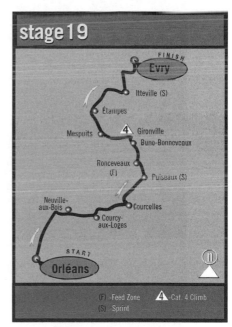

Green-jersey holder O'Grady was one rider who was very pleased that he didn't have to ride all the way to Paris. A bee got stuck in his aero' helmet during the time trial, and before the Aussie could discard it, he was stung on his temple and thigh. So the way he saw it, a short stage of less than 150km the next day was just fine.

At the same time, stage 19 was a very important one for O'Grady. He was leading Zabel by just 11 points in the green-jersey competition, and he had the incentive of becoming the second Aussie on the Paris podium (Phil Anderson won the young rider's white jersey in 1982). All he had to do was stick with his German rival (and friend), and the jersey was his, right? Well, not exactly.

Crédit Agricole knew that Zabel was the faster sprinter, so the best tactic to keep him at bay was to help form a breakaway group that could take all the points at the two intermediate sprints (at 62.5km and 125.5km) and maybe the finish (149.5km). The French team tried to get something going in the opening kilometers, as did still-winless riders like

143

Tyler's diary: Stage 19

July 28, 2001

EVRY: I'm going to cut to the chase since the word is out. This will be my last season with the U.S. Postal Service Cycling Team. In January 2002, I will be joining CSC-Tiscali, based in Denmark.

Looking back on the last seven years, I can reflect upon an incredible experience with a tremendous team composed of some of the world's greatest athletes and support staff. I turned professional with this organization in 1995 and traveled along with it all the way to Paris, where we've hoped Lance Armstrong would write history at the Tour de France. It's been an unbelievable journey, one I will always be grateful to have made.

While making a change can't help but be difficult, mine has been made easier with the support and encouragement of my friends and teammates at U.S. Postal. Although we will be on different teams next year, one thing is for certain: Our friendships and support for one another will remain.

I'm looking forward to the opportunity and new challenges the CSC-Tiscali team will offer. And, most of all, I'm thankful that the sport of cycling has and is offering me so many different experiences and so many avenues of support.

Until December 31, I will be a member of the U.S. Postal Service team, and there's a lot of work to be done before we can hang up our bikes. I'm looking forward to finishing out the season with the team that has been behind me for my entire professional career.

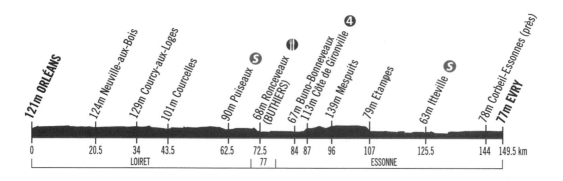

LFDJ's Durand. They tried, but their attacks were closed down by Zabel's Telekom men.

On the straight flat road leading out of Orléans, the voice of Radio Tour, former French racer Charly Mottet, was constantly warning the cars preceding the peloton: "Faster, faster—the peloton is at 60 kph!" No one could get clear at that speed.

After 40km of this insane pace, the Telekoms finally allowed an initiative by Crédit Agricole's ever-willing Voigt to take off. Problem was, they wouldn't let anyone else go after him. So the tall German, enjoying a wonderful Tour, eked out a 40-second gap before the Telekom train began winding up the pace for the first sprint. Voigt managed to hang on to take the first-place six points, while Zabel was just too fast for O'Grady in the sprint for second. The Aussie's lead was down to nine.

The next sprint was still 63km away, so Telekom wasn't too bothered when five men stole away on a narrow, winding section through a forest, 70km from the finish. However, the 1:20 they took meant nothing when the five reached windswept, wide-open fields 20km before the second sprint. And with the finish only 24km beyond the sprint, Telekom was gladly helped by the Bonjour, Festina, Domo, Lampre and Fassa Bortolo teams, all working for their fast finishers. The five leaders were caught 3km before the sprint, Zabel again outkicked O'Grady ... and the green-jersey gap was down to seven points.

The stage finished as fast as it started, because so many teams were leading out their sprinters. In the confusion, O'Grady lost Zabel's wheel, but with the savvy he learned in Aussie track racing, the green-jersey holder switched to the draft of world champion Vainsteins, squeezed through impossible gaps and threw his bike at the line.

The result though was 1. Zabel, 2. O'Grady. The Aussie's lead was down to two. One more stage, and three more sprints to go....

145

STAGE 20: CRAFTY OLD MEN

On the last stage of this ever-fascinating Tour, the previous day's battle between O'Grady and Zabel reached its logical conclusion: a sixth consecutive green jersey for the

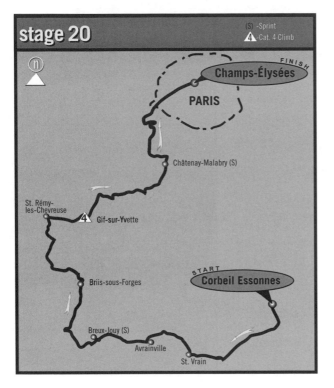

31-year-old German. The Telekom man again finished ahead of his rival on each of the day's three sprints, to finish out the overall winner by eight points. But it could have been different....

Let's go back to 1984, when Sean Kelly, like Zabel, was the green-jersey favorite every year. The rapid Irishman had taken it the previous two years, and in '84 he had an eight-point lead over Belgian Frank Hoste going into the final bend, 400 meters from the finish on the Champs-Elysées.

Speeding into that turn, with the sprinters elbowing their way forward in an attempt to chase down a late attack by the Renault team's Pascal Jules, Kelly lost his position after an alleged, subtle flick

by Hoste. Another Belgian, Eric Vanderaerden, flew by and overtook Jules just before the line to take the win, while Hoste came in third, with Kelly a couple of places back in fifth. Hoste won the jersey by four points.

There were no such antics at this year's final fanfare. There was a late break, but the

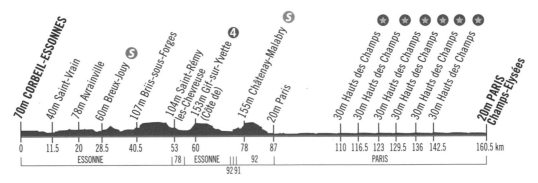

146

It was a banner day for Armstrong (above) on stage 13, when Roberto Heras (right) earned a big chunk of his high salary from Postal by setting tempo for his team leader and Ullrich (left) on the climb to Pla d'Adet.

Yes, a third yellow jersey awaited the American (below) … and within a few months twin daughters were expected to join son Luke.

With the village of Portet d'Aspet below, the peloton tackled the first of six climbs on the pivotal stage 13.

On passing the memorial to his
late teammate Fabio Casartelli,
on the Portet d'Aspet descent,
Armstrong vowed to win that
day's stage at Pla d'Adet.
In doing so, he pointed to his
departed friend, as he had done
on winning the stage to Limoges
after Casartelli's death in 1995.

Ullrich fought to the end, like here on the summit finish at Luz-Ardiden, but he could never dislodge Armstrong.

After Ullrich and Armstrong pulled the leaders up the Col du Tourmalet, Roberto Laiseka (No. 117) gained strength from his orange-clad Basque fans to pull off a fairy-tale victory at Luz-Ardiden (right).

Like a sun king drawn by his entourage,
Armstrong rode regally through the fields
of the Massif Central on the stage to Sarran.

Here pulling the pack on one of the stage 16 climbs, Tyler Hamilton
battled through days of sickness and injuries to prove his worth to
Armstrong's Postal team in the final week.

There was a second coming for Belgian Serge Baguet
at Montluçon (above), while stage win No. 4 awaited
Armstrong (left) in the next day's time trial.

Looks said it all on the faces of Armstrong and Ullrich before the stage 19 start in front of Orléans Cathedral (above), while at the finish in Evry, Erik Zabel (above right) won the stage to get the upper hand over green jersey O'Grady. The next day in Paris, Spain's team of climbers, Kelme-Costa Blanca, took the top team award for the second straight year (right).

LE TOUR
DE
FRANCE

Everywhere you looked on the Champs-Élysées, the message was the same: Lance, Lance. Lance!

CREDIT LYONNAIS
CL

LE TOUR DE FRANCE
01
BRAVO LANCE!

Even the blackboard man—who relays time splits to the racers—got into the act on the final stage.

651 BXL 78

counterattack by Jean Delatour's Brochard under the one-kilometer archway, right after joining Telekom's Vinokourov, came to nought. It did create a gap, though, and when LFDJ's Magnien surged through with Mapei's Bettini on his wheel, the astute Svorada— who had already taken the field sprint behind Baguet at Montluçon—jumped on the train. Then, as Brochard dropped back, a vital 10-meter gap was created on that same corner where Kelly was flicked those 17 years back.

The Telekoms were closing, but with 300 meters still remaining, the 32-year-old Svorada bolted past Bettini and gratefully sprinted away to his third career stage win at the Tour. Even Zabel was too far back to challenge. But the German still had to race full pelt to take second, and hold off the gutsy O'Grady, to continue his perfect run of green jerseys. As the two rivals carried on pedaling up the Champs-Élysées, Zabel and O'Grady put their arms around each other, one congratulating, the other commiserating.

Their mutual respect mirrored the shake of hands that Ullrich gave Armstrong exactly one week earlier, high in the Pyrénées at Luz-Ardiden. Both gestures also reflected the wonderful spirit in which this 88th Tour de France had been fought: a Tour won by a Texan for the third consecutive year.

Tyler's diary: Stage 20

July 29, 2001

PARIS: 3462km ridden. 20 stages completed. 10 flat stages weathered. Three medium mountain stages ascended. Four high mountain stages behind us. Two individual time trials and a prologue endured. One team time trial survived. Five mountaintop finishes achieved. Two rest days appreciated. Three-peat checked off.

The fat lady is singing. And I've never been so happy to hear her voice.

Results: Pau to Paris

WEEK 3

Stage 15: Pau - Lavaur. July 24.

1. Rik Verbrugghe (B), Lotto-Adecco, 232.5km in 5:16:21 (44.097 kph); 2. Marco Pinotti (I), Lampre-Daikin, s.t.; 3. Alessandro Petacchi (I), Fassa Bortolo, at 0:06; 4. Sylvain Chavanel (F), Bonjour; 5. Nico Mattan (B), Cofidis; 6. Nicolas Jalabert (F), CSC-Tiscali; 7. Boogerd; 8. Franck Bouyer (F), Bonjour; 9. Marco Serpellini (I), Lampre-Daikin; 10. Nardello, all s.t.

Others: 13. Julich, at 0:06; (Peloton of 125 riders at 15:07).

Overall: 1. Armstrong, 67:46:32; 2. Ullrich, at 5:05; 3. Kivilev, at 5:13; 4. Beloki, at 6:33; 5. Simon, at 10:54; 6. Gonzalez de Galdeano, at 12:04; 7. Sevilla, at 13:55; 8. Boogerd, at 16:15; 9. Botero, at 17:49; 10. Serrano, at 19:20.

Stage 16: Castelsarrasin - Sarran. July 25.

1. Voigt, 229.5km in 5:27:11 (42.086 kph); 2. McGee, at 0:05; 3. Botcharov, at 1:59; 4. Niki Sørensen (Dk), CSC-Tiscali, s.t.; 5. Luis Perez (Sp), Festina, at 2:55; 6. Stéphane Heulot (F), BigMat-Auber 93, at 3:44; 7. Eddy Seigneur (F), Jean Delatour, at 6:39; 8. Zabel, at 25:45; 9. O'Grady; 10. Nazon, all s.t.

Others: 12. Ullrich, at 25:45; **16. Armstrong;** 18. Kivilev; 20. Beloki; 29. Simon, all s.t.; **44. Hamilton, at 26:08; 47. Julich, s.t.; 92. Livingston, at 26:08; 139. Hincapie, s.t.**

Overall: 1. Armstrong, 73:39:28; 2. Ullrich, at 5:05; 3. Kivilev, at 5:13; 4. Beloki, at 6:33; 5. Simon, at 10:54; 6. Gonzalez de Galdeano, at 12:04; 7. Sevilla, at 13:55; 8. Boogerd, at 16:15; 9. Botero, at 18:12; 10. Serrano, at 19:20.

Stage 17: Brive-la-Gaillarde - Montluçon. July 26.

1. Serge Baguet, 194km in 4:13:36 (45.899 kph); 2. Jakob Piil (Dk), CSC-Tiscali, s.t.; 3. Massimiliano Lelli (I), Cofidis, at 0:05; 4. Jan Svorada (Cz), Lampre-Daikin, at 0:13; 6. Nazon; 6. Zabel; 7. O'Grady; 8. Vainsteins; 9. Petacchi; 10. Christophe Capelle (F), BigMat-Auber 93, all s.t.

Others: (121 riders in peloton, at 0:13); **133. Livingston, at 1:01.**

Overall: 1. Armstrong, 77:53:17; 2. Ullrich, at 5:05; 3. Kivilev, at 5:13; 4. Beloki, at 6:33; 5. Simon, at 10:54.

Stage 18: Montluçon - St. Amand-Montrond TT. July 27.

1. Armstrong, 61km in 1:14:16 (49.282 kph); 2. I. Gonzales de Galdeano, 1:15:40; 3. Ullrich, 1:15:55; 4. Rous, 1:16:41.16; 5. Serrano, 16:41.20; 6. Beloki, 1:16:48; 7. Julich, 1:16:53; 8. Botero, 1:16:59; 9. Vinokourov, 1:17:13; 10. J. Gutierrez, 1:17:17.

Others: 46. Hamilton, 1:22:09; 106. Hincapie, 1:25:16; 109. Livingston, 1:25:22.

Overall: 1. Armstrong, 79:07:33; 2. Ullrich, at 6:44; 3. Beloki, at 9:05; 4. Kivilev, at 9:53; 5. Gonzales de Galdeano, at 13:28; 6. Simon, at 17:22; 7. Sevilla, at 18:30; 8. Botero, at 20:55; 9. Serrano, at 21:45; 10. Boogerd, at 22:38.

Stage 19: Orléans - Evry. July 28.

1. Zabel, 149.5km in 3:12:27 (46.610 kph); 2. O'Grady; 3. Vainsteins; 4. Teutenberg; 5. Svorada; 6. Petacchi; 7. Nazon; 8. Sivakov; 9. Capelle; 10. Casper, all s.t.

Others: (72 riders in the first peloton); **90. Hamilton, at 0:41; 109. Livingston, at O:57.**

Overall: 1. Armstrong, 82:20:00; 2. Ullrich, at 6:44; 3. Beloki, at 9:05; 4. Kivilev, at 9:53; 5. Gonzales de Galdeano, at 13:28.

Stage 20: Corbeil-Essonnes - Paris (Champs-Elysées). July 29.

1. Svorada, 160.5km in 3:57:28 (40.553 kph); 2. Zabel; 3. O'Grady; 3. 4. Teutenberg; 5. Petacchi; 6. Nazon; 7. Mikhailov; 8. Casper; 9. Max Van Heeswijk (Nl), Domo-Farm Frites; 10. Capelle, all s.t.

Others: (139 riders in the peloton, all s.t.).

88th TOUR DE FRANCE. July 7-29, 2001.

1. Lance Armstrong (USA), U.S. Postal Service, 3457.7km in 86:17:28 (40.070 kph); 2. Jan Ullrich (G), Deutsche Telekom, at 6:44; 3. Joseba Beloki (Sp), ONCE-Eroski, at 9:05; 4. Andrei Kivilev (Kaz), Cofidis, at 9:53; 5. Igor Gonzalez Galdeano (Sp), ONCE-Eroski, at 13:28; 6. François Simon (F), Bonjour, at 17:22; 7. Oscar Sevilla (Sp), Kelme-Costa Blanca, at 18:30; 8. Santiago Botero (Col), Kelme-Costa Blanca, at 20:55; 9. Marcos Serrano (Sp), ONCE-Eroski, at 21:45; 10. Michaël Boogerd (Nl), Rabobank, at 22:38; 11. Didier Rous (F), Bonjour, at 24:22; 12. Iñigo Chaurreau (Sp), Euskaltel-Euskadi, at 28:09; 13. Francisco Mancebo (Sp), iBanesto.com, at 28:33; 14. Stefano Garzelli (I), Mapei-Quick Step, at 29:00; 15. Roberto Heras (Sp), U.S. Postal Service, at 30:44; 16. Alex Vinokourov (Kaz), Deutsche Telekom, at 33:55; 17. Alexander Botcharov (Rus), AG2R, at 41:15; **18. Bobby Julich (USA), Crédit Agricole, at 48:04;** 19. Laurent Jalabert (F), CSC-Tiscali, at 50:06; 20. Carlos Sastre (Sp), ONCE-Eroski, at 50:20; 21. Thomasz Brozyna (Pl), iBanesto.com, at 53:35; 22. Axel Merckx (B), Domo-Farm Frites, at 55:29; 23. Laurent Brochard (F), Jean Delatour, at 56:01; 24. Wladimir Belli (I), Fassa Bortolo, at 57:29; 25. José Enrique Gutierrez (Sp), Kelme-Costa Blanca, at 59:17; 26. Andreas Klöden (G), Deutsche Telekom, at 59:53; 27. Mario Aerts (B), Lotto-Adecco, at 1:00:06; 28. Roberto Laiseka (Sp), Euskaltel-Euskadi, at 1:02:15; 29. Jörg Jaksche (G), ONCE-Eroski, at 1:06:02; 30. Daniel Atienza (Sp), Cofidis, at 1:07:10; 31. Stéphane Goubert (F), Jean Delatour, at 1:08:40; 32. Luis Perez (Sp), Festina, at 1:11:07; 33. Michele Bartoli (I), Mapei-Quick Step, at 1:13:05; 34. David Etxebarria (Sp), Euskaltel-Euskadi, at 1:15:57; 35. Benoît Salmon (F), AG2R, at 1:17:07; 36. Stive Vermaut (B), Lotto-Adecco, at 1:20:13; 37. Felix Garcia Casas (Sp), Festina, at 1:20:33; 38. José Luis Rubiera (Sp), U.S. Postal Service, at 1:21:48; 39. Giuseppe Guerini (I), Deutsche Telekom, at 1:22:01; 40. Stéphane Heulot (F), BigMat-Auber 93, at 1:22:02; 41. Javier Pascual Rodriguez (Sp), iBanesto.com, at 1:22:37; 42. Walter Beneteau (F), Bonjour, at 1:24:28; **43. Kevin Livingston (USA), Deutsche Telekom, at 1:24:31;** 44. Leonardo Piepoli (I), iBanesto.com, at 1:26:21; 45. Guido Trentin (I), Cofidis, at 1:29:40; 46. Jens Voigt (G), Crédit Agricole, at 1:30:02; 47. Denis Menchov (Rus), iBanesto.com, at 1:31:50; 48. David Moncoutié (F), Cofidis, at 1:32:09; 49. Nicki Sørensen (Dk), CSC-Tiscali, at 1:33:14; 50. Laurent Roux (F), Jean Delatour, at 1:33:26; 51. Udo Bölts (G), Deutsche Telekom, at 1:34:10; 52. Marco Pinotti (I), Lampre-Daikin, at 1:34:29; 53. Gilles Bouvard (F), Jean Delatour, at 1:35:35; 54. Stuart O'Grady (Aus), Crédit Agricole, at 1:36:20; 55. Patrice Halgand (F), Jean Delatour, at 1:38:38; 56. Jean-Cyril Robin (F), Bonjour, at 1:39:33; 57. Daniele Nardello (I), Mapei-Quick Step, at 1:41:49; 58. Javier Pascual Llorente (Sp), Kelme-Costa Blanca, at 1:44:40; 59. Guennadi Mikhailov (Rus), Lotto-Adecco, at 1:46:23; 60. Matteo Tosatto (I), Fassa Bortolo, at 1:50:07; 61. Felix Cardenas (Col), Kelme-Costa Blanca, at 1:55:25; 62. Mikel Pradera (Sp), ONCE-Eroski, at 1:57:09; 63. Iñigo Cuesta (Sp), Cofidis, at 1:58:31; 64. Ivan Gutierrez (Sp), ONCE-Eroski, at 1:59:12; 65. Sylvain Chavanel (F), Bonjour, at 1:59:40; 66. Daniel Schnider (Swi), La Française des Jeux, at 2:00:43; 67. Massimiliano Lelli (I), Cofidis, at 2:01:26; 68. Piotr Wadecki (Pl), Domo-Farm Frites, at 2:02:03; 69. Jon Odriozola (Sp), iBanesto.com, at 2:05:23; 70. Paolo

Bettini (I), Mapei-Quick Step, at 2:05:38; **71. George Hincapie (USA), U.S. Postal Service, at 2:05:46;** 72. Geert Verheyen (B), Rabobank, at 2:05:53; 73. Haimar Zubeldia (Sp), Euskaltel-Euskadi, at 2:06:17; 74. Franck Bouyer (F), Bonjour, at 2:07:01; 75. Maarten Den Bakker (Nl), Rabobank, at 2:07:42; 76. Antonio Tauler (Sp), Kelme-Costa Blanca, at 2:08:11; 77. Alberto Lopez de Munain (Sp), Euskaltel-Euskadi, at 2:08:19; 78. Ludovic Turpin (F), AG2R, at 2:09:21; 79. Victor Hugo Peña (Col), U.S. Postal Service, at 2:10:05; 80. Sven Teutenberg (G), Festina, at 2:11:22; 81. Fabio Baldato (I), Fassa Bortolo, at 2:11:50; 82. Viatcheslav Ekimov (Rus), U.S. Postal Service, at 2:17:04; 83. Brad McGee (Aus), La Française des Jeux, at 2:17:54; 84. Michaël Blaudzun (Dk), CSC-Tiscali, at 2:22:28; 85. Serge Baguet (B), Lotto-Adecco, at 2:22:50; 86. José Angel Vidal (Sp), Kelme-Costa Blanca, at 2:23:09; 87. Pascal Lino (F), Festina, at 2:24:09; 88. Unai Etxebarria (Ven), Euskaltel-Euskadi, at 2:26:04; 89. Nicolas Vogondy (F), La Française des Jeux, at 2:27:37; 90. Servais Knaven (Nl), Domo-Farm Frites, at 2:27:51; 91. Erik Dekker (Nl), Rabobank, at 2:29:16; 92. Pol Van Hyfte (B), Lotto-Adecco, at 2:29:57; 93. Marc Lotz (Nl), Rabobank, at 2:31:02, **94. Tyler Hamilton (USA), U.S. Postal Service, at 2:31:35;** 95. Eddy Seigneur (F), Jean Delatour, at 2:34:19; 96. Erik Zabel (G), Deutsche Telekom, at 2:34:28; 97. Alessandro Petacchi (I), Fassa Bortolo, at 2:35:08; 98. Nico Mattan (B), Cofidis, at 2:35:39; 99. Nicola Loda (I), Fassa Bortolo, at 2:35:51; 100. Florent Brard (F), Festina, at 2:37:05; 101. Steffen Kjaergaard (N) U.S. Postal Service, at 2:37:24; 102. Christophe Mengin (F), La Française des Jeux, at 2:40:20; 103. Angel Castresana (Sp), Euskaltel-Euskadi, at 2:42:41, 104. Alexei Sivakov (Rus), BigMat-Auber 93, at 2:43:02; 105. Eladio Jimenez (Sp), iBanesto.com, at 2:43:08; 106. Jérôme Bernard (F), Jean Delatour, at 2:44:09; 107. Anthony Morin (F), Crédit Agricole, at 2:46:48; 108. Sébastien Demarbaix (B), AG2R, at 2:47:19; 109. Damien Nazon (F), Bonjour, at 2:48:10; 110. Raivis Belohvosciks (Lat), Lampre-Daikin, at 2:48:14; 111. Christophe Oriol (F), Jean Delatour, at 2:49:00; 112. Rik Verbrugghe (B), Lotto-Adecco, at 2:49:17; 113. Emmanuel Magnien (F), La Française des Jeux, at 2:50:07; 114. Pascal Chanteur (F), Festina, at 2:50:26; 115. Nicolas Jalabert (F), CSC-Tiscali, at 2:50:31; 116. Franck Renier (F), Bonjour, at 2:56:00; 117. Jakob Piil (Dk), CSC-Tiscali, at 2:58:06; 118. Francisco Cerezo (Sp), CSC-Tiscali, at 2:59:57; 119. Frédéric Bessy (F), Crédit Agricole, at 3:01:02; 120. Christophe Agnolutto (F), AG2R, at 3:01:24; 121. Gilles Maignan (F), AG2R, at 3:01:27; 122. Marcelino Garcia (Sp), CSC-Tiscali, at 3:05:05; 123. Christophe Capelle (F), BigMat-Auber 93, at 3:05:12; 124. Frédéric Guesdon (F), La Française des Jeux, at 3:07:12; 125. Marco Serpellini (I),

Lampre-Daikin, at 3:07:47; 126. Sébastien Talabardon (F), BigMat-Auber 93, at 3:09:02; 127. Jacky Durand (F), La Française des Jeux, at 3:09:58; 128. Matteo Frutti (I), Lampre-Daikin, at 3:13:01; 129. Jan Svorada (Cz), Lampre-Daikin, at 3:17:38; 130. Johan Verstrepen (B), Lampre-Daikin, at 3:21:26; 131. Thierry Gouvenou (F), BigMat-Auber 93, at 3:24:23; 132. Romans Vainsteins (Lat), Domo-Farm Frites, at 3:24:56; 133. Ludovic Auger (F), BigMat-Auber 93, at 3:26:02; 134. Max Van Heeswijk (Nl), Domo-Farm Frites, at 3:27:22; 135. Stéphane Bergés (F), AG2R, at 3:29:53; 136. Guillaume Auger (F), BigMat-Auber 93, at 3:30:44; 137. Sébastien Hinault (F), Crédit Agricole, at 3:33:21; 138. Olivier Perraudeau (F), Bonjour, at 3:38:00; 139. Chris Jenner (NZ), Crédit Agricole, at 3:38:21; 140. Rubens Bertogliati (Swi), Lampre-Daikin, at 3:39:05; 141. Rolf Sørensen (Dk), CSC-Tiscali, at 3:40:36; 142. Davide Bramati (I), Mapei-Quick Step, at 3:41:14; 143. Enrico Cassani (I), Domo-Farm Frites, at 3:41:46; 144. Jimmy Casper (F), La Française des Jeux, at 3:52:17.

Final points classification: 1. Erik Zabel (G), Deutsche Telekom, 252 pts; 2. Stuart O'Grady (Aus), Crédit Agricole, 244; 3. Damien Nazon (F), Bonjour, 169; 4. Alessandro Petacchi (I), Fassa Bortolo, 148; 5. Sven Teutenberg (G), Festina, 141; **6. Lance Armstrong (USA), U.S. Postal Service, 134;** 7. Jan Ullrich (G), Deutsche Telekom, 127; 8. Jan Svorada (Cz), Lampre-Daikin, 124; 9. Christophe Capelle (F), BigMat-Auber 93, 114; 10. François Simon (F), Bonjour, 108.

Final mountains classification: 1. Laurent Jalabert (F), CSC-Tiscali, 258pts; 2. Jan Ullrich (G), Deutsche Telekom, 211; 3. Laurent Roux (F), Jean Delatour, 200; **4. Lance Armstrong (USA), U.S. Postal Service, 195;** 5. Stefano Garzelli (I), Mapei-Quick Step, 164; 6. Roberto Laiseka (Sp), Euskaltel-Euskadi, 147; 7. Joseba Beloki (Sp), ONCE-Eroski, 145; 8. Alex Vinokourov (Kaz), Deutsche Telekom, 134; 9. Patrice Halgand (F), Jean Delatour, 123; 10. Oscar Sevilla (Sp), Kelme-Costa Blanca, 120.

Final team classification: 1. Kelme-Costa Blanca, 259:14:44; 2. ONCE-Eroski, at 4:59; 3. Team Deutsche Telekom, at 41:06; 4. Bonjour, at 41:49; 5. Rabobank, at 51:53, **6. U.S. Postal Service, at 54:41;** 7. Cofidis, at 1:20:41; 8. iBanesto.com, at 1:22:24; 9. Festina, at 1:45:33; 10. Jean Delatour, at 1:49:18; 11. Euskaltel-Euskadi, at 2:04:15; 12. Mapei-Quick Step, at 2:22:00; 13. Lotto-Adecco, at 2:22:22; 14. Crédit Agricole, at 2:43:06; 15. La Française des Jeux, at 2:52:43; 16. AG2R, at 2:55:13; 17. Fassa Bortolo, at 3:09:43; 18. CSC-Tiscali, at 3:17:05; 19. Domo-Farm Frites, at 4:30:53; 20. Lampre-Daikin, at 4:41:38; 21. BigMat-Auber 93, at 5:18:23.

149

PART THREE
Reflections

No. 3 for King Lance

ARMSTRONG'S OBSESSIVE APPROACH TO THE TOUR
MADE HIS THIRD VICTORY THE MOST IMPRESSIVE YET

A third consecutive Tour de France victory isn't something that should come easily, but that was the impression Lance Armstrong gave as he dominated the 2001 Tour in the manner of the legendary Eddy Merckx. From his first sprint out of the prologue start house in Dunkirk on July 7, to his triumphant ride along the Champs-Élysées with the lone-star flag of Texas 22 days later, Armstrong was king.

In regal style, he dictated the tactics of the race, commanded the peloton, and handled the media with aplomb—even when he had to answer tricky questions about his previously hidden relationship with Michele Ferrari, the controversial sports doctor who was about to be tried for alleged doping practices in an Italian courtroom. In short, the U.S. Postal Service team boss did what he wanted, said what he wanted, and came away with exactly what he wanted: a Tour hat-trick.

For the record, Armstrong won the 88th Tour de France by beating the same two riders he defeated in 2000, almost by the same margins: 6:44 over runner-up Jan Ullrich and 9:05 over third-place Joseba Beloki. If there were one surprise, noted the Texan, it was the performance of Deutsche Telekom leader Ullrich: "He was very ready, much better than I

153

thought he would be." And to his credit, the German never gave up. He attacked in the mountains, killed himself in the time trials, and tried every tactical nuance in his bag to put Armstrong at risk.

One image of this "new" Ullrich stood out. It was shortly after the finish of stage 13, the toughest of this Tour, over six formidable peaks in the Pyrénées. That stage saw Armstrong win in a late solo break, dedicate his victory to the late Fabio Casartelli, and take over the yellow jersey. It was also the stage in which Ullrich put his Telekom riders in aggressive positions, went on the attack himself, and even overcame a frightening crash.

After disappearing into his team camper van to clean up his wounds, Ullrich emerged to face a scrum of TV, radio and press microphones. He had donned team sweats and a black wool skullcap, like a boxer after taking a beating. There was a leather African talisman around his neck, the trademark silver ring in his left ear, and a look of determination in his wide-apart eyes. The square-jawed German spoke with strength and sincerity, occasionally flashing a quick smile, his perfect white teeth contrasting with his red-bronze face.

Ullrich's most insightful statement to the press that day was: "Lance is even stronger than he has been the past two years. I don't know what we can do. I will try stuff, the team will try stuff. Tomorrow is another very tough stage, and we'll try again."

It took only five minutes of Ullrich's time, but that impromptu Q&A confirmed the message he had been giving on the bike. If anyone were going to threaten Armstrong's supremacy, it was him. The Telekom leader's words were reinforced by the professional attitude his team had adopted—exemplified by its renting a helicopter to take Ullrich and his teammates directly to their hotel after this stage, instead of their having to endure a two-hour transfer down the mountain roads from Pla d'Adet to Pau.

Ullrich had prepared for this race more thoroughly than any of his previous four Tours. He gutted his way through the Giro d'Italia to bring his weight down and prepare for a vigorous training camp in the Alps. His physical capacities measured at the University of Freiburg just before the Tour were outstanding—"far better than those of 1997," said the 27-year-old German's team director and confidant Rudy Pevenage. And 1997 was the year that Ullrich cruised to his one Tour victory.

And yet Armstrong parried Ullrich's attacks with insolence. On more than one occasion, the American said, "My job is to show up and win the Tour de France." It sounded clinical, but he also spoke about the passion he has for the Tour, and his potential frailties.

"I never feel untouchable," he conceded. "Things are never always going to be perfect. Nothing is guaranteed."

That said, Armstrong and his team of counselors—team director Johan Bruyneel, coach Chris Carmichael, agent Bill Stapleton, technical consultants John Cobb and Steve Hed, and, yes, altitude training and nutrition guru Ferrari—did everything they could to guarantee victory. Armstrong himself was always seeking to gain an advantage and, more than any other rider, he was ready to push himself to his physical limits. Among the tasks he added in 2001 were an hour of stretching every day and extra abdominal exercises.

"Every year, as I get older, I work harder," said the 29-year-old Texan after his most impressive stage win: beating Ullrich by two minutes on the 13km ascent to L'Alpe d'Huez. "For me, the easiest way to judge that is by the training camps that we do. I know that we have attacked those camps harder and harder each year. I mean, it's almost like a race."

Then, scarily, he added, "I still believe there's another level that Lance Armstrong can attain, and I think that that level is going to be found in hard work."

While the Postal team's approach to the Tour didn't please everyone—"It's too American," said the European media—the results were warmly appreciated by the fans who turned out in huge numbers, particularly in Belgium, the Vosges, the Pyrénées, at the final time trial, and in Paris. Talking to those fans, you got the impression that they were seeing the Tour in a new light.

Throughout the 1990s, there was a general complaint that the Tour de France no longer had romance and had become too predictable. It was said that the flat stages were bound to end in bunch gallops, because teams such as Saeco and Mapei totally controlled the tactics to give their sprinters a shot at winning each day. As for the climbing stages, they were deemed a bore, because Miguel Induráin would take the yellow jersey in the first-week time trial and then ride defensively the rest of the way. It was also alleged that many of the more spectacular performances, such as the long solo breakaways in the mountains, could be explained by EPO use—a suspicion that even open-minded cycling fans accepted after the Festina drug-bust in 1998.

Some of those suspicions still existed in 2001. But life had become much more difficult for the cheats since the stepping up of the fight against drug abuse. That fight included complete, regular medical check-ups; surprise blood hematocrit sampling; the UCI-recognized test for EPO; out-of-competition testing; and more in-race controls.

155

Was there a new attitude toward "drug use" at the 2001 Tour? Yes, and it was evinced by the manner in which this Tour was raced. Take the case of Brad McGee, a 25-year-old former world track champion from Australia, who was competing at his first Tour. A talented athlete, he figured in several long breakaways, taking a third place at Aix-les-Bains and second at Sarran.

McGee spoke every day during the Tour with a sportswriter from *The Australian* newspaper, Rupert Guinness, who passed on the Aussie rider's reactions to the world's toughest bike race. One of McGee's more insightful comments was how much tougher the Tour was than it appeared on TV, particularly climbs like L'Alpe d'Huez. McGee finished in a daze after his second place at Sarran, having neglected to eat enough on his marathon breakaway, and he needed oxygen to be revived. The young Aussie said he abhors needles and tubes, but he learned that in order to recover from the constant physical hammering his body received during the Tour he needed help; and so, after consulting with his own doctor, he agreed to have intravenous glucose-type drips on five occasions.

More evidence that this was a Tour with minimal drug abuse was how riders who had been in a long break one day often lost time the next, or had to recover by riding in the *gruppetto*, the group of backmarkers that paces itself to finish just within the time limit on the tougher stages. Jens Voigt, the German who defeated McGee at Sarran, reported that there was often some whining in the gruppetto by riders who said the pace was too fast. Voigt would shout at such riders: "Shut up and suffer!"

Whining wasn't something that would be heard from cyclists using EPO. Even so, it would be difficult to endorse the comments made by the UCI in its post-Tour communiqué that EPO was no longer a problem in elite-level cycling. But there *was* evidence that this form of blood-doping was less prevalent: The UCI reported that the Tour peloton's average hematocrit level was 43.7 percent, well below the 50-percent danger level.

Skeptics said that one reason for the reduced use of EPO was the growing utilization of so-called altitude tents, which can help increase an athlete's hematocrit count while also increasing the total volume of his blood. Tour winner Lance Armstrong was one rider who acknowledged that he used an altitude tent, and he added that Dr. Ferrari was one of the experts who had helped him obtain the maximum training benefit from using it.

Continuing his association with Ferrari may not have been smart, particularly in view of the Italian doctor's being investigated for allegedly supplying athletes with EPO in the

1990s. But the Texan was not the first Tour winner to benefit from Ferrari's advice. Before he won the first of his five consecutive Tours, Induráin worked with Dr. Ferrari, who helped the big Spanish rider lose enough weight to become a Tour contender.

Whomever you wanted to believe, it was hard not to agree that there had been changes in the peloton's attitude toward drugs. As a result, the 2001 Tour was less controlled, giving rise to a more old-fashioned style of racing. The crowds appreciated the Tour's new diversity and romanticism … and its many unexpected stories. Besides the four stage wins scored by an invulnerable Armstrong, the race's unforgettable moments included:

- the double punch in Antwerp by Rabobank's Erik Dekker and Marc Wauters that resulted in Wauters wearing the yellow jersey into his hometown the next day;
- the intense 50-kph pace set by the Postal and ONCE teams in pursuit of a dangerous nine-man break across the Ardennes, which caused more than half the field to lose 18-plus minutes;
- the underdog win by Crédit Agricole in the wet, drama-filled team time trial, and the unbridled howl of triumph from a resurgent Bobby Julich;
- the 14-man break through a cold rain that finished a half-hour ahead of the pack at Pontarlier, and thrust the names of Andrei Kivilev of Kazakhstan and François Simon of France into the public consciousness;
- the storybook stage wins of Colombian Felix Cardenas of Kelme-Costa Blanca and Basque Roberto Laiseka of Euskaltel-Euskadi in the Pyrénées;
- the frightening crash on a descent in the Massif Central that sent six men to the hospital, including early race leader Wauters and outstanding Swiss-American debutant Sven Montgomery of La Française des Jeux;
- the remarkable stage win by Lotto-Adecco's Serge Baguet, who last year came back to pro cycling after three years of working full-time in the building trade;
- and the final weekend's green-jersey battle between Aussie Stuart O'Grady and his eventual conqueror Erik Zabel, who thus took the points title for a record sixth consecutive year.

From the French perspective, the Tour rediscovered its folklore roots with the improbable yellow-jersey reign of Bonjour's Simon; the prologue victory and eventual ignominious exit of Festina's Christophe Moreau; and the aggression, two stage wins and polka-dot jersey of CSC-Tiscali's Laurent Jalabert—whom the public affectionately adopted as Jalala the Panda.

157

While all three of those 30-something Frenchmen were close to the end of their careers, the 88th Tour also heralded the arrival of a new generation of Hispanic racers. ONCE's Beloki, 27, may have been the current leader of this talented troupe, but not far behind was his multitalented teammate Igor Gonzalez de Galdeano, also 27, while the winner of the white jersey as best young rider, Kelme's Oscar Sevilla, 24, would surely be a major contender in the years to come.

One other Spanish rider whose potential seemed untapped was Laiseka, even though he was already 32. In his Tour debut, he was perhaps the best pure climber of the race, producing outstanding rides on four of the five mountaintop finishes. But what all these riders had to face was the prospect of Armstrong continuing his domination for another three years ... if he wanted to.

Regarding the 2001 Tour, the radiant American said the day before the finish, "I'll leave an honest man, a happy man and, hopefully, tomorrow a winner." Not just any winner, but a three-times-in-a-row winner, who added, "I have a lot left. I love this event. Even a little heated press conference on the rest day ... is probably what I wanted. I'll be around for years, [as long as] I have this passion. When it goes, I'll get out very quickly."

For the moment, though, the legend of the man-who-came-back-from-cancer didn't appear to be ending any time soon.

On Top of His Game

WITH A THIRD CONSECUTIVE TOUR DE FRANCE WIN
BEHIND HIM, LANCE ARMSTRONG WAS READY TO TALK

L istening to Lance Armstrong speak in August 2001, you got the sense that in a not-so-distant past, when Texas Rangers rode horses, he would have been a gunslinger. Not a raw, do-it-for-kicks Billy the Kid, but a character like Paladin, portrayed by Richard Boone, the all-in-black hero of the mythical TV Western, "Have Gun, Will Travel." Like Paladin, the man called Lance is very intelligent, has a veneer of sophistication, and shoots from the hip. Only, Lance uses words, not bullets.

Quick on the draw in this interview, the 29-year-old Texan had just given the world another virtuoso performance, as he dominated the 2001 Tour de France in his "take no prisoners" style. With gunslinger panache, he won the toughest mountain stages *and* flaunted his superiority in both of the long time trials—something that not even Miguel Induráin, Greg LeMond, Bernard Hinault or Jacques Anquetil did in a single Tour. In fact, the last rider to "do a Lance" was an explosive Laurent Fignon in 1984, when Hinault was the foe whom the winner baited and beat.

Jan Ullrich was the man Armstrong shot down in 2001, but the stoic German still insisted that he'd beat the American in a future Tour. That was his plan; Armstrong had others. When asked the obvious question—"Are you going for the record of five victories?"—at his press conference in Evry, on the eve of the Tour's final stage, the Texan gave a very Lance-type answer: "If I'm sitting here next year and I find I no longer have the passion, I will be gone and you'll never see me again."

"I'm not chasing a record," he added. "And I'm definitely not coming back for second place. At the moment, I'm chasing No. 4 ... if we get through tomorrow."

Armstrong got through "tomorrow"—stage 20 into Paris—when he crossed the finish line in 70th place on the Champs-Elysées, ready to savor his third consecutive Tour triumph: pulling on the 35th yellow jersey of his career atop the winner's podium; carrying the lone-star flag of Texas past the Arc de Triomphe on his team's victory parade; and being the guest of honor at the third annual U.S. Postal Service team banquet in the grandiose Orsay Museum.

Two days later, Armstrong was competing in Switzerland at the invitation-only Across Lausanne hill climb. And the next morning, August 1, with wife Kristin and son Luke, he flew to New York. After arriving in the Big Apple, the Tour champion's appearance schedule was maniacal. That evening, he recorded a TV spot for "The Late Show with Letterman" and threw the opening pitch at the New York Yankees–Texas Rangers baseball game. The next morning, Armstrong was up early to appear on three breakfast TV programs: "Today," "Early Show" and "Live with Regis & Kelly." Then came a ceremony on the steps of the main New York Post Office for his team sponsor, followed by taped interviews with Fox Sports' Jim Rome and public television's Charlie Rose.

Armstrong said he felt a different reaction from the public regarding his latest success than he did in previous years. Talking from his Austin home on August 6, he said, "It seems to me that people are understanding the event more and more. I think the Outdoor Life coverage was enormously successful, compared to what people thought it would be. Which is good for us, good for the fans ... even for people that just have no idea. Everybody knows that live sports are better than tape-delayed sports. I think that was very helpful for people to follow the event.

"Whenever we had dinner [in New York], people were very friendly, complimentary and congratulatory. For us, it's neither here nor there, but I think for our sport it's good, very good, that some regular person in a restaurant can put two and two together."

Of the TV talk shows he did, Armstrong most enjoyed his appearance on Charlie Rose. "It was a lot of fun, a different sort of thing," he said. "The morning shows are four or five minutes. Charlie Rose is a full hour, just a conversation, uninterrupted, no-commercials television ... good format to have a real discussion."

When asked if there been any hard questions, Armstrong hesitated before replying, "Uuuh ... in my opinion there's no such thing as a hard question. When you're honest and you're innocent, there's no such thing as a hard question. They may appear to be hard ... you know, of long delivery and somebody watching my face, that's a hard question. And if you're a liar and a cheat, that would be hard to answer, but I have no problem in answering questions honestly."

Armstrong knew that he would have to answer many "hard" questions raised by recent newspaper articles on both sides of the Atlantic, especially those that included remarks made by the only other American to win three Tours de France, Greg LeMond. After saying he was "devastated" to read about Armstrong working with Italy's so-called "doping doctor," Michele Ferrari, as a consultant for high-altitude training and nutrition, LeMond told *The Sunday Times* of London: "In a general sense, if Lance is clean, it is the greatest comeback in the history of sport. If he isn't, it would be the greatest fraud."

"I was surprised to see the comments," said Armstrong, choosing his words carefully. "I consider Greg to be a very good friend, and that made it even more surprising. When you think you have a friend, [who] happens to be a legend in your sport as well, and if you see something like that, it's obviously a little ... a little alarming. I thought the best thing to do was to just call him and see what's up. But there's not much to say, I'm disappointed. I wouldn't have said those things...."

Intimating that LeMond's comments might have sprung from competitive feelings, Armstrong went on: "People will always ride faster. Regardless of what I do in cycling, there's gonna be another American that comes along and does something better, something faster—marks or standards or records or speeds. That's evolution in sport, that's evolution in society, and that's normal ... and I'm perfectly, um, willing to accept that. So, I don't know. I was surprised...."

Did he think that LeMond understood his use of Ferrari a little better after their conversation? "I dunno," Armstrong replied hurriedly. "I dunno ... I still respect Greg a lot. You cannot take away what he's done for our sport, and what he's done for me as a person, as an athlete.... He was the first cyclist in America to have the great story. He did a lot. He put the sport on the map, and I owe him a lot in that, so ... I'll end my comments with that, and whatever he says or thinks is his business. But we owe him a lot."

Then, after a long pause, the second American cyclist with a great story stated, "I prefer not to take the low road."

A few days after this interview, LeMond too decided that he didn't want to take the low road and issued a written statement, saying his remarks to the press had been taken out of context. "I sincerely regret that some of my remarks ... seemed to question the veracity of Lance's performances," LeMond said. "I want to be clear that I believe Lance to be a great champion and I do not believe, in any way, that he has ever used any performance-enhancing substances. I believe his performances are the result of the same hard work, dedication and focus that were mine 10 years ago."

Despite LeMond's retraction, his remarks did trigger a barrage of media questions. Armstrong went on to address these issues, like the *Newsweek* item that said: "Lance Armstrong's challengers insist he's on drugs."

The Tour winner commented, "I understand that based on articles like that [in *The Sunday Times*], people might say, 'Hmm, you have to ask the question.' And that's why I don't blame most people for writing the articles, because it's newsworthy."

"But," he continued, sighing and pausing, "it's our sport. It's absolutely our sport. And that's the unfortunate thing. But look at cycling, man. Nobody else can say that they've done what cycling's done. Look at an event like the Tour, three weeks long. And you look at the controls that are in place, and the amount of controls that the UCI did, and Society du Tour de France did, and random controls ... 10 athletes a day. Say, for example, somebody wanted to take a risk and use EPO, there's no way ... because anyone who did would have to be incredibly stupid."

Armstrong said he wished that journalists who so willingly write about doping in cycling would also give publicity to the good things that are happening in the sport, such as the UCI's report from the 2001 Tour de France that the peloton's average hematocrit level was 43.7 percent—well below the 50-percent level where EPO use is suspected.

Maintaining a steady hematocrit level is one of the keys to recovery during a race as long and demanding as the Tour. And it's now acknowledged that, despite its potentially deadly side-effects, EPO was the drug widely used by athletes, particularly cyclists, in the 1990s to maintain a high hematocrit level. That's why there were so many batches of EPO in the Festina team car busted by French police on its way to the start of the 1998 Tour.

Times have changed. In 2001, top athletes—including Armstrong—were using altitude tents, which can simulate sleeping at an elevation of 14,000 feet, and thus replace red blood cells faster than occurs at sea level. Asked if he used one during the Tour, the Texan said, "Sporadically in the beginning." But, he explained, there are drawbacks to using an altitude tent, as it precludes the use of air conditioning. "First of all, it's hot," he said. "It's hard to do in a race because you sleep well, but you don't recover as well.… [I used it for] all of the Tour of Switzerland, the entire Tour of Switzerland, and at the other times I was in St. Moritz, before and after the Tour of Switzerland."

Would an altitude tent one day play a part in Armstrong's plan to attack the world hour record? And more to the point, when would he make his attempt on the record that both Merckx and Induráin attacked after winning the Tour? "Definitely not this year," he replied. "Don't know the plans … there are no definitive dates."

But when would he like to do it? "Good question. I don't think it's opportune to do it right after the Tour. And the Tour falls in the middle of everything. It's a difficult, difficult question. Don't know.

"I know that it's appealing and that at one point it will be done … I mean, will be attempted. I shouldn't even say.…

"Before that, there will definitely be testing to find out if I can ride the track fast enough. I'm unfortunate that I have no track experience. I've probably ridden 20 kilometers in my entire life on the track, so I could be worthless.

"Soon, we have to scout the locations where we do it, build the track [he was thinking of an indoor track at altitude], and see if people are interested in funding something like that. It's a big.… If you build it, it's not something you can do overnight."

So, no world hour record attempt in 2001, and no world's either, right? "Nope." But when asked if he ever intended doing the world road championships again, Armstrong asked, rhetorically, "Isn't it in Canada in a couple of years?"

Yes, in 2003, the road world's will be held in Hamilton, Ontario, and the road race is slated for a tough course that local Steve Bauer, a world's medalist in the 1980s, helped design. With two climbs up the Niagara Escarpment every lap, it is a course that would play to Armstrong's strengths.

By October 2003, Armstrong might have won the Tour five times, and his participation in a world championship in North America would attract massive publicity. So, would he race the Hamilton world's? "I don't know, I'll have to think about it," he said, thoughtfully.

When he *did* think about it, Armstrong would realize that winning a second world championship, 10 years after his first rainbow jersey, would put him on a par with LeMond—something that might give him a big incentive. And it would be another coup for a rugged champion, a gunslinger who's proud of his conquests.

Lance Armstrong's also very proud of his family, as he revealed when he brought this interview to an abrupt end. "Okay, Kristin just pulled in," he said with an excited lift in his voice. "The Boss, Luke the Boss is here. I gotta go...."

Questions, Questions and More Questions

LANCE ARMSTRONG FOUND OUT DURING THE 2001 TOUR
THAT THE MEDIA'S INFATUATION WITH LINKING HIS NAME
TO DOPING IN CYCLING SIMPLY WON'T GO AWAY

During most of his post-2001 Tour interviews, Lance Armstrong tried to explain, and perhaps understand, the media's focus on the apparently insurmountable problem of drugs in cycling. It's a long story, and not one confined to cycling. Indeed, the use of performance-enhancing drugs has become something of an "arms race" in sport in general, with new substances and new techniques staying one or two steps ahead of new rules and new detection methods. It is a problem that especially plagues those sports that demand incredible endurance, such as soccer, elite cross-country ski racing and distance running. But it is cycling that has been the focus of attention for the last few years, and the reason for that can be distilled down to one source: the Festina affair of 1998.

To be sure, drugs have been a part of cycling since the sport began in the 19th century. Competitors in the early six-day track races allegedly chewed coca leaves and ingested strychnine as boosters. And Tour de France riders in the early 20th century were said to have rubbed cocaine in their eyes simply to stay awake during the brutally long 400-plus-kilometer stages conjured up in the event's early editions. Even after Tour organizers cut

165

stage distances to a "more humane" 200-plus kilometers, speed and endurance then became so critical that riders continued to seek a pharmaceutical boost.

Armstrong knew that. He also knew none of that history—even the untimely death of Tom Simpson in 1967 from cardiac failure triggered in part by amphetamines—had moved the doping issue to center stage. That is, until the year before Armstrong's first Tour win.

The tale of the drug scandal that tore apart the 1998 Tour de France has been well documented: the early-morning police stop of a Festina team car; the discovery of more than 400 vials of EPO, growth hormone and amphetamines; the ejection of the team from the Tour; the police searches; more ejections, more searches … trials, prison sentences … and the inevitable book contracts that followed.

Ever since that July morning when French police stopped Festina soigneur Willy Voet's Tour-issued Fiat, cycling in general and the Société du Tour de France in particular have struggled to put the scandal behind them. Just a year after the Festina affair—and barely a month after 1998 Tour winner Marco Pantani was sullied by a blood-test scandal at the Giro d'Italia—Tour director Jean-Marie Leblanc began talking in terms of a new beginning, a "Tour of redemption" even. But a newly skeptical press wasn't biting.

And into that fray walked Armstrong. Recently recovered from cancer and the new yellow-jersey holder, the Texan was not universally hailed as a hero. Rather, he was immediately challenged by the post-Festina media, which claimed that his performances could not be possible without the aid of pharmaceuticals. Armstrong made it clear that he wouldn't tolerate questions on doping, and his relationship with the media quickly soured.

Two years later, in April 2001, Armstrong conceded that he "made the mistake of going into a shell and refusing to talk to a lot of people because I was so offended. You know, I have had a lot of time to think about this, and I realize that that's just not a good idea. It's better to just talk about it. And I understand why people were more suspicious if you went inside, if you were in your bus, if you didn't talk to the journalists. It was my fault; I just didn't know that at the time."

Perhaps the nadir of Armstrong's relationship with the media came during the 2000 Tour. In search of a story, a crew from France 3 television surreptitiously followed a U.S. Postal Service team car, and filmed the team doctor and chiropractor disposing of a plastic garbage bag, which was later found to contain packaging from syringes, used bandages and gauze, as well as used bottles from a collection of 14 medications. None of the substances were included on the Union Cycliste Internationale's or International Olympic Committee's banned list, but among them was a Norwegian-made drug derived from calves' blood known as Actovegin. This bovine hemo-derivative was said to enhance glycogen uptake and improve the transport of oxygen to the blood cells. Though both benefits would certainly boost athletic performance, the product was not a banned substance.

The U.S. Postal squad quickly issued a statement insisting that no one on the team had used banned substances. It was 10 days before the denial included "hypothetically helpful" medications that may not have yet appeared on the banned-substance list. The team issued copies of the manifest submitted to border police at the start of the Tour, showing Actovegin among the list of substances reported in the paperwork. A later press statement said that the Actovegin in the seized bag was used for the treatment of abrasions and the personal medication of a staff member suffering from diabetes—both appropriate and acceptable uses.

Appropriate or not, the TV crew's video and the contents of the now-infamous trash bag were sent to police officials in Paris for analysis. Those authorities repeatedly promised to release test results, but even a month after the end of the 2001 Tour, the report had yet to be released. And this was in spite of the fact that three months before the Tour Armstrong had held a news conference in Paris, when he revealed that, according to the official investigator, all tests on the riders' urine samples were negative. At the time, Armstrong said he remained hopeful that he and the sport could get beyond the cloud of suspicion and simply get back to the business of racing bicycles. But that was before he reconnected with the award-winning Irish journalist, David Walsh.

Walsh, a sportswriter and columnist for *The Sunday Times* of London, has long used his space in Britain's most-respected newspaper as a forum to fight the use of performance-enhancing drugs in sport. He was among the first to raise questions of propriety about the Olympic-medal-winning performances of Irish swimmer Michelle De Bruin in 1996. He and other De Bruin critics were eventually proven to be right.

Walsh first wrote extensively about Armstrong in his book *Inside the Tour de France*, a collection of character profiles and stories from the 1993 Tour. Among those featured was Armstrong, then a brash 21-year-old rookie on the Motorola team contesting his first Tour. It was a generally sympathetic piece and the two seemed to have a genuinely friendly relationship. But that was 1993.

167

Six years later, after Armstrong's illness and recovery, and after the devastating revelations that emerged from the Festina scandal, Walsh found himself at the 1999 Tour and wondering if anyone could truly excel in cycling without cheating. It was a theme that reappeared in his columns throughout 1999 and 2000—particularly at Tour time. But Walsh was looking for something more definitive than simply raising questions as the 2001 Tour approached. He wanted answers.

Toward that end, Walsh began a six-month project that saw him compile a seemingly disparate collection of interviews, police observations and even hotel records into a compelling, but circumstantial, case against Armstrong. The American learned of the effort and in April rang Walsh on his mobile phone to invite him to France for a face-to-face interview. What ensued was a tense two-hour meeting—conducted in the presence of Armstrong's friend, agent and attorney Bill Stapleton—that left both rider and writer frustrated and more than a little angry.

Armstrong continued to insist that Walsh's energies and questions were misdirected, pointing to the "proof" that he was indeed a clean rider. "We run a clean program, we work hard, we've been submitted to every test they've got," Armstrong told Walsh.

Walsh, however, was not convinced and raised the question of the Italian sports doctor, Michele Ferrari. Right or wrong, Ferrari's name, when mentioned in connection with cycling, usually elicited the same response that the name "Nixon" might have when mentioned in political circles. He was the sort of man about whom everyone had an opinion. Part of the problem was certainly Ferrari's own fault. In 1994, he had publicly argued that the red-blood-cell-boosting drug, Epogen (EPO), was "no more harmful than five liters of orange juice." The comments triggered a wave of criticism and caused him to become the subject of an ongoing investigation. Ferrari was, at the time of the Walsh interview, facing trial on charges of "sporting fraud" because of his alleged reliance on performance-enhancing drugs to aid an elite list of clients, including former Postal team rider Kevin Livingston, one of Armstrong's best friends in their hometown of Austin, Texas. Walsh wanted to know if Armstrong, too, had worked with the doctor.

"I did know Michele Ferrari," Armstrong told Walsh.

"How did you get to know him?" the reporter asked.

"In cycling, everybody ... when you go to races, you see people," Armstrong explained. "There [are] trainers, doctors, I know every team's doctor. It's a small community."

"Did you ever visit him?" Walsh asked.

"Have I been tested by him, gone and been there and consulted on certain things?" Armstrong responded. "Perhaps."

It was that last "perhaps," Walsh later said, that set him off to try and document if and when Armstrong ever visited the Italian doctor. That effort delayed by more than two months the publication of Walsh's piece in *The Sunday Times*.

As part of their investigation, Italian police had been monitoring Ferrari and keeping track of visitors to his office. By late June, Walsh had compiled a list detailing the dates of visits, and even the hotels in which Armstrong had stayed. According to those records, Armstrong had indeed traveled to Ferrari's hometown on several occasions, including a brief visit just before the Sydney Olympics and another on the eve of the 2001 Tour of Switzerland. Four days before the prologue in Dunkirk and five days before publication of the article, Walsh e-mailed those details to Stapleton for comment. Though he received no direct response, Armstrong did go public with the details of his relationship with Ferrari in an interview with the Italian sports daily, *La Gazzetta dello Sport*.

The *Gazzetta* story appeared on Saturday, July 7, the day the Tour de France started in Dunkirk. It described Armstrong's plans to attack the prestigious world hour record. "Between now and the end of the year I'm going to try to break the world hour record. I will decide when after the Tour, and I'll count on the advice of Michele Ferrari—an expert in records," Armstrong told the paper.

It seemed an odd revelation, especially on the dawn of the Tour, and left many wondering why Armstrong opted to discuss a relationship with a physician with such a reputation. It wasn't until the next day, when *The Sunday Times* feature story, "Saddled by suspicion," hit the newsstands, that the *Gazzetta* item began to make sense.

In a full-page article, Walsh attempted to answer the question of whether anyone can excel in a sport so rife with drugs and remain clean. "Can a clean rider beat those on drugs?" Walsh asked. The writer included interviews with an unnamed former Motorola team rider, who suggested that Armstrong sought EPO as far back as 1995, characterizing the then-young Texan as being the "spokesman" for the rest of the team regarding the subject of EPO. The article also included comments by former U.S. Postal Service team physician Prentice Steffan, who left the team one year before Armstrong signed on. Steffan, later the doctor for the American team, Mercury, suggested his departure from

Postal was triggered by a refusal "to do all that could be done" to help his riders excel after a poor performance in the 1996 Tour of Switzerland.

Steffan said that, at the time of his dismissal, he raised the issue of doping with Mark Gorski, the general manager of the Postal team. Steffan said he never got a direct response, though he did receive a letter threatening a lawsuit if he ever went public with the charges.

On the Sunday evening following stage 1 of the 2001 Tour, Armstrong issued a written statement saying that Ferrari's role had been limited to consultation "on dieting, altitude preparation, hypoxic training and the use of altitude tents, which are all natural methods of improvement." Armstrong added that he had little reason to advertise the relationship because of the "irresponsible comments [Ferrari] made in 1994 regarding EPO." The statement reiterated that Armstrong had never discussed using EPO with Ferrari.

Armstrong did not specifically address the allegations raised by the unnamed former teammate or by Steffan, though he did ask to be allowed to address all of those issues in a press conference that a spokesman said would come no sooner than Verdun, after stage 4 of the Tour. Gorski, however, did make himself available to reporters that Sunday evening and characterized Steffan's comments as "lies." "His statements are false, and they were false five years ago, and I'm really disappointed that he's decided to bring them up again," said Gorski.

But it wasn't Steffan's comments or even those of the former Motorola rider that triggered the most negative response. Indeed, it was Armstrong's admission of his working relationship with the Italian doctor that caused the most controversy. It raised questions that followed Armstrong through the entire Tour, causing even race director Leblanc to question the propriety of the relationship.

"Armstong is a respected rider, but he is not loved," Leblanc told the French newspaper *Le Journal du Dimanche*. "He doesn't speak French, and he exudes little warmth. Two gorillas [Armstrong's bodyguards] look after him at the village and the finish. He lives with suspicion, and these latest revelations about Dr. Ferrari have only added to the doubts."

Despite Leblanc's concerns, despite Walsh's efforts, despite the lingering questions, despite the Ferrari trial due to open in the fall of 2001, and despite the pending French police report on the Postal team, Armstrong described his relationship with the media in 2001 as "improved."

Maybe it was improved. Or maybe, finally, he was just getting used to it.

Tackling the Tour's Time Trials

TECHNOLOGY AND TECHNIQUE AGAIN
PLAYED A HUGE ROLE IN THE
TEAM AND INDIVIDUAL TIME-TRIAL STAGES

Going into the Tour de France, all the contenders knew that their performances in the various races against the clock—prologue, team time trial, uphill time trial and long time trial—would play a key role in their overall placings. That's why their teams paid special attention to the bikes and equipment used in these four stages. Whether that included putting riders and bikes in wind tunnels during the winter, shaving ounces off certain accessories or developing a rider's pedaling cadence, technology was king.

Here's a look at some of the intriguing products and projects that teams encompassed during the 2001 Tour.

TTT Winner

French-made Look time-trial bikes, which took a black eye in the late 1990s with some failures of weak forks, pulled off the ultimate Tour victory: an entire team winning a stage on them. There were more Look bikes in this Tour than any other make, as four teams (Crédit Agricole, Kelme, BigMat and CSC-Tiscali) were riding them. That put Look ahead

171

of two Italian framebuilders: Pinarello, which had three teams (Telekom, iBanesto.com and Fassa Bortolo); and Colnago, which had two (Rabobank and Mapei). But who could have predicted how well some of the Look-mounted teams would do against the powerhouses riding Pinarellos and Colnagos? That was particularly true in the stage 5 team time trial won by Crédit Agricole.

The Look KG 396 CLM frame, molded in one piece out of carbon fiber, was the same design as the KG 396 frame that won six Olympic track medals (four of them gold) in Sydney. (CLM stands for *"contre la montre,"* French for "against the clock.") Look claimed that the frame and fork weighed between 2.4kg and 2.7kg (5.3-5.9 pounds). The fork hinged off the front of the frame, mounting above and below the head tube, and presented a sharp edge to the wind. Crédit Agricole's aero' bikes were equipped with Cinelli bars and Fir deep-section, spoked front wheels and flat rear discs.

The riders in green and white looked to be more together in terms of equipment, as well as in riding speed, than all but a couple of teams. They all wore shoe covers and aero' helmets, and the team car was loaded with spare time-trial bikes. Many of the other teams had riders with bare heads, caps and headbands among those in aero' helmets; a mixture of riders with and without shoe covers; a mixture of different types of wheels; and support cars loaded with standard road bikes.

ONCE, which finished second to Crédit Agricole, was another together squad. Its team vehicle bristled with spare time-trial bikes equipped in the same way as the ones being used in the stage. The Spanish team's sloping-top-tube Giant TCF bikes were fitted with HED3 front wheels and Campagnolo Ghibli rear discs. The bike's aluminum frames had the trademark Giant adjustable stems and aero' seatposts held in place by double binder bolts pointed in opposing directions, while its bars were Cinelli down-slung wings.

Uphill Time Trial

The winning formula for time trialing is generally a simple one: use high power coupled with low wind resistance. In other words, strong riders with a minimal frontal surface area will go faster on a flat course. But that all changes when the grade steepens. Greater emphasis then has to be given to light bikes rather than aerodynamic efficiency. So for stage 11 of the Tour de France, the mountain time trial from Grenoble to Chamrousse, nearly every rider used a standard road bike with road bars—but each team used a different approach to reducing the weight of the equipment while retaining its aerodynamic qualities.

Many had taken note of what Lance Armstrong—legendary for his attention to equipment detail—had used at the uphill time trial in the preceding Tour of Switzerland: his regular climbing bike equipped with a custom-made clip-on bar and special wheels and cogs. And knowing he was being watched before the start in Grenoble, the U.S. Postal star played a little poker by warming up on his low-profile time-trial bike wearing an aero' helmet: a subterfuge designed to make his opponents wonder if they should reconsider their equipment choices. Armstrong, of course, changed bikes before he reported to the start, but he did keep his aero' helmet on for the early, flatter kilometers until throwing it off when the hard climbing began.

Armstrong's climbing bike, like that of his Postal team lieutenants Tyler Hamilton, Roberto Heras, Victor Hugo Peña and José Luis Rubiera, was a Trek with a gray finish, silver front end and a straight-bladed fork. The frame, sold as the Trek 5900 Superlight, was built from an expensive carbon-fiber fabric that weighed 110 grams per square meter, substantially less than the 120 fabric of the U.S. framebuilder's standard 5500 OCLV road bikes. Trek engineers claimed that the Superlight was just as strong as the 5500 frame since it used the same amount of carbon. The frame itself weighed around 1 kilogram, and the fork, with an aluminum steering tube, had a claimed weight of 345 grams. The steering tube was slightly conical, as the headset had a 1-1/8-inch top bearing and a 1-3/8-inch bottom bearing. Savvy tech types recognized this as a Klein design, and indeed Trek, which also owns Klein, had adopted some of Gary Klein's ideas to make the bike lighter while maintaining rigidity with this oversized steering tube.

The aero' bar clipped onto Armstrong's Deda Newton road bar was created to Armstrong's specifications by Louisiana aero' guru John Cobb. Armstrong wanted an aero' position and aero' wheels, but he did not want to cramp his climbing style by lugging a heavy bar and wheels, and he did not want to give up any potential hand positions. He felt that the available clip-on options for a road bar were too heavy and took up valuable real estate on top of the bar where his hands might want to be when climbing.

Cobb built the bar by creating a different mounting system for a pair of Profile Carbon-X extensions. "Over the years, Lance has decided he likes his wrists to be at a certain angle, so I had to mount the extensions under his bar and his elbow pads over it to get

173

that angle," said Cobb. "I couldn't use the original Profile parts, because the extensions would mount on the wrong side of the bar and the pads would be too low and wide."

The elbow pads were set higher above the bars and further forward and inward than normal so that Armstrong could grab the bar near the stem when climbing. The pads supported his arms just behind the wrists. According to Cobb: "He likes to pull hard on the bars, and the way I set up the pads, he can't rest on them, he can only pull against them. The bar ended up weighing 300 grams, the extensions are adjustable for length and rotation, and there is a tiny bit of elbow-pad adjustment."

The Postal star opted for Lightweight brand wheels, which were made by two craftsmen in Munich, Germany, using carbon hubs, rims and braking surfaces connected by carbon-Kevlar spokes. These were virtually the same wheels that Bjarne Riis used when he won the Tour in 1996, and by Bobby Julich during his third-place finish in 1998. They weighed about 1050 grams per pair.

After feeling that the 23-tooth cog he had on L'Alpe d'Huez the day before was too low and the 21 was too high, Armstrong chose a 12-22 cassette for the Chamrousse time trial to go with his 39-54 chainrings on 175mm Shimano Dura-Ace cranks. The larger cogs were blue aluminum gears made by CSH, and the two-tooth jumps were between the 15, 17 and 19 cogs. That way, his lowest cogs were 19, 20, 21 and 22, and Armstrong said he used all of them. As for brakes and shifters, he had a Dura-Ace STI combination brake lever and shifter on the right side; on the left, he had an old Dura-Ace brake lever and a down-tube front shifter to save some weight. However, Armstrong's interest in light weight and high technology did not lead him to switch from his old Shimano Look pedals or Selle San Marco Concor Light saddle.

As for rival Jan Ullrich, he rode his climbing bike—a tuned version of his Pinarello Prince to save a kilogram over the one that he used on the road stages—with a clip-on bar. The frame had the Prince carbon fork and seat-stay wishbone, but the aluminum main tubes had thinner walls, and the down tube was smaller in diameter. Ullrich's climbing style is to stay seated, so the lost torsional rigidity was not an issue for him. His clip-on had wider elbow pads than Armstrong's, which prevented the German from holding the tops of the bars.

Like Armstrong, Ullrich used a down-tube front shifter to save 100 grams in parts and cable length. His brake lever looked like a Campagnolo ErgoPower carbon Record lever because it was, but the shift lever and some guts had been removed. His saddle was a lighter version of his normal Selle Italia Turbo, with carbon rails and aluminum reinforcement of the clamping section. His bottom bracket had a lighter titanium spindle than normal. His wheels were full-carbon rims that strongly resembled Ambrosio XCarbo rims laced to black Campagnolo straight-pull-spoke hubs so they looked like Campagnolo Bora wheels. Telekom officials were tight-lipped about the rims, as Campagnolo was one of the team's equipment sponsors, and the rims were clearly not from Campagnolo. The team used this type of wheel, coupled with Corima cork brake pads for the carbon braking surfaces, in all the Tour's road races and time trials, but the ones on Ullrich's climbing bike were lighter still, with thinner and lighter spokes.

Despite the fine-tuning seen on Ullrich's and Armstrong's bikes, one man did well with virtually no time-trial refinements. This was Euskaltel-Euskadi's Roberto Laiseka, who rode to an eye-popping fourth place in the Chamrousse time trial (second fastest on the main climb) on a bike with no aero' bar; and he didn't even wear shoe covers. Laiseka rode a Dura-Ace-equipped aluminum Orbea frame fitted with Mavic SSC SL wheels and Vittoria Corsa CX tires—the same bike, completely unchanged, that he rode in the regular mountain stages. His deficit on the stage's third-place finisher, Joseba Beloki of ONCE-Eroski, was 40 seconds—probably too much time for him to have made up in the opening 13.5km had he used an aero' bar.

CSC-Tiscali's Laurent Jalabert—who would go on to win the King of the Mountains title—used a new carbon-fiber sloping-top-tube Look frame with 650C (26-inch) Lightweight all-carbon wheels and standard bars with clip-ons and no elbow pads. This frame was called the "Escalade," and Jalabert's 48cm version was considerably smaller at both the seat tube and the head tube than his normal 55cm frame, since it had only 5cm of slope, meaning that the head tube was still 2cm lower than his normal Look. He made up these differences with a long seatpost and an up-sloping stem. Jalabert's complete Escalade (without the clip-on bar) was claimed to weigh 16.5 pounds, 0.8 pounds under his normal road bike and about a pound over the UCI's 7kg minimum-weight requirement, although this was without the Lightweight wheels. The frame and fork together were claimed to weigh three pounds (1.36kg). Third-placed Beloki also used 26-inch wheels and a sloping-top-tube frame—an aluminum Giant—and aero' clip-ons. The smaller wheels' lower rotating weight made around twice as much difference as weight lost on the frame and other components.

In the time trial's 21st place, Jonathan Vaughters was the second highest-placed American. He and his Crédit Agricole teammates Bobby Julich and Stuart O'Grady rode Look carbon frames and forks with unmarked Mavic carbon Cosmic wheels and Cinelli Spinaci clip-ons on their Cinelli road bars. Vaughters added Cinelli strap-on elbow pads.

Cofidis's Andrei Kivilev tried to keep his dreams of the yellow jersey alive on a Columbus aluminum MBK with a Columbus carbon fork and seat-stay wishbone, an ITM clip-on without elbow pads, and a Campagnolo Bora rear wheel and Nucleon front wheel with Vittoria Crono CS tires.

Kelme's Oscar Sevilla and Santiago Botero placed fifth and seventh, respectively, on Look frames with Look carbon forks. But where Botero's frame was carbon and had a level top tube, Sevilla's was aluminum with a sloping top tube. Where the bigger Botero was using 172.5mm Dura-Ace cranks, the smaller Sevilla had 175s. Where Botero used a standard ITM clip-on with elbow pads, Sevilla used an ITM Spinaci-style bar without elbow pads. Both used Shimano carbon wheels, 12-23 cogsets and 41-53 chainrings.

Axel Merckx of Domo-Farm Frites managed to place in the top 50 on a pair of Lightweight wheels and clip-on bars atop an aluminum frame from his father, Eddy Merckx. The rider in the yellow jersey, Pascal Simon of Bonjour, rode a Time frame and fork with Spinergy Rev-X wheels, Michelin tires and Deda bars and clip-on. He lost seven minutes to Armstrong that day. The rider then in the best climber's polka-dot jersey, Laurent Roux of Jean Delatour, rode standard Shimano wheels, and standard 3T Forgie stem and bars with no clip-on, on his aluminum Cyfac bike. He conceded about the same amount of time as Simon.

For both the riders and their mechanics, the uphill time trial was a stage to look for any advantage they could find. And the consensus was clear: Make the bike as light as possible for the climb, and add a clip-on for the flatter parts.

Armstrong's Cadence

When, the day before the Chamrousse time trial, Armstrong rolled away on L'Alpe d'Huez and gained time on his rivals in large gobs, he spun his 39x23 and 39x21 at around 90 to 100 revs per minute. His rapid climbing cadence is somewhat unique in recent cycling history, as not since the days of "Angel of the Mountains" Charly Gaul had long-time race followers seen someone climb away from his rivals spinning 15 to 20 rpm faster than any of them. Not that those trailing in Armstrong's wake were under-performing: the 70- to 75-rpm climbing cadence of Ullrich and Beloki was completely standard. In fact, Ullrich pedaled the same way when he won the Tour in 1997, riding smoothly in the saddle up L'Alpe d'Huez inexorably dropping second-placed Richard Virenque, who was thrashing about, constantly out of the saddle. The difference was that race followers were in awe of the German that day, watching him trounce his rivals. In 2001, Ullrich was the one who was in awe of Armstrong.

Comparing their differing styles, Armstrong's personal training guru, Chris Carmichael, said, "A big guy like Ullrich probably needs to use a bigger gear, since he has bigger muscles. It's very individual. For Lance, the higher cadence works because he has an efficient pedal stroke and it allows him to go as fast while his watts per pedal stroke are lower. On the flip side, it takes better aerobic conditioning to pedal at higher cadence. And you have to train a lot at high cadence to develop efficiency. Most people are more efficient at 80 rpm than they are at 90 rpm."

Carmichael and Armstrong worked for years on improving the Texan's pedaling efficiency. Watching his feet swing so elegantly through each stroke, ankling from flat to toe-down and back 90 times per minute, was like seeing an artist in action. In 2001, Armstrong had added an hour or so of daily stretching as part of his preparation. He said about this new regime: "Longer muscles are stronger muscles." They are also more supple muscles that allow fluid leg motion at high rotational speed.

Furthermore, Armstrong had developed his aerobic fitness beyond anything that any cyclist has perhaps done before. It allowed him to spin away from very strong men like they were juniors. After Roux was caught on Alpe d'Huez by Armstrong at the end of an all-day breakaway, the Frenchman, clearly impressed, remarked, "When he passed me, I had the impression that it was a motorcycle at my side. It was beautiful to see."

Facts and Stats

Number of starters: 189.

Number of finishers: 144 (17 more than 1999).

Only team with nine finishers: Bonjour.

Average speed: 40.070 kph (second fastest in history).

Top sprinter: Telekom's Erik Zabel (a record sixth green jersey).

King of the Mountains: CSC-Tiscali's Laurent Jalabert (by 47 points over Jan Ullrich).

Top team: Kelme-Costa Blanca (by 4:59 over ONCE-Eroski)

Best rider 25 or under: Kelme's Oscar Sevilla (by 10:03 over 2000 winner Francesco Mancebo).

Most aggressive rider: CSC-Tiscali's Laurent Jalabert (by 39 points over Laurent Roux).

Top cash winners: U.S. Postal Service $367,000; Telekom $283,000; ONCE-Eroski $206,000.

Top stage winners: Armstrong (4), Zabel (3), Jalabert (2).

Yellow jerseys: Christophe Moreau (2 days), Marc Wauters (1 day), Stuart O'Grady (6 days), Jens Voigt (1 day), François Simon (3 days), Lance Armstrong (8 days).

Glossary of Cycling Terms

Bonus sprints On every stage of the Tour de France, the organizers designate sprints at two or three intermediate points along the course. At each sprint, the first rider over the line scores six points for the green-jersey competition (and has six seconds deducted from his overall time); the second gets four points (and four seconds); the third, two points (and two seconds).

Break (or breakaway) A rider or group of riders that escapes from the main field after making a successful attack is called a break or breakaway.

Draft To gain the maximum shelter (or draft) from air resistance or the wind, it is best to ride directly behind or slightly to the side of the rider in front. Riding in a draft saves approximately 30 percent in expended energy compared with riding alone.

Echelons When the wind is blowing from the side on flat roads and the racing is fast, the riders form echelons (like flying geese) to gain the maximum draft from each other. The echelon rotates because the riders on the leeward side move forward, and those on the windy side move back. The echelon can only be as wide as the road, so a field of 150 racers may split into several echelons, angled into the wind.

Feed zone At about half-distance on every stage, the Tour organizers designate a feed zone (usually about a kilometer long). A vehicle from each team drives ahead of the race and parks in the feed zone, where team personnel fill canvas bags (a.k.a. musettes) with food and drinks, to later hand up to their riders as they pass through the designated area.

General Classification (or G.C.) The general classification is the order of the riders on overall time, computed by adding together each rider's stage times (less time bonuses). If you don't understand the concept, think of a golf tournament, where scores are added together after each round, and the lowest score leads. At the Tour de France, the leader on G.C. wears the yellow jersey.

Grand tours The collective name for the world's only three-week stage races: the Tour de France, the Giro d'Italia and the Vuelta a España.

Green jersey The green jersey is worn by the leader of the points competition. Points are awarded at intermediate sprints (see "Bonus sprints") and at the finish of each stage. For so-called flat stages, each of the first 25 finishers scores points (35 points for first place, down to one point for 25th). For mountain stages, only the top 15 score points (20 points for first, down to one for 15th). And just the top 10 score points in individual time trials (15 points for first, down to one for 10th).

Gruppetto The group of riders that forms at the rear of the field on mountain stages, and which moves at a constant pace to finish within the day's time limit (see "Time cut"), is called the *gruppetto* (the Italian word for "a small group"). The gruppetto is sometimes called the *autobus* or laughing group.

Individual time trials Often called the race of truth, an individual time trial sees each rider racing alone against the clock, and the one with the fastest time wins. At the Tour, riders start at one-minute intervals in the prologue time trial, at two-minute intervals (one minute for the first half of the starters) in the first long time trial, and at two-minute intervals (three minutes for the final 20 riders) in the final time trial. Riders start in reverse order of the overall classification standings.

Leadout Heading into a mass-rider finish, you will often see the teammate of a sprinter racing flat out at the head of the field. He is the leadout man. The purpose of the leadout is twofold: to stop a rider from another team making a late attack; and to allow the sprinter to ride in the draft of his leadout man until he's ready to unleash a final effort.

Mountain climb categories There are no set rules on how an organizer can categorize a hill or mountain climb. For the Tour de France climbers' competition, five categories are used, as follows:

▷ the easiest is a Cat. 4, which is typically less than 2km long and about 5-percent grade, or up to 5km at a 2- to 3-percent grade.

▷ a Cat. 3 can be shorter than 5km but steeper than a Cat. 4, maybe 6 or 7 percent; somewhat longer, more than 5km, with a grade of 5-percent; or even as long as 14km if less than 4 percent.

▷ a Cat. 2 is anywhere between 4km at 8 percent, and 18km at 4 percent.

▷ a Cat. 1, once the highest category, can be anything from 7.5km at 8 percent to 23km at 5 percent.

▷ exceptionally tough climbs are given an *hors-categorie* (or above-category) rating. This could either be a Cat. 1-type climb of 10km or longer whose summit is the finish of the stage, or one that is 12km long at 7.5 percent or steeper, or up to 25km long at 6 percent or steeper.

Peloton The peloton is a French word (literally "platoon") used to describe the main field of riders, also called the pack or main bunch.

Polka-dot jersey The white-and-red polka-dot jersey is worn by the leader of the climbers' competition. Points are awarded on every categorized climb, ranging from five points for being first across a Cat. 4 climb, 10 points on a Cat. 3, 20 points on a Cat. 2, 30 points on a Cat. 1, and up to 40 points for taking first on an *hors-categorie* climb.

Prologue A prologue is an individual time trial held in the afternoon and evening before stage 1 of the Tour. The distance of a prologue is limited to 8km or less, and is normally held on a street circuit.

Teams Top professional teams are named after their main sponsor, and they usually have between 12 and 20 riders on their season roster. Nine of these riders are chosen to start the Tour de France. In 2001, the organizers selected 21 teams to compete in the Tour (see "Wild cards").

Team time trial Similar to the individual version, a team time trial sees each team (as opposed to individuals) race separately against the clock, with the fastest team winning the stage. For the Tour, with its nine-man teams, the time of the fifth rider across the finish line is the one that counts. Teams start at five-minute intervals.

Time bonuses Besides the time bonuses earned at intermediate sprints, the first three across the finish line of each stage (except for time trials) are awarded time bonuses of respectively 20 seconds, 12 seconds and six seconds—which are deducted from their overall race times.

Time cut On every stage of the Tour de France, each rider has to finish within a certain percentage of the winner's time to remain in the race. Riders not making this time cut are eliminated from the Tour. Time-cut percentages vary considerably: Time trials carry the highest margin of 25 percent; mountain stages are usually around 10 percent; and flat stages have a low of 5 percent (depending on the average speed).

Wild cards In January each year, 15 teams automatically qualify for the Tour de France (based on world team rankings and performances in the previous year's three grand tours); the remaining teams are selected in May by the race organizer, the Société du Tour de France. These last selections are called wild cards, and in 2001 the Société chose six wild-card teams, to make up the field of 21 teams.

Yellow jersey (maillot jaune) The yellow jersey (or *maillot jaune* in French) is worn by the leader on overall time (see "General Classification"). It is yellow because when it was introduced in 1919 the organizer and main sponsor of the Tour was the daily sports newspaper *L'Auto*, which was printed on yellow paper.

About the Authors

John Wilcockson visited the Tour de France for the first time as a fan in 1963, riding his bike 200km a day, and managing to catch sight of the race on key mountain climbs, the time trials and several finishes. Five years later, he reported the Tour as a professional journalist and has now followed the event 32 times. Prior to joining *VeloNews* in 1988, Wilcockson was the editor of four other cycling magazines, and for 10 years was the cycling correspondent of *The Times* and *Sunday Times* in London. He has written six books on cycling, not including the four editions of the VeloPress Tour book. His *John Wilcockson's World of Cycling* is available from VeloPress. Wilcockson is currently the editorial director of *VeloNews* and lives in Boulder, Colorado, with his wife, Rivvy Neshama.

Bryan Jew reported the Tour de France for the second time in 2001—covering the race from start to finish as the lead reporter for velonews.com and driving the *VeloNews* press car. He has also covered the Giro d'Italia, Vuelta a España, Paris-Roubaix, Liège-Bastogne-Liège, Tour of Flanders and the world road championships. Jew is the senior writer for *VeloNews* and lives in Boulder, Colorado, with his wife, Kori.

Charles Pelkey has followed the Tour de France four times, and this is his fourth year of contributing to the VeloPress book on the Tour. Pelkey is a former amateur bike racer and has enjoyed a long and varied media career—working as a political reporter, a U.S. senate press secretary, and even a late-night jazz disc jockey. He has been the technical editor of *VeloNews* since 1994, and lives in Golden, Colorado, with his wife, Diana Denison, and their children, Philip and Annika.

Lennard Zinn has followed the Tour de France four times, and this is the first time he has contributed to the VeloPress book on the Tour. Zinn is a former Olymipic development amateur bike racer, sometime cross-country skier and professional frame builder. He has been the senior technical writer for *VeloNews* since 1989, and lives in Boulder, Colorado, with his wife, Sonny, and their two daughters, Emily and Sarah.

Other Books by VeloPress®

The CTS Collection: Training Tips for Cyclists and Triathletes *from Carmichael Training Systems, featuring Chris Carmichael; Foreword by Lance Armstrong.*
Lance Armstrong's coach offers education, tips, perspective, and motivation about improving performance for both cyclists and triathletes.
Paperback • 7 x 10 • 232 pp. • black-and-white photos • 1-931382-02-6 • P-CTS • $21.95

Graham Watson: 20 Years of Cycling Photography
A visual feast of four-color photographs highlighting some of the finest and most heartbreaking moments in European road racing. Graham Watson, one of cycling's foremost photographers, captures some of cycling's greatest heroes.
Hardcover • 11 x 11 • 224 pp. • 1-884737-84-6 • P-WAT • $49.95

Maillot Jaune: The Tour de France Yellow Jersey *by Jean-Paul Ollivier*
A tribute to all 227 cyclists who have had the honor of wearing the yellow jersey in the past 82 years—some for just a day, some day after day. Sumptuously illustrated with hundreds of black-and-white and full-color photos.
Hardcover • 8 1/2 x 11 • 192 pp. • 1-884737-98-6 • P-MAJ • $39.95

John Wilcockson's World of Cycling
This wonderful book brings the world of bicycle racing alive through the eyes and experiences of veteran *VeloNews* editor John Wilcockson. Wilcockson has covered practically every major bicycle race around the globe for 30 years, and his writing is a joy for any cycling fan.
Paperback • 6 x 9 • 336 pp. • 1-884737-77-3 • P-WPB • $18.95

Zinn & the Art of Road Bike Maintenance *by Lennard Zinn*
Whether you're an experienced wrench or a repair novice, master framebuilder and *VeloNews* technical writer Lennard Zinn's easy step-by-step instructions and clear explanations make the sometimes baffling world of bike maintenance so clear you'll wonder why you've avoided mechanics all this time.
Paperback • 8 1/2 x 11 • 296 pp. • 1-884737-70-6 • P-ZYR • $19.95

VELO
press®

Tel: 800/234-8356
Fax: 303/444-6788
E-mail: velopress@7dogs.com
Web: velopress.com
VeloPress books are also available from your favorite bookstore or bike shop.